W9-BJP-273

SUNDAYS IN AMERICA

SUNDAYS IN AMERICA

A Yearlong Road Trip
in Search of Christian Faith

SUZANNE STREMPEK SHEA

BEACON PRESS · BOSTON

BEACON PRESS
25 Beacon Street
Boston, Massachusetts 02108–2892
www.beacon.org

Beacon Press books
are published under the auspices of
the Unitarian Universalist Association of Congregations.

Printed in the United States of America

11 10 09 08 8 7 6 5 4 3 2 1

This book is printed on acid-free paper that meets the uncoated paper ANSI/NISO specifications for permanence as revised in 1992.

Text design by Tag Savage and composition by Susan E. Kelly at Wilsted & Taylor Publishing Services.

Library of Congress Cataloging-in-Publication Data

Shea, Suzanne Strempek.
Sundays in America : a yearlong road trip in search of Christian faith / Suzanne Strempek Shea.
p. cm.
ISBN 978-0-8070-7224-0
1. Christianity—United States. 2. United States—Church history. I. Title.
BR515.S44 2008
277.3'083—dc22 2007039110

In thanksgiving for the blessings that were my maternal grandparents, Stanley and Mary (Krolik) Milewski

INTRODUCTION

The route to church on each and every Sunday morning of my childhood was the same. From my seat in the back of the family's blue Chevrolet, in the manner I still practice on journeys that take me down the same roads over and again, I gazed at favorite sights: the patch of scary jungly woods behind my great-aunt's purple-shingled duplex, the exact pointy meeting place of the Ware and Quaboag rivers that run beneath the green-railed bridge we crossed to get to Main Street, and the dazzling white clapboard church at the top of the hill just after the village center. This was not the church to which we were headed. Ours was another half mile or so up the road. I wasn't certain what type of church the white one was, but I knew from an early age that it was not Catholic. So I always felt sorry for the people I saw walking up its stairs. As nice as they might look all dressed in Sunday best, as kind and good as they might be every day of the week, the sad truth was, they were going to hell.

That was the fate of Protestants, I was taught at my parochial grammar school, located next to what the Sunday liturgy reminded me was the "one holy, catholic, and apostolic church." The folks entering any other type might believe in God, but they somehow had the rest all wrong. The details weren't ever explained, but the big point was made: they were doomed, and if we kids ever so much as set foot inside one of their churches, so were we. Oh, and only *after* the ceiling caved in. I'm not sure that the nun who told me this was the same one who told my First Communion class about the man who kept the wafer in his mouth until he got home, where he sliced the host in half, causing it to bleed furiously and drown his entire town. But she had the same way of telling a story that would stick, one that would keep me far from the doorways of non-Catholic churches, and my pity upon those who did enter.

In the thirty-five years since my last year of parochial school, I've stepped inside only a handful of Protestant churches. My job as a reporter and my life as an adult brought a few occasions that found me walking through doorways and always, always giving a look ceilingward. I came away with no big impressions except that my pity for congregants' fates had been replaced by a pity for the lack of decor in their surroundings. Raised in a church thick with frescoes, friezes, paintings, and statues, I found sad the expanses of plain walls, the bland or nonexistent altars.

So I never had any great desire to tour the non-Catholic world until 2005, when Pope John Paul II died. I viewed his televised wake incessantly. Sitting on the couch at home, I stared at the screen. I drove to my mother's and watched it with her. Back home, I flipped it on again. Waking at night to use the bathroom, I clicked on the TV, and he was still there.

Certainly, Pope John Paul II had been an enormous presence in both my Roman Catholic religion and my Polish American ethnic community, where in 1978 bells rang literally and metaphorically at the news that a man from our ancestral homeland had been elected, and similar celebrations marked each anniversary, milestone, crisis, and renewal in his twenty-six-year papacy. There's no denying that he had a big hand in bringing an end to Communism in Poland, and on a personal note, I'd always thought he resembled my maternal grandfather, so I had several additional reasons to be struck by his passing.

But his mourners really were what grabbed me. Innumerable, jamming the streets for miles, singing, sobbing, smiling, praying, silent, focused. Humanity being what it is, enough of them were there just to say they'd been there and to snap a picture of his corpse. But the majority looked crushed. As a Catholic who in recent years had experienced a spiritual disconnect, I felt a true homesickness for that level of passion.

When you're born, your parents give you maybe three things that might last. Unless you go into showbiz or crime—or, hey, the papacy—the name you're given is the one you keep. And where you're born is often where you stay. What you're told is the third thing: your basic beliefs, some sort of faith. Certainly, we all have our periods of rebellion, but a child brought up to revere the sun and the earth might just feel guided by them for the rest of her life. The one instructed to look inward for comfort and guidance just might do that for good. The one told about an all-powerful guy in the sky might look up in good times and bad. I was given the guy in the sky, and I've stuck with him for forty-seven years now.

In one of my earliest memories, I am sitting with that pope-resembling maternal grandfather—my *dziadziu*—in his living room downstairs. He is pointing to the ceiling and teaching me the word for God. "*Boże*," he says over and again. "*Boże*." His finger aims in the direction of a round knob that decorated the center of the ceiling, covering the hole where a lamp once hung. *Dziadziu* is telling me "God," but I am thinking "knob." It took a while for me to finally catch on—maybe getting it when he gave me the same lesson outdoors, beneath the infinite sky—but the word was the same, as was the idea. That up there, somewhere, past our view, is a heavenly father who loves and guides us and in time will make sense of everything, so there's no need for you to go worrying, just go out and play. God and I might have had our disagreements, but I've never stopped loving and believing in him, and over the years I have pulled him a lot closer, seating him next to me as I fly off on vacation, across from me as I nervously await a dental appointment, in the front row as I begin a book reading. For me, he's a lot clearer when I can lay eyes on him, and as challenging as it can be at times, I try to remember that all I need to do to get a glimpse of him is look at any person I encounter.

But for most of my life, my view of God was a bit more by the book. I attended church, and those four decades of Sundays were an opportunity to sit and be grateful for all the good things in my life.

As crazy busy as the rest of a week could get, and as tangled as my do-nine-things-at-once personality could make me, I counted on church as a place where I'd be forced to sit and ponder the past seven days. But in my forties, cloudy forces like those drawn on a weather map converged to create a version of the private soul storm most people encounter at some point in adulthood.

While I held on to my parents' gift of God, it was his house that I came to find problematic. Like most things made by the hand of humans, it has its flaws, and for me they came to the greatest light at the same time I was having a few issues of my own.

In the 1990s, my husband spent four years investigating and reporting for our local newspaper the case of a priest who was a prime suspect in the murder of a local altar boy. Tommy's work was among the earliest to bring a clerical sex-abuse case into print, and over the years that followed, the problem was found to be a blight in churches not just across our state but throughout the world. Discovery of the deception practiced by so very many of the men in charge of my religion made me look anew at the place that was my spiritual home. Crashing into that wave of disgust and disappointment was an urgent need to look at the choices in my life. Because, for the first time, my health was in danger.

At forty-one I was diagnosed with breast cancer. Some people run to religion when they're ill; I went in the opposite direction. Fear of death propelled me, as did anger that the tidy little cart of my life had been upset. I returned home from Mass one Saturday evening to a phone message from a friend asking if I was OK—somebody had told her they'd seen me crying in church. Though displayed in a public place in my little village, my anguish had been meant only for God. I continued to attend church, but only when services weren't being held, sinking into the peace of the silent space that began to feel right for me at the time—as it continued to over the four years that followed. Right up to those April nights in 2005 when I found myself glued to coverage of the pope's wake, and suddenly very much wanting what those in St. Peter's Square had.

The essence of what it was about those crowds in Rome that so drew me was the devotion I saw in their faces. I began to wonder why they'd be so focused on this one man and religion, when there are so many others to choose from. I had never had to choose, or thought to choose, or been interested in choosing. But now, four years after floating away from organized religion, I got the idea that I might want to go on a pilgrimage of sorts, tour a few other houses of worship, finally find out just what goes on in those churches I grew up forbidden to enter, and understand what makes for devotion to a religious community. Rather than sit quietly by myself in an empty church, I would, for a day, be part of a congregation once again.

"Write about it." Tommy was making the suggestion he does each time something really thrills, intrigues, or bothers me. I'm a writer by trade, so the comment made sense. And never one to do things by halves, I decided to make the few more than a few. So I'm headed off to a year of weekly services in non–Roman Catholic churches, focusing on Protestant denominations among the choices in the wide world of worship because they are the ones I've always wondered about. I want to know what makes Methodists different from Dunkers, Shakers from Quakers, Seventh-Day Adventists from Foursquare Gospelists, and what in general makes these and the rest of America's estimated twenty-five hundred Protestant denominations Protestant in the first place. I want to learn what makes other Christian churches different from the Catholic one in which I was raised. I fully realize there's an entire world of religion, but I'm skipping such majors as Judaism and Islam to focus on the many forms of the "banned" Christian faiths of my childhood.

My goal is to experience the services as a worshipper who's just wandering inside, rather than as a special guest on a mission. I won't phone ahead and ask for a press kit, nor will I mention my project while there. I want to get the first-timer's first impression, and will rely on a single visit to harvest that. So it's with a pilgrim's prayer that I begin my year of stepping inside traditional tiny chapels and increasingly popular megachurches, and houses of worship of all sizes in between, experiencing what they have to offer beneath ceilings that, with God's help, will hold.

PART ONE: SPRING

New Mount Zion Baptist Church, New York, New York

Colorado Springs Cowboy Church, Colorado Springs, Colorado

First Baptist Church, Spartanburg, South Carolina

Arch Street Friends Meeting House, Philadelphia, Pennsylvania

First Church of Christ, Scientist, Boston, Massachusetts

St. Spyridon Greek Orthodox Church, Newport, Rhode Island

Cadet Chapel, United States Military Academy, West Point, New York

Trinity Evangelical Church, Peterborough, New Hampshire

Trinity Episcopal Church by-the-Sea, Kihei, Maui, Hawaii

South Royalton Ward Meetinghouse, South Royalton, Vermont

St. Sebastian Catholic Church, Baltimore, Maryland

NEW MOUNT ZION BAPTIST CHURCH

NEW YORK, NEW YORK

"Happy Resurrection Sunday!"

The greeting is a new one for me, but far from the most unusual thing about this particular morning.

Yes, it is the Sunday on which Christians celebrate Jesus's Resurrection, but I'm used to hearing plain old "Happy Easter." At the church in which I was raised, add to that *"Wesołego Alleluja!"* and *"Chrystus zmartwychwstał!"* But I'm not in Polish America anymore. Ten minutes earlier, the Manhattan Transit Authority's Number 2 subway delivered Tommy and me forty-five minutes north from our hotel in trendy Tribeca to 135th Street in Harlem. Tommy's Celtic DNA usually makes him the least pigmented person in a roomful of even the most blinding Caucasians, but right now both he and I are the palest people around.

The contrast is not unexpected. I had wanted this Easter morning to be the polar opposite of my traditional church experience, in location, building, congregants, and worship. So on Holy Saturday, Tommy and I traveled south three and a half hours by train, leaving our quiet New England village of 1,992 for a city teeming with 8 million. Rather than attend Catholic Mass at a middle-class, 99 percent Caucasian, Polish American church one mile up the street, where the biggest neighborhood problem is the installation of a sewer pipe slowing traffic outside its doors, I would visit a Baptist church ministering to an economically challenged, largely African

American community in which, one late afternoon earlier this week just a couple of blocks away, a homeless woman had been murdered on the street. Songs, prayers, and readings delivered in Polish would be traded for English; Eastern European pomp for swaying, shouting, and drum banging.

And it was the beat that told us we were headed in the right direction. "I think I hear music," Tommy said as we turned off Seventh Avenue at the Met Foodmart and started up 140th, walking past a playground in progress and a row of neat brick apartment houses. Across from a senior center stood the eighty-one-year-old New Mount Zion Baptist Church, a small sandstone-colored brick building sandwiched between two more sets of apartments. I felt a zip of excitement. This slender, unassuming church with one of its two doors already open would be the start of my pilgrimage. Where would I stand in a year? What would I carry in my head and heart and soul by then? I took in the triptych-style stained-glass window rising two stories above the open door; the white cross jutting perpendicular to announce New Mount Zion to all who pass; the roof that rises to a crossless point, its apex framing a round-topped opening revealing a patch of Caribbean-blue sky. Cars edged the front walk, where half a dozen adults stood chatting, dressed in the kind of glitzy attire I am more used to seeing on parents of the bride than on people headed to church—even on such an auspicious morn.

When I'd phoned the previous week to ask how early we might need to arrive to get a seat, the receptionist had answered with a peppy, "This is the day the Lord has made, let us rejoice and be glad in it!" and gave the 10:45 starting time. I was surprised when she said I need not arrive any more than fifteen minutes early. For Polish Catholics, Easter is the biggest holiday on the church calendar, topping even Christmas. I'm accustomed to arriving a good forty-five minutes ahead of time on a day that sees wall-to-wall crowds, including worshippers who might have stayed away the rest of the year but who are here today doing what's known as Easter duty. To this day, a version of the same Easter procession in which I walked four decades ago in my red-and-green grammar school uniform and First Communion veil still helps mark the morning, as Confraternity of Christian Doctrine students join the choir, societies, altar servers, and priest in circling the church to resounding hymns brought over from the old country: *"Wstał Pan Chrystus," "Wesoły Nam Dzień Dziś Nastał."* When it comes to this morning's service, I have no idea what to expect. My just-as-white-and-just-as-Polish-Catholic cousin Joanne, whose marriage to a Jamaican man inspired her to investigate a range of black cultural experiences, recommended New Mount Zion after a service there drove her both to musical rapture and soul-sprung tears. Whatever was going to happen for me, I wanted to experience it inside the building, rather than in front of the flat-panel TV screen in the entryway. So Tommy and I stepped through the doorway to our first "Happy Resurrection Day!" I'd responded with the familiar "Happy Easter," as I'd not yet sat through the two-hour-and-fifteen-minute service in which I'd learn the term to use.

It was not the first lesson of this trip. The day before, I discovered that it's not such a great idea to hang your belongings in that little closet at the front of the Amtrak car. Because, in the excitement of arrival in New York City, it's easy to breeze right past that closet without retrieving your stuff, which means that, come Resurrection Day, you may be walking into church wearing your baggy green L.L. Bean raincoat rather than your nicest blazer. Would that normally matter? Not in the churches I know. Catholic chic has changed drastically in my lifetime, the meaning of Sunday best morphing from suits and ties for men and nylons and dresses and even gloves for women, to a unisex combo of baggy Levi's and Red Sox hoodies. Attire certainly can be a way of honoring your creator, but in this day and age of shrinking church attendance, might it not be more important to celebrate that someone has shown up at all rather than that she's shown up in Gucci? Not so at New Mount Zion, where rows of women in pastel suits embellished with pearls, lace, embroidery, and sequins adjust the angles of their wide-brimmed flower-bedecked hats with hands swathed in matching-color gloves, and men in suits of sherbety tones, spotless white, and dramatic black remove fedoras as they step over the threshold with mirror-finish shoes. Even the toddlers are decked out: the boys seem ready for a day on Wall Street in their three-piece suits; the girls in layers of fluff and yards of ribbon are treasures from a confectioner's window. Tommy and I, in black corduroys and blue skirt, respectively, move self-consciously, our matching green ripstop nylon making loud sawing sounds. We quickly choose a pew—third from the back in the right-hand-most of three sections of seats—and just as quickly are greeted again.

"Welcome! Happy Resurrection Sunday!" This from a fortyish woman in the aisle, glowing in a night-cream-pink suit with flowing bell-shaped cuffs. "Welcome to New Mount Zion!"

"Greetings! Praise Jesus!" This from an older lady in disco-gold dress and jacket, who sidesteps her way between pews.

"Happy Resurrection Sunday! We're glad you're here." This from a middle-aged woman curiously attired as a nurse. Fitted white dress, matching hose and shoes, a white skullcap pinned to her hair with white bobby pins. From above her left breast dangles a badge, silver, with the words NEW MOUNT ZION, and a name—JOHNSON. Her white-gloved hands grasp ours solidly. Nurse Johnson then steps the few yards to the back of the church, where she joins three other women in matching dress.

Never have Tommy or I been made so instantly welcome in a church. Or comfortable. These pews are upholstered—an odd luxury to Catholic haunches used to hard wooden benches. You could easily relax here for a few hours without having to shift around—or even get up for a Kleenex: full boxes await on every windowsill, a fresh sheet puffed out like the wing of a dove. And the absence of kneelers makes for a novel amount of legroom. As I settle in, the sun's rays brighten the white walls, accented with blond wood, and turn up the contrast on the four pairs of stained-glass windows that pop color along each side wall, beginning at the main level, continuing up through the balcony and ending in a peak just beneath an arching dark wood ceiling. My focus lingers there. I check for cracks announcing our presence, as I will in each and every church I attend this year. I see none—but it's early yet. I turn my attention to the front of the building. In my church, that's the location of the big altar on which stand life-size statues of Saints Peter and Paul flanking a similarly sized Jesus. When we students were assembled in the church and the nun in charge went into the sacristy, it was rumored she climbed inside the Saint Paul to spy on bad behavior.

Up front at New Mount Zion, there's not a statue to be seen. Instead, a pair of wide wooden organs bookend a drum kit cozy in its Plexiglas surround. One level up, behind a metal railing through which half a dozen lilies throw their thickly scented blossoms, hangs a choir loft of a space, a big wooden pulpit at its center. The loft is empty right now, but there's a feeling that the start is near. More and more worshippers file in, some women in furs, several carrying tambourines, many holding Bibles the size of the Manhattan phone book. For the unequipped, tucked into the wooden pocket in the back of each pew are red hardcover copies of the New International Version of the Bible and the *New National Baptist Hymnal* used by what is currently the second-largest religious group in the country, with an estimated membership of 90 million worldwide—47 million of them in the U.S.A.; that's one in five Americans. This post-Reformation movement was founded in Holland in 1609 by John Smyth, a former Anglican priest who preached the "believer's baptism" of total water immersion at the age of informed adulthood, rather than the symbolic splash on the forehead in spiritually unconscious infancy. Second only to the Roman Catholic Church in American membership, and second worldwide to the Pentecostals, whose ranks are zooming due to evangelism in Asia, Africa, Latin America, and eastern Europe, this country's fifty Baptist organizations include the divisions of Southern, American, and Conservative.

Pretty sure I'm not going to know any of the words, I ask Tommy if he can reach a copy of the hymnal. The woman in the pew in front of us turns and asks, "What you need, baby?" Pretty sure she knows all the words, she hands me hers.

I browse the program we were given at the door, seven unstapled pages behind a cover color photo of the sun rising and the words "Christ is risen Alleluia!" Page 1 is the order of worship, which lists the prayers, hymns, announcements, and the theme for the sermon: "Turning Grief into Joy."

A cloud of white suits walks slowly up the aisle. This is the choir—men and women of all ages—lining up as the Reverend Dr. Carl L. Washington Jr. lifts a microphone at the front of the church. He wears an ornate long-sleeved black coat that flows to the ground with a few interruptions of decorative white stripes and piping. He looks to be in his late fifties, balding, mustachioed, and tall, and maybe it is the slimming black, but he is rotund in a way you don't notice until he angles sideways. He speaks loudly and deeply and sincerely: "We give thanks to the Lord for the gifts he brings. For his mercy endures forever." Here he slows—"Spirit of the living God" —then pauses before imploring, "fall fresh on me."

His delivery is dramatic and effective, the words given their own time and emphasis, as if he placed them each inside individual boats for the trip to our ears. The organ hums softly before the choir repeats three times in drawn-out majesty: *Spi-rit of the liv-ing God, fa-all fresh on me.*

The organ kicks in at a punchy pace and heads throughout the church nod as the choir fills the front and faces the congregation in three long, loose lines. The congregation, now standing, claps, shimmies, raises arms, agitates tambourines. From the balcony on down, throughout the church, nearly everyone sings along: *Be praised forever. Be praised forever. Be praised forever, and ever more . . .*

I'm sold. This is, in short, fun. You can move. You can be moved. If you remembered ahead of time to bring it along, you can beat on your own bongo. Tommy and I exchange the same delighted smiles and wide eyes we do at the start of a concert we weren't sure would be any good. This is the most noise I've ever heard in a church. And it is very cool noise. Especially because none of it is scripted—thanks to John Smyth, who decried as sinful any worship involving a text. At Mass, I'm used to holding a missalette and following along, reading in not-too-jazzed monotone the lines prefaced by the prompt "ALL." Here, I am one of maybe 350, allowed and encouraged to shout whatever the heck I am moved to shout—not that I have yet. For now I stand and marvel as the song concludes to applause and "Praise Jesus!" and "Glory!" and "Amen!" Pastor Washington invites us to join in the Lord's Prayer, which is the same Our Father I've been saying all my life, except for veering off to a "for-thine-is-the-Kingdom-and-the-power-and-the-glory" ending, where I'm used to a conclusion of "and lead us not into temptation, but deliver us from evil. Amen."

The ending used here, from the 1662 Anglican Book of Common Prayer, jolts me anew to my setting. I glance heavenward. The ceiling remains intact. The choir launches into a song in which *praise him* and *lift him up* are repeated many times. From their seats throughout the main floor, various women take to their feet and jostle tambourines. Maybe twenty additional people choose to stand. You move as the spirit sparks you, sitting or cheering; there is nothing stating that all should respond with a hum or a thank you, Jesus, or an amen. Response issues from the congregants, with conviction and in celebration.

As the choir begins to step from side to side in time with the slowed, trilling organ, a middle-aged woman in the right-hand section of the choir begins to sing. Her voice is at once enormous and intimate, and a ringer for Phoebe Snow's. *Li-ving, he loved me,* she tells us. *Dy-ing, he saved me . . .* The choir backs her but she needs no help or filler. The congregation is seated now and the beauty of her voice is melting us into the seat cushions. Three rows ahead, a man nods to the slow beat, and even from behind I can sense his sadness. He sticks out as one of the relatively few adult males present among the hundreds of women and children, and women and teens—most of the teens female—in the congregation. The pastor now appears on the second tier, joined to his right by a younger, thin, and totally bald man in a dark brocade tunic, and to his rear by another of the women in the nurse's outfits, with a traditional peaked cap right out of *Doctor Kildaire*. Things look serious—these men have their own medical crew. But their messages are delivered as joyously as those of the rest of the morning. Guests are asked to stand, and twenty-two do, Tommy and I and a man in the balcony the only whites. Faces turn, smile. We are applauded. More shouts: "Welcome to Zion!"

Next comes the sort of housekeeping I'm used to hearing at the beginning of a Mass. The death of a niece in South Carolina is mentioned, and those who reached out to two bereaved families in the past week are thanked. A Christian education trip to Buffalo will leave the following morning. "I just want to remind you who are going to Buffalo to be on time," the pastor says. "We're leaving at five thirty, y'all, Amen?"

"Amen," the congregation answers.

Presentations of floral bouquets are made to two of the oldest women in the congregation. Mother Maxwell and Mother Tally stand as teen boys sweetly deliver the gifts. In the program I notice that the list of ill and shut-in church members includes names prefaced with the designations "minister," "trustee," and "sister." In my Catholic upbringing, "sister" means nun. But I've been called Sister Shea by a black friend who grants her female friends that title. On this list, Sister Dorothy Nibbs, Sister Mable Runchess, and Sister Louvenia Kelly maybe aren't sisters, but they are indeed Sisters.

Whatever your title, in this church you are expected to tithe. That's a major topic in the bulletin; page 4 covers the practice, defined as an "external, material testimony of God's ownership of the material and spiritual things of our lives." The fact that you can find the word "tithe" in Genesis 14, and in twenty-eight subsequent Old Testament locations, is noted, as is the fact that *tithe* translates from Hebrew and Greek to "tenth." Which boils down to an expectation to donate to the church a tenth of one's time, talent, and, yes, finances.

I'd never heard much about the topic in my church, other than the word mentioned in a few Gospel readings. But collections have been taken at every Mass I've attended, via a basket at the end of a long stick that an usher spooned through each pew. Here, congregants walk row by row to a small table in front of the drum kit and deposit their donations onto a brass plate.

The pastor then takes to the pulpit and gives a scripture reading, a mere two lines that end with, "And we do not know where they have laid him." He throws in "Amen?" And we all respond "Amen!" Because I'm accustomed to a Mass that includes readings from both the Old and New Testaments, with a little commercial break of a responsorial psalm in between, this seems brief. But I find out that it simply allows for additional sermon time. Like wardrobes, Catholic sermons have changed in my lifetime, from lengthy and preachy to short and some form of sweet. The faithful might want to attend Mass, but they also in the same day want to attend a meal out, a movie, a half-off sale at the mall. I know this because I've been guilty, guilty, and, finally, guilty of all the above. But there is no rush at New Mount Zion, where the pastor now invites everyone to stand, "For this is the time for prayer."

Congregants take to their feet and step toward the aisle—into it if they were at the end of a pew. The woman in gold who'd greeted us earlier is back, holding her hand out to Tommy, who is flipping through his program. Thinking she wants to read it, he offers her the copy. She shakes her head and gestures smilingly for him to accompany her.

Tommy takes her hand and becomes a link in the chain of energy that is running through the building. He reaches for my left hand. My right dangles without a thing to do, so I look behind me just as I feel someone take hold of it. In the last few right-hand pews of New Mount Zion Church, both a physical and spiritual connection runs through our small circle of strangers, who don't seem to be that any longer. "Right now, Lord, I'm asking you to bless the bereaved families, because they need you," a woman at the front of the church is imploring into the microphone. "We're asking you to come to us. Go into the hospitals, onto the street corners, every place."

Hands part only to pass along tissues. The lone man several rows up hangs his head. Suddenly, a woman in a salmon-colored suit near the end of his pew is overcome, gripping the edge of the pew and wavering as a nurse and two nearby women catch her. She sobs as they gingerly walk her to the back of the church, then encircle and hold her, praying: "I love you, Jesus. I love you, Jesus." At the front of the church, the Phoebe Snow woman returns. *I'm born again,* she sings, *free from sin, because of the blood.*

The choir chimes in. The woman in salmon, repaired now, claps as she returns to her seat, just in time for the sermon. "We stand outside the tombs of life, weeping over lost hope, lost dreams, lost meanings," Pastor Washington begins.

"Mmm-hmms" reverberate.

"Wouldn't you feel strange if you went to the cemetery days after you buried a loved one? And found the grave empty?"

"Yes!"

"If you lived in the twenty-first century, you would go back to the one you had entrusted with the care of your loved one, and you wouldn't go back there smiling, because your grief would have been turned to sorrow because you know you were there when they put him in the ground. The story of Mary Magdalene is the story of how God turns grief into joy. How God opens tombs."

"Mmm-hmm!"

Nurse Johnson advances to distribute fans to several older women halfway up the aisle as the pastor tells the story of Mary Magdalene's home of Magdala. "It was known for its wealth and its immorality," he says. "Its wealth and its immorality." He pauses before adding, "Mary coulda come from New York, y'all!"

Applause.

Next to the pastor, the younger minister is hopping, clapping. It is a delight to witness the joy he expresses, as it is to see that he is able to jump around in a church without anyone shooting him a dirty look. Others join him, sporadically leaping from their seats to applaud or wave. One young woman from the choir pogos.

I'm struck by the layers of the sermon. We're getting a retelling of the two lines of the Gospel, but we're also getting history.

"She was the first to hear the angelic announcement: 'He is not here but he has risen.' "

"Mmm-hmm!"

"That first person was a woman. A woman, y'all. Rescued from a life of open shame." Then there's another pause, and just in case there's any doubt, he adds, "She was a whore, y'all. That's what she was. She was grateful to the man who had plucked her back from the living dead, and she joined the group that followed him. He singled her out as the first to share the astounding news, 'I have seen the Lord.' He entrusted that to a previously obscure woman and one who, by first-century standards, was least qualified."

The reverend has his theory for the choice. "Imagine—God gave the Word to a woman," he says. "Because all the men were hiding." Then he gives a shot to the absent males. "Same thing happening here this morning. The men are at home waiting for Mary to come home and tell 'em what happened."

"Aha!"

He alternately reads from a prepared text and riffs on an idea. As the minutes pass, he increases in energy as well as volume. "Amen," shouts one of the nurses in the back. "Keep it real!"

A few rows ahead, the lone man is turned to the window at his right.

"I want to pause this morning to tell you that welfare will not turn your grief into joy. Winning the megalottery will not turn your grief into joy. Getting a better job will not turn your grief into joy. Making the wrong right will. I came here on Resurrection Sunday. The God that I serve has already turned my grief into joy."

More and more people take to their feet, raise arms. At the pulpit, the nurse hands a towel to the younger preacher, who passes it to the reverend, who mops his face and then drapes the cloth around his neck, boxerlike.

"This is the most depressed country in the world," he says emphatically. "With all that we have we cannot be satisfied. We have people who own BMWs driving off bridges. People with houses in the Hamptons molesting their own children. Having Jesus in your life is the only way to make sense of this world."

There is whooping, applause, shouts of "Praise Him" and "Right!" The reverend's reply: "I invite you all to Jesus."

This has to be the "born again" moment recognized by evangelical Protestants but not an issue in the Catholic world, where you're baptized as an infant and that'll do you. These folks follow John 3:5, in which Jesus says, "Truly, truly, I say to you, unless one is born of water and the Spirit, he cannot enter the Kingdom of God."

People answering the call begin to rise. A man and a woman. A mother and toddler. A chubby young man. The reverend coaches them forward, calling in a now-raw voice, "Look at Jesus. He'll turn it. He'll turn it."

I look at the man a few rows ahead. Like most of us he is on his feet, but he is wracked with sobs, his face in both hands, still turned toward the window as if he might vanish through it. I think of Cousin Joanne weeping in these seats. The sight of this man is what triggers my tears. What has brought him to this point? Which of the reverend's comments has so affected him? No nurses tend to him as they earlier had rushed to the worshipper at the end of his row. The white-suited woman to his left doesn't acknowledge his anguish. Perhaps he is a stranger to her. Or perhaps she knows him too well.

"Lookit Jesus, lookit Jesus," the reverend continues, now on the ground floor, greeting the tearful parade walking toward the front of the church, up a few steps, and through a side door to the right of the organs. I wonder what they'll be doing back there, but I'm not so curious as to join them. I remain seated, watching the man a few rows ahead, wishing I could do something for him. The pastor tells us, "The people in front of you have problems, too. Everyone has been a sinner. Nobody's exempt. When you really get saved, you don't care what people know."

"Jesus!" shouts a woman.

"Jesus!" echoes someone else.

The man is absolutely in turmoil now. Still, no one extends a hand.

"If you come up today, you won't be an Easter Christian," the reverend says. "I used to be one of those. I came on Mother's Day because it made my ma happy. Easter because it was expected. Not on Father's Day—I sent a big monetary gift and that made him happy. Not on Christmas, either. I showed up on New Year's Day because I thought it was good luck. Let me tell you, your luck can run out."

"Amen!"

"There are many who are unsaved. They just been in church all their life. They don't understand that not accepting Jesus is just as bad as not going to church at all."

The choir starts up: *God has been, God has been, God has been so good to me.*

The door to the right of the organ opens and those who'd disappeared a few moments before are returning. There is booming applause and the organ cranks in volume. The man at the window raises both hands in the air, shaking. I can't tell from behind him if his grief has been transformed to joy, but it's the most unburdened he's appeared this morning. The pastor stands among those who've returned. Names are announced. Five who've just been born again, ten who'll be back for baptism within the month. All are weeping.

"Somebody has to shout hallelujah!" invites the pastor. In keeping with how this morning started, he reminds members of their duty: "These are the newest babies in our families. I don't want any of you to leave here without introducing yourself to them. Amen?"

"Amen."

To a jumble of organ music, the reverend calls out, "The God that I serve has already turned my grief into joy. Picked me up and turned me around . . . Have I got a witness in the house who can say he has turned my grief to joy?"

He's yelling now. Feverishly intense. "How can you sit there when the Lord has healed you, delivered you, set you free?"

There is applause, hallelujahs.

"Mary's message to us is joy!"

Fans shuttle the air.

"If the Lord lifted you up this morning, started you on your way, gave you eyes to see, ears to hear, legs to walk, a voice to talk, shout yeaaaahhh!"

"Yeaaaahhh!"

"If the Lord kept you all week, lay awake for you when everybody else stayed away, shout yeaaaahhh!"

The response is off the meter. The pastor is drenched. Some of his words are fuzzed by the volume being shot into the microphone, but there is no doubt about the message. "He's all right, I tell you! He's all right. Anybody here know he's all right? Say 'He's all right!' "

We say it, shout it.

"He's all right! Look at somebody real quick and say 'He's all right!' "

I look at Tommy. On this Resurrection Sunday, he is all right, and so am I. Skyward I lift my eyes a final time. The ceiling of this Protestant church is intact above these 350, including two who were raised to never step beneath it. It's as solid as the faith that fills this place, and that can't help but start to work its way into every soul that's open even a hair. I know I can feel it washing into mine. And I wonder if that's what all those childhood warnings were about—the fear that another church might offer such a balm? I don't know what to say at this early stage. Except that when the reverend asks "Amen?" I answer—no, I shout—"Amen!"

COLORADO SPRINGS COWBOY CHURCH

COLORADO SPRINGS, COLORADO

The sign at the front door of the Pro Rodeo Hall of Fame warns me not to "eat, drink, smoke, or chew." I pass it for another nearby green-on-white placard pointing a helpful arrow toward a courtyard with a tourist's-dream view of Pikes Peak. To the right, a woman and a boy circle lassos over their heads. To the left, a man in a cowboy hat, dress shirt, jeans, and boots chomps a doughnut. Passing a metal-fenced corral, a cowboy-hatted woman walks toward the hall's Hal Littrell World Champions' Pavilion. I follow her inside, to this morning's service of the Colorado Springs Cowboy Church.

In the 1800s, this cactus-root ministry got its very informal start on the range. Though the original aim of the Cowboy Church was to serve the spiritual needs of cowboys as well as ranchers, farmers, and rodeo types, the lure of the buckaroo lifestyle has drawn many whose only horsepower is beneath the hoods of their SUVs. The church's roaming preachers more recently have led services in the civic centers and state fair buildings of the modern rodeo circuit. Prayers for a fixed home were answered in the early 1980s, with Billy Bob's Texas nightclub in Fort Worth, said to be the site of the first modern cowboy church, where world champion calf roper Jeff Copenhaver preached to a few hundred people every Sunday night. An estimated two hundred cowboy churches exist in the United States. Additional communities meet in Canada and Mexico, and as "outback churches" in Australia. In a fittingly maverick way, few are connected to any distinct branch of Christianity, and membership numbers are unknown.

I am thrilled by the church's name, having spent my childhood in one of two uniforms—that of Sts. Peter and Paul grammar school and the American cowgirl, switching each weekday afternoon from plaid jumper, clip-on bow tie, and beanie to fringed shirt, jeans, boots, five-gallon hat, and Annie Oakley holster.

"Make her wear something else!" I remember my older sister pleading to my parents.

Happily for me they didn't, and dressed for the Wild West I accompanied my family everywhere short of church. This morning, that childhood getup would have fit right in at the church I'm visiting while at a writing conference literally two blocks away. Wardrobe is Marlboro Man, many worshippers in big-belt-buckled jeans, neat long-sleeved plaid shirts with pearly snaps and piping, and, of course, cowboy hats and boots, even though the slogan is "All are welcome—with or without boots!" A woman in a good-guy white hat calls out, "Welcome to the Cowboy Church!" as she leaves a couple of three-year-olds to play on Navajo rugs encircled by folding chairs.

"Welcome to the Cowboy Church," says an older man at the coffee urn. I ask him how many worshippers might be expected and he tells me, "Some days twenty-five, some days forty. They straggle in. Just like a bunch of cowboys."

"I wanted to come here because I always wanted to be a cowboy," I excitedly tell a woman at the pastry tray.

"We get lots of that," she answers flatly.

The church's population of actual cowboys? "One," she calculates. "That one there. He has thirty-five acres."

In ball cap and hiking shoes, he's also the only one not wearing a shred of traditional attire.

I wander to the literature table set up in front of windows giving a wide view of the Rockies that, to this easterner, look like giant photographs taped up for my pleasure. Rough and brown-gray, their creases are contrasted by jags of snow leading to Pikes Peak.

Immediately before me is God's Box, a heavy-looking dark wood bread-loaf-size container ready for the nearby envelopes marked TITHER and printed with the passage "The tenth shall be holy unto the Lord—Lev. 27:32." I wonder why the chairs aren't facing this mountain view instead of the dark end of the room, where guitar chords are twanging out our invitation to the 10:59 service.

From the last row of the right-hand-most section of one hundred white plastic gray-metal-legged chairs, their backs stamped with the word LIFETIME, I take in a stone fireplace lit from above by a giant chandelier made of pointy animal horns. An American flag stands to the left of the fireplace. A movie screen on the opposite side glows with "Howdy! Welcome to Colorado Springs Cowboy Church" and an image of a cowboy, horse, and cloth-wrapped cross backlit by the sun. At a pulpit made of rough-hewn wood draped with a woven blanket on which a Bible rests, a trim thirtyish black-hatted guy holds a guitar. His name is Brian. His wife, Lynn, in another good-guy white hat, is at the electric keyboard. Another man in a hat sits at the electric drums. A third takes up the bass.

The congregation stands. Headwear is removed.

"We thank you very much for this church," prays Brian, "that you have chosen brothers and sisters for us to walk with for the weekend."

"Amen," somebody says, and hats are replaced.

Brian can sing quite well, and we follow him, prompted by the words displayed in green on the screen: *As for me and my house, we will serve the Lord.*

This is another church in which people aren't afraid to sing. We number twenty now, and we are loud and following the rockish beat. The manner in which we're scattered about the room makes for a less intimate experience than last week's, but there's no lack of intensity from the regulars, who shut eyes tightly and raise hands in praise and prayer.

"Amen! I love working for God!" Brian concludes brightly. "You know, we're all called to serve God. Maybe you don't get to preach. But if you do what God says, you will find that your life gets better."

A young man claims the chair two to my right. Between us rests his Bible, its black zip cover printed with the emblem of the Fellowship of Christian Cowboys.

"Let the weak say 'I am strong,' " Brian starts as he strums slowly and softly. The lyrics are projected over a photograph of a waterfall. The teen boy who was lassoing outside is now minding the little kids in the corral of chairs. A teen girl enters the hall with what might be her grandmother. The girl carries a Bible and an iPod with fluorescent orange earpieces.

Lynn steps from the keyboard to the pulpit to offer announcements. A clothing drive has resulted in a wealth of Wranglers in sizes for both men and women. Someone taps my shoulder.

"I'm David," says a tall, dark-featured man in white hat and shirt, jeans and boots. He offers a Bible, a little cowboy-themed one open to Matthew.

"You can keep this," he tells me.

Published by the Colorado Springs–based International Bible Society, my gift is a New Testament titled *The Way for Cowboys,* and it is tiny enough for back pocket or bootleg. The cover photo is a saddle and lasso slung over a fence, and the contents include cowboy/faith-flavored stories from rodeo types, among them country singing star Reba McEntire's look-alike baby sister, Susie Luchsinger, who preaches at cowboy services.

"Kids of all ages dream of being a cowboy," the first few pages don't need to remind me. "No time clocks to punch, no tests in school, no concrete jungle of high-rise buildings, no blaring horns, no traffic jams. Just a good horse and wide-open spaces."

I close the Bible to listen as Brian speaks on the parable of the workers in the vineyard. The congregation has straggled to twenty-eight, all white but for an Asian teen boy, as Brian talks about how much the vineyard owner should pay those who worked the longest. David stands at the back of the room, dramatically silhouetted against the bright windows and the monstrous Rockies. The wind rattles the glass behind him. Brian reads about the vineyard owner telling his foreman to assemble the workers at the end of the day. "Pay them their wages, beginning with the last ones hired and going on to the first." Brian stops. "Anybody here have a problem with this?"

"It's unfair," says a woman seated in front of the one actual cowboy.

"That's right," Brian says. "Justice. The workers had a problem with it, too. Think about it—he was going to reward those who had shown up just before evening. They're not the first people you'd want to reward. Really, it's a terrible parable. We've got people who obviously do not deserve to get paid a day's wage. This is a big old insult to those who were there all day. Anybody upset?"

Heads and hats nod.

"But it's a parable about servanthood. And what do we learn? The key message is servanthood. The servanthood here is not the servant's, it's the master of the house's. What he saw was not what the workers deserved, but what they needed. So the last will be first, and the first will be last."

For me, it's a twist on this parable I've heard hundreds of times, a story that's always had me focus on the good fortune of the last-minute workers, getting in just under the wire, rather than on the reason the owner was so generous. It's also a twist on the thin expectations I had held for this oddly named church meeting in an oddly named space. As I nod goodbye to David and leave the service just before benediction to catch my plane, I'm hit by the reminder not to prejudge; that, in itself, is as much a Sunday-morning lesson as the one given from the pulpit.

FIRST BAPTIST CHURCH

SPARTANBURG, SOUTH CAROLINA

While selecting the houses of worship I would attend on my yearlong pilgrimage, I wanted to include some that featured female preachers.

"How about Billy Graham's daughter?" Tommy asked.

"He has one?" was my answer.

Yes, the world-famous eighty-one-year-old evangelist has not just one but three daughters in his brood of five. The second-oldest, fifty-two-year-old Anne Graham Lotz, a wife and a mother of three, has devoted thirty years to her own brand of the family business—though she'll be the first to note that she's not an evangelist, but an assistant in what she calls the "process postliberation from sin." Through her AnGeL Ministries, Anne makes approximately one hundred fee-free appearances annually, traveling the world to speak, preach, lead revivals, and generally talk up the love of God and committing one's life to him. Her ministry operates on a budget of $1.5

million and offers programs including "A Passionate Pursuit," three-day retreats for women honing their faith. As my AGL-savvy friend Elisabeth put it, "She is the alpha female of born-again women in America." I am not AGL savvy. But early on in life I was BG smart, because my grandparents were Billy Graham fans.

Anne's father was on my grandparents' Zenith every week of my childhood, it seemed, broadcast from exotic locales, his rugged face and mane filling the screen as he delivered his message in a hilly southern accent to football fields full of praying, singing, weeping faithful. I knew he wasn't Catholic, a dead giveaway being the lack of priests, altar boys, or altar itself. I wasn't interested in the seriousness of his presentations, but I was curious about the attention shown by my *babci* and *dziadziu*, who added themselves electronically to the approximately 210 million Graham preached to in more than 185 countries and territories over a fifty-five-year career that has included being spiritual adviser to every U.S. president since Eisenhower. Anne Graham Lotz is similarly on the go, and this Sunday she is at a Southern Baptist Convention church in Spartanburg, South Carolina.

The SBC would be hard to ignore while trolling the waters of Christianity. Though this country holds three times as many Catholics as Southern Baptists, SBC congregations outnumber those of any other faith. Organized in 1845 in Augusta, Georgia, it claims 16 million members in more than forty-two thousand U.S. churches. Congregations adhere to the Southern Baptist mission to proclaim the Gospel to the entire world. As is the case with other Baptist churches, the process of joining includes acceptance of Jesus as Savior and Lord, and baptism by immersion.

As the name suggests, the SBC is biggest in the South, where Baptists arrived at the end of the seventeenth century and where the Convention's domination has figured in local and state legislation, including prohibition of legalized gambling and alcohol sales. Its headquarters in Nashville is no Vatican: like other Baptist churches, SBC churches are autonomous. Apparently, they also can be very large. The enormous brick of First Baptist Spartanburg, or FBS, as it's known, takes up most of a city block. The steeple is the tallest thing in the area, if you ignore the pancake-colored high-rise across the street housing Denny's Corporate Headquarters. A walk around the FBS complex offers glimpses of a three-thousand-seat sanctuary, a library, classrooms, and a playground featuring a green-roofed plastic structure with a yellow-on-red sign proclaiming JESUS LOVES ME.

At 7:30 a.m. I follow a stream of worshippers through the church's front door. For the third consecutive weekend, I am instantly greeted. First by two older men, then, as I'm taking a bulletin from a third, I hear a small, formal voice saying, "I'm Ruby Powell. I'd be very pleased if you sat with me."

Ruby doesn't seem to be an official greeter—no nametag on her purple faux-suede skirt suit. But she's a pro at sussing out a newcomer and making her feel less obvious. We're not halfway up one of the two beige-carpeted aisles and Ruby's already saying she'd be very pleased if I attended Sunday school class.

To me, the term "Sunday school" has always meant the place Protestant kids went because, unlike my parochial school, their public schools did not include religious education.

"How old are the children you teach?"

"I don't teach," she chuckles. "I'm a student." Then she gestures to the left—"This is mine"—and we slip into a white-painted pew and onto a cushy blue-gray seat pad.

Along the ecru walls, detailed Bible scenes have been translated into stained glass, sweeping the eye back to the large balcony on which two men fuss with what looks like the controls of a PA system. Overhead, six enormous glass chandeliers light the space, assisted by modern fixtures aimed at the stage. Several video cameras point in the same direction.

According to Ruby, a twenty-five-year member of FBS, six thousand people worship here at the three Sunday services, beginning with the 8:00 a.m. Classic Worship that Ruby, well past retirement age, prefers due to its traditional hymns and presentation. A 9:30 and 10:50 Celebration Worship follow, more contemporary services making use of the instruments peeking from behind the greenery on the wide stage in front of us. Again, no altar, just a podium in front of that foliage and between pairs of large and comfortable-looking wood-framed chairs. Behind the plants, five elevated rows of wooden armchairs run the width of the stage. Above, a giant movie screen oddly shares space with a hand-lettered sign, WELCOME RACING FANS. Or maybe not so oddly: I am in NASCAR territory, judging from the racing theme of most every T-shirt and jacket I've seen since arriving in town. Black-and-white-checkered pennants festoon the back wall of the stage and carry the eye down to the door of an actual racecar (#98) just past the organ and baby grand.

To explain, Ruby points to an insert in her bulletin, which bears a photograph of the Earth and is titled "When God Speaks." Inside, the *Encourager Weekly Update* is headlined "Race to Win," the title of the 5:00 p.m. performance of the children's choir. Upcoming events include activities by seven ministries, including the adult New Friends BBQ, the men's rafting trip on the Nantahala River, and the students' second annual Tailgatin' Event—"Free Food! And Talk'n Football!" Guest speaker: Kevin Hynes, chaplain of the University of Georgia Bulldogs.

I flip the sheet to find "Let Us Pray Together," and lists of those at which to aim those prayers, complete with their current locations in hospitals and rehabilitation centers. "Christian Sympathy" is extended to the families of three recently deceased individuals, and twenty-one names float beneath the heading "Please Pray for Our Active Service Personnel."

Elsewhere, the bulletin announces a Man to Man Prayer Breakfast; DivorceCare; and a request for new king- and standard-size pillowcases, followed by an explanation: "These will be made into adorable church dresses and given to girls during our Kentucky mission trip. The cuter the pattern, the cuter the dress."

"This is a busy place," I say, and Ruby nods.

"Some people say 'I don't want to join First Baptist, it's too big.' But it's just that many more people to love you," she says, and grabs my right wrist in a hug.

When I tell Ruby that I'm here to hear Anne Graham Lotz, she laments, "I wish I knew you were coming. I would have brought you up to Billy Graham's house. We could have gone yesterday." She also would have put me up. She's used to being a hostess, Ruby tells me, working at the church's house for missionaries. "I change the beds, stock the pantry. I wish I knew you were coming!"

Two of Ruby's friends, toting Bibles and binders like so many others, take seats behind us, and I'm introduced, while up front, fifty choir members in blue robes file from stage right. The rest of the attire in the sanctuary is Sunday best. Not as grand as New Mount Zion, but nothing like the ready-for-ropin' of the Cowboy Church. Grooming is immaculate; many of the women sport Laura Bush bobs.

At the center of the stage, a choir leader stands and directs. The title "I Stand in Awe" floats onto the movie screen. Fittingly, the congregation stands. The choir's voices are full and rich and professional and if anyone else is singing they can't be heard.

From a doorway to the left of the stage, a string of men and women proceed to seats in the first few rows. I spot Anne Graham Lotz, even though I know her only from Internet photos, where she looks like her father in a silver-blond wig.

"That's Pastor Don," Ruby narrates as a dark-suited man takes his place to the left of the choir director. I know it's early and I might be looped from travel, but his accent appears to be a blend of southern and Australian as heads bow and he says, "We gather together on this Lord's Day to be with you in spirit and in truth."

Senior Pastor Don Wilton has been preaching for a dozen years at FBS. For the past two, his sermons have been shared with an additional 150,000 via *The Encouraging Word* television ministry, and an even wider audience since Easter of 2005, when FBS hit cable's Inspiration Network.

I will later learn that Pastor Don is a native of South Africa whose teaching experience includes stints at Billy Graham Schools of Evangelism worldwide, and whose travels include preaching at five hundred revivals and crusades in Africa alone. He's now preaching in a state that's roughly 30 percent African American, though in this service I spot among the crowd of approximately nine hundred only one person of color—a black man in the center of the choir.

Pastor Don also is the 2006 president of the South Carolina Baptist Convention, having been elected at the same meeting that passed a resolution favoring that alternatives to evolution, including intelligent design, be taught in public schools and endorsed a proposed constitutional amendment banning gay marriage. He warmly greets us with a prayer, talking about the past week, of a missionary group ministering in maximum-security prisons all the way to St. Louis and back. I see smiles from congregants, but hear no "Amens" or "Right ons."

"What a blessing to have Anne Graham Lotz here today," Pastor Don says. He recounts spending yesterday with Billy Graham, and Billy Graham telling him, "You know, Anne is the best preacher in the family." Then Pastor Don inserts a commercial: "Tomorrow, Anne will be at Christian Supply. She might have a few minutes to sign a few books." This makes sense to me only later, when I find out that FBS is Anne's last stop in a two-month, ten-city book tour promoting the latest of her twenty-three titles, *I Saw the Lord: A Wakeup Call for Your Heart*.

A new hymn, "Holy Lord of Hosts," begins: *In the year King Uzziah died*... Three churches into this experience, I am struck by the amount of biblical knowledge possessed by Protestants. I have no clue who King Uzziah is. And though anybody could tuck some old-time king's name into a song, I'd bet that everyone in this church could tell me who he actually was.

After a collection is taken up by men with brass badges and brass plates, Anne Graham Lotz makes her way to the pulpit. She wears a white tunic and tan skirt and brown backless shoes with pointy toes. She thanks the choir for the beautiful hymn. She says that coming to this church is a privilege. She wonders about the car stuff on stage and expresses the hope of being clued in later. Then she launches into a prayer.

"You are the God of the wind, the rain, you are the savior and we love you ... come down in our midst and let this be a fresh experience with you. We want this to be more than just church."

Her sermon is on wakeup calls. Another thing I will learn later, courtesy of the copy of *I Saw the Lord* purchased down the hall for 25 percent off, is that AGL is giving us the first chapter of the book she's here to promote. But at this point there's no reference to the book, no clunky advertisement feel to her presentation.

Anne recounts a morning on which she was to have started leading a three-day conference, but missed the bell. "If you sleep through your alarm, you'll miss something vitally important," she tells us. To Anne, September 11, Hurricane Katrina, recent droughts, all have been wakeup calls. More personally, divorce, the death of a loved one, the diagnosis of disease have further popped open her eyes.

"We don't like the alarm," she says. "We don't like what it's saying . . . He's trying to use you and me for the Kingdom of God, but we're sleeping." There's a mention of Isaiah, Chapter 6. Ruby picks up her Bible, a large-print edition. I take a copy from the seat pocket, which contains red hardcover New International Versions of the Bible and green hardcover hymnals.

Anne Graham Lotz once toyed with modeling but much earlier in life knew her true path. When she was around ten, she watched Cecil B. DeMille's original silent film *The King of Kings* and, particularly moved by the Crucifixion scene, decided to follow Jesus. With her command of the pulpit, she seems a natural to have taken over her retiring father's role. But because her church adheres to scriptural rules denying women equal religious authority, brother Franklin Graham, forty-eight and a ringer for a forty-eight-year-old Billy Graham, landed the job. The way Anne put it to the *New York Times*, "God has forbidden me to be ordained or be a senior preacher."

But that doesn't mean she can't preach, which she does, mentioning a son diagnosed with cancer and a friend lost to an almost instantly fatal illness. "It made heaven feel so close but life so temporary and eternity just a breath away."

Anne says many tragedies lurk in lives, including financial problems, family pressures, and addiction, then asks, "What happened to you?"

No one answers. But inwardly throughout this space there must be at least a few screams.

And Anne is here to say the screaming is okay.

"When you and I have been shaken, it's appropriate for a child of God to look up, say 'Lord, are you trying to get our attention?' "

Again she poses a question: "What has caused you to doubt that Jesus is seated on the throne? When my twenty-eight-year-old son called to say he had cancer, I fell back on the knowledge that Jesus is seated on the throne."

There are some nods, but still no verbalized agreements. Three weeks into these visits and I find myself missing the pastor-congregation back-and-forth of New Mount Zion. It's such a great idea and I'm wondering why every branch of faith isn't in on it. Ruby is lovely and open but there's a staid feeling from the majority of her fellow congregants. I try to picture one or two shouting "Keep it real" as Anne notes that loving God is easy when you have money in the bank and a good hair day. But when life throws the opposite, she adds, "and you're still praising Jesus, the world stands up and says, 'I want to know *her* Jesus.' "

She turns to Isaiah, bemoaning sinners. "Isaiah says woe to those ... woe to those ... We could say the same today." She singles out those "promoting the homosexual agenda, abortionists killing off the next generation, an athletic team accused of rape, a minister's wife charged with murder."

Here it is, all around me, and I'm glad I know my way to the door. This is take-no-prisoners fundamentalism, an ultraconservative movement born a century ago at Princeton Theological Seminary that stresses rigid belief in every letter of every word of the Bible, rejection of opposing views, and disdain for the secular. Anne is a follower who supports the death penalty. In 1984 she prayed with a convicted murderer whose execution was drawing near, but the experience did not sway her.

" 'Woe to you,' I could say. But chapter six, verse five, what did he say? 'Woe to me!' " Anne wants us to judge ourselves first. Under any steeple, that sounds like a good idea.

"Who are you blaming for your sins? Parents? Neighbors? Employers?" She pauses. "You've lost all excuses. All defenses. I'm not a victim when it comes to the yoke of sin. I am a sinner ... James says if you've ever sinned once in your life, you've committed all the sins in the world."

That's another Bible quote I've never heard. But I suppose Catholic guilt covers that—you already feel like you've done everything without James verifying it.

We are asked to quietly stand in admission of sins, and people begin to take to their feet. To my right, Ruby rises slowly. I'm wondering what a woman like this might be guilty of—forgetting the loaf of Wonder when stocking the mission house pantry? I shrug. I've done plenty. I stand, if only to gain a better view.

"Some of you are still seated," Anne reports. "Fine. You might be totally right with the Lord." I crane my neck to see what the perfect among us look like. I see no one. "God's message to you this morning . . . Stop it!"

She invites us to join in some spiritual housecleaning: "I confess to you my"—here there is a pause to silently fill in your particular problem—"and believe that Jesus died on the cross for that sin."

Then she concludes, "We are your people. We want to be a reflection of Jesus to a lost, dying world that's blessed to know him."

Pastor Don takes the pulpit. "What God wants from us is not our building or our money," he tells us. "What he wants is you and me. He doesn't want our ability, he wants our availability."

Behind him, the choir director is beaming. Anne Graham Lotz exits stage left.

After an altar call during which two women step forth to receive Jesus Christ as their personal Savior and Lord, Ruby gestures for us to leave our seats. When I do, I have to stop myself from genuflecting. There is no such custom here. But there is that muscle memory upon leaving a long bench in a house of worship and heading out for some fresh air.

I wonder what my grandparents would have thought of this morning. I guess they would have joined me in liking Ruby very much, and they would have gotten a kick out of seeing Billy's daughter. And even though they weren't the twist-and-shout type of worshippers, I'm betting that they would have gone along with my wish that a little more joy be evidenced, on stage and in the pews. That, as Anne had prayed and I had hoped on this Sunday morning, church could have been more than just a place to be humbled and lectured at.

ARCH STREET FRIENDS MEETING HOUSE

PHILADELPHIA, PENNSYLVANIA

An elderly gentleman in suit and bow tie walks in. Will he be the one to get this rolling? Apparently not; he does nothing more than take a seat.

A young man in a blue blazer and khakis strides in next. Will it be he? No, he simply claims the far end of the bench in front of me.

My frame of reference for the start of a worship service is the arrival of a male in symbol-bedecked floor-length garb, so I'm looking for any man who's dressed a bit more grandly than in the assortment of jeans, shorts, and hiking pants I see so far.

But this isn't home, so maybe the person to look for is a woman. An older one in a blue suit enters the room. But she, too, just sits.

I forgot my watch, so I have no idea of the time. But after maybe ten minutes I figure it out: the worship is already happening.

Here. Now. Among this group of forty or so adults sitting silently on antique wooden benches that edge the room and fill its center. This is a Quaker meeting.

I have traveled 264 miles to do nothing here in the mecca of Quakerism, the Arch Street Friends Meeting House in downtown Philadelphia. Built in 1804, it's not only the world's largest Friends meetinghouse, but the oldest still in use in a state that got its start as a haven for these faithful.

In mid-seventeenth-century England, a seeker named George Fox was sampling religions when he came to the belief that the inner voice of God needs no intermediary. The flood that joined his Religious Society of Friends felt that ordained leaders and consecrated buildings were likewise extraneous. The "Friends of the Light" also saw no point in tithing or swearing oaths, or treating anyone as less than or greater than equal. Not surprisingly, this insulted the crown, which incarcerated thousands of Friends and couldn't have been satisfied when the terms were served without rancor or a change of heart.

By 1677, the faith had spread throughout the U.K. and continental Europe. Members soon acquired a nickname—"Quakers," a taunt thrown at them due to the ecstatic trembling some experienced during worship—and an influential, wealthy champion—William Penn, who bent the ear of King Charles II. Penn suggested that a place of the Quakers' own, far removed from England, might be a good idea for all, and the result was the granting of a very faraway place indeed, Pennsylvania. In 1682 Penn founded the colony as a "Holy Experiment," a verdant laboratory for the testing of religious and civil liberties. All faiths were welcome, but Quakers initially represented the greatest numbers and held the most sway.

Quakers have used the Arch Street site since 1693. Penn originally set it aside as a cemetery, which in fact it became when yellow fever epidemics necessitated mass burials. The symmetrical brick building with peaked center roof and yellow trim was constructed atop those graves in the early 1800s. Just after I entered this morning, modern-day member Mike offered me a tour of the most historic part of the meetinghouse. I followed him into a large square balconied space that recalled a courtroom but was free of tables, desks, and rails. Long wooden benches faced the center, which was filled with more benches. Along the soft green walls, five windows illuminated the main level, and another five lit the balcony.

Arch Street's is traditionally a silent worship, Mike had explained, noting that meetings in some parts of the country are led by pastors. Here, he said, I'll find no liturgy, no prayers, no songs, no statues, and few holidays observed. I didn't know that, but then there's a lot I don't know about Quakers. I've read that Joan Baez is a Quaker, and so was Richard Nixon. I learn lots more today, including that we can credit Quakers with some basics of our society: asylums for care of the insane; decent prisons; and a system of commerce with fixed fees and prices.

The Nobel Peace Prize–winning American Friends Service Committee, founded in 1917 to give conscientious objectors a way to serve civilian victims of war, is rooted in the Quakers' belief that love can squelch any societal ill. Members today work on a variety of sociopolitical fronts, including the war in Iraq, the Palestinian-Israeli conflict, and rights for immigrants, gays, bisexuals, and transgendered people.

However, as is the case whenever more than one person is present, a variety of views are held. Fifty-two percent of draft-eligible Quakers served in World War II, and supporters of the Iraq war exist in today's communities. Members hold many translations of the word "God"—if they indeed believe—and homosexuality is not cool with everyone. Still, all in all, an open-minded Christian might be more at home on a bench here than on the ones I've occupied the past few Sunday mornings.

This meetinghouse stands a block from the U.S. Mint, which is across the street from Benjamin Franklin's grave, which is kitty-corner from the National Constitution Center, which has a nice view of the roof of Independence Hall another few blocks away. History abounds; a sign in front of the meetinghouse informs, PHILADELPHIA'S RELIGIOUS HISTORY IS THE NATION'S. The City of Brotherly Love is also the birthplace of the Methodist, German Reformed, Episcopal, and African Methodist Episcopal churches in America. The first African American bishop was named here, the Hebrew Bible was first translated into English here, the first General Assembly of the Presbyterian Church in America was held here, and, in the 1730s, the one and only place in the entire British Empire where a Catholic Mass could be celebrated in public was right here.

Mike, blond, Caucasian, fiftyish, wearing khakis and dress shoes, a tie around the neck of his parochial-school-type white shirt, was a Catholic before he started "hanging with the Quakers," as he put it, five years ago, joining a membership numbering 338,219 worldwide and 152,856 nationally, with 11,000 or so of those right here in Philly. Mike explained that he was attracted by the religion's political views, then added, "I love the Quaker spice." I pictured a kicky, fancy-free membership, but Mike was giving me the acronym for Simplicity, Peace, Integrity, Community, and Equality. Then he showed me the door. Because the service was about to begin.

"Be still and know that I am God," reads the "Invitation to Worship" sheet I have been given. "We gather in silence, endeavoring to submit ourselves wholly to the Divine spirit, which we believe is accessible to every attentive mind."

This meeting room is similar to the one Mike had shown me,

containing the same arrangement of antique benches, but it is more modern and maybe a third of the size. Mike had estimated a typical crowd at forty-five to seventy-five, and those scattered around the room range in age from early twenties to elderly. I have all to myself the last of the benches just to the left of the entrance.

Beneath a ceiling texture-painted white, the walls bear only three plain glass windows offering a view of leafy branches. As if paid to perform, birds begin to sing while inside the only sounds are an electrical hum layered over exhalations, throat clearings, nose blowings, and a few aquatic belly sounds.

I stare at my feet. At the tan rug. I look around. Lots of eyes are closed. No heads turn. One woman stares at some sort of coin between her thumbs. The young woman in front of me in a red jogging top twirls her hair with the fingers of her left hand. I put down my notebook. My hands automatically fold. I unfold them. I look around. I refold. "Pray for peace" was the text I received last night from Mary Ellen, whom I met on my first day of full-time newspaper work and who in the twenty-six years since has added only goodness to my life. She's still working at the paper and covers all manners of tragedy yet manages in her personal life to focus on the positive in this world. I take her request.

Peace, I say silently with every breath. *Peace. Peace. Peace.* A man with frizzy dreads that octopus down to his waist enters from my right and takes a seat against the far wall. I am supposed to be thinking *Peace* but instead I think *Hair.* I've traveled to Philly with my friend Susan, whose husband, Dominick, is being treated for cancer and recently shaved his head after half a dozen years beneath a toupee. He has found the lack of hair freeing. I think of him sitting at home with his little found-in-the-middle-of-the-road dog, Bette, which makes me think of my little pound dog, Tiny, and how Tiny has been so lonesome since I rushed our big lively and suddenly ill Zelda dog to the twenty-four-hour vet at 5:00 a.m. and she died ten minutes later. Now I'm sitting here in Philadelphia one day short of four weeks after that morning, being quiet and thinking, *Zelda died and I feel horrible.* I get back to *Peace. Peace. Peace.* And think how there is none in Iraq and how one of the soldiers who returned to the town next to mine was so haunted that he hanged himself in his family's basement. I think *Peace* for his family. *Peace* for him. *Peace*. I am staring at my feet and I notice a pair of black leather clogs has settled to my left, on the feet of a blond woman, maybe twenty-five, who sits with eyes closed. I gaze ahead to a Joe-Strummer-like guy, dark slicked-back hair, generous sideburns, black T-shirt and jeans, sitting next to a young woman with electric red hair, also wearing black. I'm studying them when a guy to my left bolts to his feet and begins to speak. The sound cracks the room.

"Hope is a state of the heart and not a state of the world," he begins.

I estimate that we've been sitting here for about twenty minutes before he began to hold forth about the dark, how he once had lived in denial of that darkness.

I glance at the paper I was given on the way in. "Those who speak should be brief, and those who listen should do so in quiet attention." I wonder about the Quaker definition of "brief." But there's no need for me to get unpeaceful, as this man soon enough sits. I look down at my shoes again. The black vegan Mary Janes I ordered from a store in Amherst because, as a vegetarian, I no longer want to wear leather and I've tried cheapo Kmart plastic shoes but they hurt. I push my feet against the wooden footrest running the length of the bench in front of me. Another week with no kneelers. The wood is so worn, the patterns of the grain are in relief. I study them as I did the grain in the pews of my youth, now seeing a fluttery jellyfish in front of me. Then a wing. The wing reminds me of the birds outside. Birds remind me of nature, which we constantly assault. I think of my train ride in this morning from my friend Tanya's suburban home and its front yard wild with the blooming azalea bushes that Susan is right now sketching. Just past Temple University, the surprising freshness of green poked through the soil of community gardens, and gardens make me think of my maternal *babci*, whose family arrived from Poland to this very port city. She was the most faith-filled person I've ever met. Her answer to any difficulty was prayer, and a steely confidence that God would provide. I say *Peace* to her. *Peace*. I realize my eyes are closed. I open them to forty-five people now, all white except for one black woman and, just like at the Cowboy Church, a lone Asian teen. I hear a snore but not a second one. It's not a stretch to imagine everyone's prayers floating like Vicks VapoRub fumes from their heads, through the textured ceiling and up to the historic air above, up farther, to where *Dziadziu* told me God is.

A woman in black, who's been sitting next to the guy who spoke maybe twenty minutes before, is suddenly on her feet. "It's one thing to say that God is in every man and woman," she tells us, then adds that it's something else to weed through not only what every man or woman might be like, but also your judgment of them. She is right on, and, just as importantly, brief.

The guy in front of me, who appears to be with the hair twirler next to him, scratches his neck and coins somewhere on him clink. A car horn sounds. I try to listen for something from within. My eyes move to the footrest again, to a knot that looks like waves folding from the prow of a boat.

Suddenly the girl to my left extends her hand toward me. "Hi!"

The guy with the hair twirler turns around. "Good morning," he says as we shake.

It seems we've all awoken at the same moment. And now we're back in the world we left an hour before.

Across the room, a dark-haired man in a blue shirt who introduces himself as Kurt stands and asks visitors to make themselves known. There are ten of us, including Ben in front of me, from a place with the great name of Fishtown, and Mara the hair-twirler, from West Philly. Everyone receives a loud "Welcome."

Mike stands to announce that the Peace and Social Concerns Meeting will be held the next Sunday, and that he just wants to say he can't remember such a beautiful spring. "When I was a child, I can remember the freshness of the air and the clarity of the clouds. I just want us to be present to our experience of the planet as we've been given it."

Maybe that's what I want to do with all of these churches. To be present to the experience as it unfolds on each particular Sunday. And at this one, sitting in silence in a group, not chanting or repeating or singing, not standing or kneeling, just sitting and being, has felt wonderfully powerful. For someone who's never gotten past a few seconds of meditation, I'm really surprised by how time has flown, and how rich was this experience, a longer and quieter version of one of the things I like best about Mass—quiet time to reflect, renew, realize. I have a feeling that this experience will stay with me.

I rise from my bench. I thank Mike, who invites me to return. I walk out the door into his air and clouds, through the opening in the brick wall to the door of the nearby Starbucks, where the black tea I order bears the label Awake: on this morning, an apt name for both the leaves and the state of being.

FIRST CHURCH OF CHRIST, SCIENTIST

BOSTON, MASSACHUSETTS

For this Mother's Day morning, I had wanted to visit Andrews Methodist Episcopal Church in Grafton, West Virginia, where the inaugural celebration of the holiday was held in 1908. But that church is now the International Mother's Day Shrine—no services, visits by appointment only. So I hopped to Plan B—the original "Mother Church" of the Church of Christ, Scientist. Home of a faith founded by a female.

That woman, Mary Baker Eddy, was born in 1821 in Bow, New Hampshire, and grew up highly religious. In her 1875 book, *Science and Health*, she tells of accepting the Gospel accounts of Jesus's life, but of drawing a line between him as man and as Christ. Eddy's perhaps best-known belief is that sickness can be vanquished by one's becoming aware of God's power and love, rather than looking to mortal healers. Hence the quote that greets me in the wide marble-pillared lobby:

> IF THE CHRISTIAN SCIENTIST REACHES HIS PATIENT THROUGH DIVINE LOVE, HE WILL ACCOMPLISH THE HEALING WORK AT ONE VISIT, AND THE DISEASE WILL VANISH

INTO ITS NATIVE NOTHINGNESS LIKE DEW BEFORE THE MORNING SUNSHINE.

MARY B. G. EDDY

Born in Boston in 1879, the faith spread through the English-speaking world and Germany. Membership is an estimated four hundred thousand, with a Quaker-like one hundred thousand members in the United States. The Mother Church was built in 1895 on a fourteen-acre triangle of what is now the city's tony Back Bay, a ninety-minute drive from my home. Designed to seat one thousand, the original structure was enlarged a dozen years later by a domed extension seating three thousand.

A month before my visit, the church announced financial problems that would necessitate cutting its annual $190 million budget by almost half and its staff by 40 percent, and emptying two of the three buildings that comprise its headquarters. I now stand in the church's enormous extension, alone; this is the first time in five weeks I've not been greeted or escorted at a house of worship. And I kind of miss the fuss. Even this past week, because I jotted my contact information on a visitor's card, I received two letters from my new friends in Spartanburg—Ruby, who wrote in her Palmer penmanship to say, "I am so glad I was privileged to meet you," and Pastor Don, who hand-signed a printed note card thanking me for my visit.

In the spacious and echoing lobby occupied by four other people, I study a table of literature. Topics touted on the *Christian Science Sentinel* magazine covers include "The Healer in You" and "Anyone Can Be a Healer." I'm all for healing, especially after experiencing a potentially fatal disease six years ago. But I'm not sure that just anyone can bring it about—I can hardly apply a Band-Aid so that it sticks. As a cancer patient, I enrolled in yoga classes and Reiki sessions, but my big money was on the success of the prescribed surgery and treatments. This recollection is the morning's first inkling that I would not make a great Christian Scientist. I walk to the left of the coat-check window, where another table of literature displays a Bible, a copy of *Science and Health*, and a booklet of weekly Bible lessons, with dozens of this trio of titles offered in languages including Danish, French, Polish, and Japanese. Unguided, I find the door to the sanctuary but go looking for the restrooms. They're through a lounge area that doesn't miss the chance to offer yet more reading material, with handy copies of the French translation *Science et Sante, The Christian Science Hymnal*, and *Science and Health with Key to the Scriptures*.

I look for but do not see any copies of what is perhaps the church's best-known publication, the *Christian Science Monitor*, an international six-time Pulitzer Prize–winning weekday newspaper founded in 1908 by Eddy at age eighty-seven. A target of the press—including the *New York World*, owned by Joseph Pulitzer himself—Eddy made her paper's aim "to injure no man, but to bless all mankind." In 1883 she wrote, "Looking over the newspapers of the day, one naturally reflects that it is dangerous to live, so loaded with disease seems the very air. These descriptions carry fears to many minds, to be depicted in some future time upon the body. A periodical of our own will counteract to some extent this public nuisance; for through our paper we shall be able to reach many homes with healing, purifying thought."

At Eddy's request, one religious article appears in each issue of the *Monitor*, the extent of the church's presence in the paper. The remaining column inches of Eddy's paper are filled with the hard realities of modern life as experienced in all corners of the globe, written primarily by staffers based in eleven countries rather than picked up from the wire services. *Monitor* reporter Jill Carroll literally made headlines after her January 2006 kidnapping in Baghdad and release after nearly three months.

Bells ring as I ascend a marble staircase leading to an expansive and breathtaking sanctuary. Seats face an elaborate stage. Three wide sections of golden organ pipes fill the center section of the front wall and a marble balcony juts from the middle of it, holding a pair of wide wooden lecterns, a row of seating behind them. Beneath a planet-high dome I count maybe a hundred other worshippers, most in rain gear; I can gauge the level of formal dress only by the few who've removed their coats. I see Spartanburg suits, jackets, and ties in a gathering that's two-thirds female with an average age of fifty. I also see Spartanburg skin—nearly. There are maybe three blacks here, and a few Asians. There also are a few balconies, and the sections that I am able to scan are empty. Down on the floor, two teens are present. No young children anywhere.

Beneath each wooden pew is a shelf holding *The Christian Science Hymnal* and a copy of *Science and Health*. I reach for the hymnal as we take to our feet to sing number 14, which I see titled only as "Potsdam": *Arise arise and see / on thee hath dawned the day / God is thy sun and Christ thy light / be thou a steadfast ray.*

I like the idea of being a ray, shining and warming things. I nestle into the mossy green seat cushion and reach for *Science and Health* ("Over 10 million copies sold," boasts the cover). "To-day is big with blessings," the preface informs me. I check congregant expressions for signs of rejoicing at this news. Serious faces abound. Including those on the two women and one man who now proceed from their seats at the front of my section, up the stairs to the little front balcony. The man and the older woman stand at each of the pulpits. The younger woman takes a seat behind them.

Maybe twenty-five more people have arrived in the sanctuary by this point. We are ants in this giant space, which makes the visitor wonder where are the other thousands for whom this space was built. Are they at a Mennonite service as part of their own quests? Have they found this faith out of step with the modern world? Are they bringing a potted azalea to Ma? There's no one nearby to ask, as I'm alone on my bench. Three women sit in the row behind me, but so far to the right, they're in their own universe. To us all, Lyle Young, blond and neat in word and movement, offers "a warm welcome to the Mother Church, the first Church of Christ, Scientist, in Boston. And a warm welcome to those who might be listening over the Internet."

Lyle reads scripture that I can see in my head: Baby Moses in the floating basket, a queen's servant plucking him to safety. A man takes a seat directly to my left though he has several hundred others to choose from. He's just in time for Lyle's direction that we all pray silently. This brings me back to last week, sitting with the Quakers and asking for peace. Mary Ellen's direction this week was to pray for a safe journey—she's leaving tonight for her annual trip to Ireland—so I do that as I imagine her plane flying without incident, and her driving easily on all those wrong-way roads.

The Lord's Prayer is next, done with something the program calls "spiritual interpretation." This means Christiane West Little, the older woman up front, reads "Our Father which art in heaven," followed by Lyle's "Our Father-Mother God, all-harmonious," the corresponding line from Eddy's writing.

"Hallowed be thy name," continues Christiane.

"Adorable One," Lyle answers.

"And lead us not into temptation, but deliver us from evil."

"And God leadeth us not into temptation, but delivereth us from sin, disease, and death."

The back-and-forth takes us through the entire prayer, complete with its "other" ending. Another hymn begins, in which we're reminded that the dark leads to a cloudless day. The man to my left is silent. I try to follow along and hear no other voice, we're all so spread out in this massive building and so few against the power of that giant organ.

Lyle then reads the notices, including that June 2 is the next time new members will be accepted into the community. May 31 is the application deadline, which on this second Sunday of the month seems like a slim amount of time for a committee's decision. Applications can be found in this building or, says Lyle, "Go to Church of Christ, Scientist, dot-org."

Julia Wade, blue suit, strawberry blond shoulder-length hair, steps forward for her solo, a female-themed "Women of Destiny." There is applause when she finishes this tune that Helen Reddy could have turned into a hit, and Lyle is back again. "Friends," he says, "The Bible and the Christian Science textbook are our only teachers. These comprise our sermon."

We're at "Subject of the Lesson-Sermon, and reading of the Golden Text." Today's subject: "Mortals and Immortals."

Christiane, in her gray bob, reads from Romans. Then Lyle gives mirroring passages, using very old English. I'm sorry, but I'm just not getting it. Christiane is reading the passages about this biblical figure begetting that one. There is a lot of conception, and references to harlots. Uriah the Hittite is mentioned, and I'm betting that the King Uzziah crowd would be able to recite along.

But I can't. Bored, I flip through *Science and Health*. Page 177 tells me that "the human mind produces what is termed organic diseases certainly as it produces hysteria, and it must be relinquished of all its errors, sicknesses and sins." The guy in my row looks at his own copy. Maybe ten minutes later, we pick up our heads. The lineage of David has been drawn for us, and, as earnestly as Lyle and Christiane spoke, I couldn't tell you a word of it. The absence of kids seems less of a mystery now. I'm finding the service excruciatingly bland and can only imagine the ordeal it would be for a child, and the fits of protest that have resulted in parents just going it alone this morning.

A collection is taken into green velvet bags while worshippers chitchat with neighbors. A benediction is a blessed fast surprise, then the organ plays a final piece and the three walk off the stage. That is it. A tidy hour in wording and mind-set from another time. Yet I sit. I wait. I want something to sink in. The walls' words on health and healing remind that we all have an expiration date, and I grab that as today's souvenir. Mine was not six years ago. I remain on the planet this Mother's Day, with both a living mother and a living mother-in-law to visit. I remember those blessings, and those plans, and exit without being given a farewell in any language.

ST. SPYRIDON GREEK ORTHODOX CHURCH

NEWPORT, RHODE ISLAND

"Uh, this Mass, it's going to be in English, right?"

"It's a liturgy," Mary corrects kindly. "And no, it's in Greek."

I don't know a word of Greek. Mary's vocabulary isn't a whole lot better. But she is a recent convert to Greek Orthodoxy, the religion practiced by her Greek American husband, Mike. That's just one of the reasons I've asked her to join me today. Mary was raised

Catholic and has been my friend since the eighth grade. Like mine, her allegiance to our home church was lost at the news of clergy sex-abuse scandals. "I just couldn't give the church another penny," she tells me on our trip down, before recounting her own religion touring, which led to her walking into a Greek Orthodox church near her Boston-area home a few years ago and simply feeling at peace. Last year she was chrismated, receiving the Orthodox sacrament of confirmation, and she is now a practicing member and my guide for this morning.

In 1896 four Greek fishermen arrived in Newport to make their living on the water. Friends and family followed, all faithful to the Greek Orthodox Church. First they assembled at the city's Quaker meetinghouse, then at a United Baptist church, and then at an Episcopalian one, before purchasing St. Spyridon's in 1924.

Named for a fourth-century Cypriot shepherd imprisoned for his faith, blinded in one eye, and condemned to life in a mine, the church sits on touristy Thames Street, hard by storefronts peddling wizard figurines and BITE ME LIVE BAIT T-shirts. St. Spyridon's customers are the locals among the approximately 1.5 million Greek Orthodox in America, 250 million worldwide. As Mary and I enter, I'm instantly reminded of the ethnic Polish Catholic churches in which Mary and I were raised. Now, like back then, a dollar is shoved into my hand. But by Mary rather than my parents.

Cigarette-thin foot-long white tapers stand in a box of sand just inside the door. I light one, place the dollar in a basket, and say a prayer for Mary's health. She is at the halfway point between breast cancer surgery and radiation. I was once at this same point, and I know that more than a few people—Mary included—mentioned my name while talking to God back then. She would walk across glass for those she loves, then do it a second time on all fours. As she has for me, for her family, and for the patients she cares for as a nurse practitioner. I want to stand in that entryway and make my prayer well-worded and strong, but Mary is leading me to a framed icon of Madonna and child. She kisses it before opening the door to the sanctuary.

Art! After five Sundays in decoration-free churches I feel like a parched desert wanderer handed a sport-sized bottle of thawing

Evian. A red-carpeted aisle leads past a dozen rows of pews to a wall of large paintings. Many saints, Virgin Mary and child. Above them is a line of a dozen smaller biblical scenes, the Last Supper in the center above an archway inside which a white-vestmented priest stands at an altar singing a cappella. Every few minutes a parishioner walks to the front of the church and places a large red jar candle beneath one of the paintings. Fancy electrified glass lamps glow above each image, and red and white bows resembling horse-show awards are clipped to every fixture, including the enormous crystal chandelier hanging from the salmon-colored ceiling. Below, an elaborately patterned Persian rug stretches across the bottom of the three stairs leading to the alcove. At each side of it glows a trident of candles. A stand holds a pair of icons that worshippers occasionally step forth to kiss.

To the left is an elaborately carved wooden pulpit, and to the left of that is the choir, an older man and four blue-robed women, middle-aged and up, gathered in front of an enormous painting of the Nativity. The church holds no statues. Three-dimensional images of holy figures are not allowed, following the commandment prohibiting idol worship. Icons, on the other hand, are simply paid reverence. But I'm not complaining—at least there's something to look at.

The priest sings *For peace and salvation* and the choir answers *Kyrie eleison*, which I know as "Lord, have mercy," from the Old Latin, and also, because this is how my mind works, from the '80s pop hit by Mr. Mister. In our seats six rows from the front, Mary and I try to follow along. The benches are old and sturdy dark wood and, for the first time in six weeks, unpadded. Their seatback pockets contain missalettes, the left-hand pages in Greek and the right in English.

On the Arch-Street-to-New-Mount-Zion scale, attire is somewhere in the very upper half. A well-dressed young family takes a seat in front of us: mother, father, twelve-year-old girl, boy about six. They stand as the priest and now a cantor continue, blessing themselves when the spirit hits them. Mary does, too. She uses thumb and first and second fingers of the right hand to touch forehead, sternum, right shoulder, then left one, the final two movements being the opposite of the direction I use. "Do it any time you like," she instructs, as those around us stop and start their blessings as if their arms are moved by independent gusts.

The Orthodox Church consists of communities recognizing the spiritual preeminence of the Ecumenical Patriarch of Constantinople. Among their other commonalities is allowing priests to marry at any point before ordination as a deacon. Our priest is the Reverend Presbyter Anthony S. Evangelatos, according to the black-on-white four-page bulletin that also informs me that St. Spyridon's stewardship program encourages free-will offerings, therefore no collection will be taken. I'm about to learn more but the liturgy seems to be officially starting. Father Anthony carries a large golden book around the altar, then disappears. I hold onto the seat in front of me as I feel transported by the small choir's chanting in Greek. This certainly isn't Polish America. It's not even America. There's an ocean outside the window, but it's the Mediterranean, showing off the blue that over here we only see on swimming pool liners. Mary and I are somewhere in Greece and have ducked into this little church. And here the liturgy begins as one of the saint paintings to the left opens and out walk four altar boys in gold brocade robes. The priest appears again, following them up the aisle and stopping in the alcove.

As he passes, I get my first good look at Father Anthony, approximately fifty, sturdy and with dark features, his head and beard thick with graying hair. In a pretty good voice he sings, *Whosoever is thirsty let them come to me and drink. Christ our God, glory to you.*

The cantor responds in heavily accented English. The choir leader sings something, too. His voice takes Mary and me on another trip, perhaps to eons ago, standing outside a cave delivering the sound he's making—baritone, ancient, mournful. When I return to the present, he's a modern-day man perhaps in his seventies, gray hair slicked back, glasses, blue robe, making these time-shifting sounds while leaning on an elbow and looking bored.

Let us pray to the Lord, sings Father Anthony.

Some people sit, so Mary and I do. Some do not. I look in the book. No page gives me any direction for position. Nor does Mary, who shrugs. We stay seated as a reading is prefaced by the priest singing the politely worded *Let us be attentive*. A man near the cantor and out of my line of sight reads about Paul's journey to Damascus.

The order of prayers, songs, and readings is similar to that of a Catholic Mass. We stand for the Gospel as Father Anthony sings the story about the Samarian woman at the well. A cappella again, with every line starting the first few words on a low note and singing the concluding ones just a little higher.

More worshippers arrive. "They come in when they want to," Mary whispers. Another procession begins from the secret door to the left. The altar boys return, one walking backward and swinging the censer in the path of Father Anthony, who holds a chalice with a hand shrouded in red cloth. People bow or bless themselves as he passes. The father in front of us takes his son's hand and helps him touch the priest's robe.

Back in his alcove, Father Anthony leads us in reciting the creed. We pray the familiar "Holy, holy, holy." The choir sings. The cantor advises us, *Rejoice, your son has risen from the grave on the third day.* Blessings are asked upon the world, the community, the archbishop and bishop. Mary and I are not sure of the page. The man in front of us leans back to say, "It's not all in there."

The Lord's Prayer concludes with that other ending before the priest steps to the pulpit and asks us to be seated. "*Christos anesti!*" says Father Anthony.

"*Christos anesti,*" says everyone, including Mary, who actually knows this "Christ is risen" greeting.

Father Anthony tells us that this is the fifth Sunday of Holy Pascha. Eastern Orthodox Easter was celebrated April 23, one week after the Easter the rest of Christianity celebrated. The Julian calendar, rather than the usual millennium-older Gregorian calendar, is used for calculating the date of Easter in this religion.

Orthodox churches sprang from the church of the Byzantine Empire, and tensions between Rome and Constantinople led to a split, the Great Schism of 1054. But the process that divided Chalcedonian Christianity into its Western form and Eastern Orthodoxy was a gradual drift. Sparking the change was the pope's claim of authority over the Eastern patriarchs, and disputes over language in the

Nicene Creed. This resulting church is the one in which Mary and I sit listening to Father Anthony tell us about Helen and Constantine, whose feast day is today.

"Here are people the church considers on par with the holy apostles," he says in one of the few times he will speak, rather than sing. "They believed in the truth of Christ and spread the Gospel throughout the pagan world.

"This is the beauty in the Orthodox faith, that we have a clear history."

The fast sermon ends with, "God bless all of you, have a most blessed week," and another "*Christos anesti*." We stand and Father Anthony returns to the alcove. More prayers and responses follow, then he faces us, holding a chalice in his left hand, a spoon in his other. Communicants make their way up the aisle. *For his mercy endures forever*, the cantor sings.

Adults, children, babies in arms receive a spoonful of the contents of the chalice—warm water, wine, and *prosforon*, a leavened bread baked each week by a church member.

When it is Mary's turn to receive, Father Anthony hesitates. Perhaps because this blue-eyed stranger's face, with its fair skin fringed by blond hair, is very un-Greek, he asks sternly, "Are you Orthodox?"

A bit taken aback in this holy moment, Mary replies that she is. Father Anthony extends the spoon.

"FOR HOLY COMMUNION," announces the very last paragraph in the bulletin, "We respectfully request that all non-Orthodox Christians refrain from partaking of Holy Communion during the Divine Liturgy . . . Only people who have been baptized or chrismated into the Orthodox faith may receive Holy Communion."

What the rest of us can help ourselves to is the leftover bread known as *antidoron*, Greek for "instead of the gift." At the end of the service, anyone may walk to the altar and receive a piece, a practice inspired by the early Christians giving bread to the needy as a bonus for coming to hear Christ.

But we're not at that point yet.

The final fifteen minutes of the liturgy are given to prayers in memory of a late parishioner, then some housekeeping, and only after that do worshippers queue.

"Kiss his hand and he'll give you a piece of bread," Mary explains.

I don't even know the guy. But I like bread.

"You're visiting?" Father Anthony asks Mary in the tone of an officer who's just pulled her over. Mary gives the name of her parish, of her pastor—actually a friend of Father A's. He smiles then. Nods. He extends his hand palm down. Mary kisses the back. The hand opens, the bread is offered.

Father asks me gruffly, "You're with her?"

"I'm with Mary."

He extends his closed hand. Upturned. The fingers open. Two pieces of bread await. I get mine without having to give a kiss, and without a smile.

I leave disappointed. The artwork, the music, the processions, the incense, the choir, all were familiar, and all are some of my favorite parts of a Catholic Mass. But the vital joy that should be the centerpiece of any "celebration" of any liturgy was the big missing piece. Mary agrees, happy to have made this journey if only to be reminded how lucky she is that the church she's found hasn't lost that heart.

Outside, the sun is bright, the tourists are thick on the sidewalk. We stand on the front steps eating our bread. It's basic and grainy, the way I like it. But too dry. I don't think I'd want another piece. Yet if I didn't have a bite of this one, how would I ever have known?

CADET CHAPEL, UNITED STATES MILITARY ACADEMY

WEST POINT, NEW YORK

In preparation for church services, I've been asked to open my heart. Now I can say that I've also been asked to open my trunk.

As will you if you're headed to any of the five houses of worship at the United States Military Academy at West Point.

Roll up to Thayer Gate at the far end of Main Street in tiny, tired Highland Falls, New York, and take out your driver's license. Because the man with the holster will want to see that before he lets you through.

To the next checkpoint.

There, you'll be asked to step from your car. To open the trunk. Then to drive slowly over those sharp forky tire-eaters. Now you are officially on the campus of the oldest military academy in the United States.

Twenty-four hours before my passage through Thayer Gate, President George W. Bush spoke to the 861 graduates of the Class of 2006. During the two-hour commencement ceremony in massive Michie Stadium, he lauded the first class to enter the academy since September 11, 2001, and vowed, "Americans will not wait to be attacked again."

That class included 131 women, 47 African Americans, 65 Asian Americans, 50 Latinos, and 2 Native Americans; they earned bachelor of science degrees and second lieutenant commissions, and they now must serve a minimum of five years of active duty, then three in the reserves. Applause was frequent a mile away from Thayer Gate, where hundreds protested the war, assembling around an enormous inflatable rat bearing a sign that read IMPEACH G. W. BUSH.

By the time Tommy and I arrive, the rat is history. The stadium stands empty. But just down the hill, a crowd is gathering at the entrance to the Cadet Chapel.

It's Memorial Day weekend, so I suppose a church at a beach or a mall might have been fitting for this Sunday. But I wanted to visit one that was sure to regard the fallen soldiers we're supposed to be honoring. Thus our three-hour drive west to the Hudson River Valley, and this 1910 chapel constructed from the granite on which the campus stands.

Built to resemble a fourteenth-century English church, with a few military battlements tossed in, the building is stunning. It's also familiar to the countless millions who've watched *The Wizard of Oz*. According to urban legend, it was the inspiration for the castle of the Wicked Witch of the West. But I spot no flying monkeys as we enter for the 10:30 a.m. service the Web site describes generically as Protestant. We join worshippers in suits and in running togs, plus cadets in their gray trousers, short-sleeved white shirts, nameplate over right breast, colored bar pin over left, moving swiftly in their shiny black shoes, white hats tucked respectfully beneath arms.

A choir of six is rehearsing at the end of the 210-foot center cement aisle. The seats are filling, though it helps that the back half of the pews for fifteen hundred is roped off with clothesline. Tommy and I choose a bench on the left-hand side, beneath a row of battle flags and a few of the 192 stained glass windows lining each side of the chapel. The largest window rises above the altar, featuring the archangel Michael—patron saint of soldiers—crushing the dragon of evil. The choir moves to seats at the right of the archangel, and two middle-aged men in suits and a young woman in a sundress walk to the front, bow their heads, and like the rest of us are shaken by the volume of the 23,500 pipes belonging to what is one of the largest church organs in the world. A man with dark hair and a light suit takes to the pulpit. "We're glad to be here with you today," he says, adding just as a pigeon flies over us, "and ignore the pigeons flying over us."

A man and woman in their early thirties take the seats in front of us and lean in like they're at a romantic film. Maybe they have nothing to do with the military. But the man wears the very short haircut I see on so many males here, and his shoulders start somewhere in Ohio and end in that seat in front of us. I guess that the couple's closeness has the impetus of a deadline.

The pigeon has found a roost and "Praise to the Lord, the Almighty" has been sung by the choir and congregants, all of us using lyrics in the *Book of Worship*, subtitled *A Collection of Hymns and Worship Resources for Military Personnel of the United States of America*, 611 songs including "Lord, Guard and Guide the Men Who Fly" and "Bless Thou the Astronauts." The young woman asks us to be seated for the scripture reading from Isaiah 55. I am leafing through the songbook when I should be listening, but I do catch and save this line and lovely image: *All the trees of the field will clap their hands.*

I scan the front of the church. No one up there wears any sort of vestment, so I still don't know who the minister is. The dark-haired man returns to the front for what the program says are "Prayers of the People."

"We are once again reminded of the significance of this academy to our nation," he says, and asks a special blessing on the firsties, lingo for seniors. "Mold and prepare them spiritually for the next chapter in their lives... Their work is difficult, their sacrifices are great, their feelings are real."

He also asks us to pray for the commander in chief, that he be granted wisdom in every decision. And he asks a blessing on Chaplain Darrell Thomsen, who'll be preaching today. We're invited to consider financially supporting one cadet who will be traveling to Colorado Springs to intern with Focus on the Family, a widely followed conservative evangelical Christian nonprofit aimed at aiding and strengthening families through practices including school prayer and corporal punishment.

Then we recognize yesterday's graduates. Eight stand, all but two in uniform. We join them in the Cadet Prayer pasted inside the hymnal and asking for honest dealing, correct choices, and help maintaining "the ideals of West Point in doing our duty to Thee and to our Country." Finally, we're asked to greet one another. In a much more exuberant and lengthy version of the sign of peace at a Catholic Mass, and a reminder of our Resurrection Sunday in Harlem that even now seems long ago, worshippers roam the church, greet friends, seek out strangers. The man in front of us turns and shakes my hand with the grip of a blood pressure cuff. The hellos go on for more than five minutes, during which the two dozen kids in attendance depart for the Children's Church one floor below.

There's another quick reading by the young woman, Joel 2's "Even now, declares the Lord, return to me with all your heart, with fasting and weeping and mourning."

I watch the man and woman in front of us nuzzle and I take in the theme from most of the churches I've visited since Easter: *Return. Come back. Be real.*

The man in the lighter suit takes to the pulpit. He's U.S. Army Chaplain Major Darrell Thomsen, former infantry mortar man, current resident of the little granite cottage attached to the back of the chapel. His message: "The Best Is Yet to Come."

"If we walk without God, this life is as good as it gets," he says, after a pause adding, "If we walk with him, the best is yet to come."

This means going willingly, Chaplain Darrell says. He recalls seeing a little boy unquestioningly trailing his father's every step on a visit to the zoo. "Lord, forgive me," Darrell prayed. "I don't walk with you like that, but you show me it's possible."

Ours needs also to be a walk of conviction, Chaplain Darrell points out. "Let me ask you this: Why are you here today?"

No one answers.

"To what?" Chaplain Darrell prompts.

"To worship," says the big guy in front of me, not very loudly. Chaplain Darrell nods, then advises that we pray without ceasing, not an original suggestion but it always sounded like an interesting challenge. It must have seemed that way to Chaplain Darrell, too, because he says, "I finally figured out what Paul meant by that. It's being aware of the presence of the Almighty at all times. At the heights. At the depths, everywhere in between . . .

"Sometimes we get distracted, draw away, get caught at work, at home, have physical struggles and the lowest lows, and we go, 'I'm lost, I can't find Him.' I tell you: God has never taken his eyes off his children. God says, 'Acknowledge that you walked away. Acknowledge, repent, return, and you can enjoy and embrace again—we'll walk together.' If we don't walk with God, this life is as good as it gets. If we do, the best is yet to come."

The sermon is over, and it's the best I've heard since Resurrection Sunday. Chaplain Darrell's friendly and matter-of-fact delivery delivered goods that were another appreciated reminder—as simple as the nudge to ask for help. To remember that we're never alone.

But I'm still waiting for some mention of Memorial Day. This is the United States Military Academy, statues to deceased war heroes at every turn. The program states that some of the flowers on the altar have been donated in memory of First Lieutenant Laura Walker, USMA Class of 2003. She'd hardly left this place. Why not mention her?

But why should the subject of death be brought up here when the government forbids publication or broadcast of images of caskets returning home from Iraq, and whose commander in chief has yet to attend a single funeral for any of the 2,474 soldiers killed there in the 1,170 days the war has been waged as of this writing?

Tommy and I walk down the hill. Past the Catholic Church where cadets in bow ties and short jackets head to Mass. We take a left and cross the street to the cemetery.

Many of the markers are the white round-topped type you see in pictures of Arlington. Some of the newer ones are grander, big and shiny. At one of those, a large black rectangle beneath a tree, an older man and woman stand before a stone for a young soldier named Peter. The man holds a jug of Poland Spring with which the woman dampens a hank of paper towels. Slowly, she wipes the surface.

Tommy and I wander toward the back of the grounds. And that's when I spot it. One of those Arlington styles, the third in a row with patches of still-growing-in grass indicating these graves are fresh. Beneath the engraved cross is:

LAURA M. WALKER
1LT
US ARMY
AFGHANISTAN
JUNE 16, 1981
AUG. 18, 2005
CLASS OF 2003
USMA

Small stones rest on top of the marker, evidence of a visit, as are the two flags, a drying floral arrangement, and one as new as this day, bold white lilies and blue columbine.

Laura Margaret Walker was twenty-four when an improvised explosive device detonated beneath her vehicle during operations near Delak.

She was the twenty-sixth of the thirty-four West Point grads killed since September 11.

In her brief life she resided in three countries and eighteen cities and studied in ten schools before graduating from high school in

Belgium and earning a bachelor's degree in political science and systems engineering from West Point.

Though her career choice is not one that ever would cross my mind, we had interests in common, I would learn later, through an online search. She enjoyed photography and had some images published, in *Stars and Stripes*. She was dreaming of attending graduate school for journalism. She taught yoga. One Web site photo shows her astride a horse.

She was buried in the cemetery past which she used to run, and down the hill from the Cadet Chapel at West Point. Where, on this Memorial Day weekend Sunday, at the Cadet Chapel's Protestant service, not a word about the dead was uttered.

TRINITY EVANGELICAL CHURCH

PETERBOROUGH, NEW HAMPSHIRE

Its slogan might be "Live free or die," but "conservative" is the word that brought me to New Hampshire this morning.

I wanted to visit a church so labeled in what's just been designated one of the ten most liberal states. My pick, Trinity Evangelical Church, is a member of the Conservative Congregational Christian Conference. This autonomous denomination of 256 churches was begun in 1948 by Congregational Church members and officials disturbed by the great numbers in their faith who they believed furthered or accepted liberal views in areas including theology, culture, and politics. This conservative church just happens to be in Peterborough, a picture-postcard town of six thousand, considered by many to be the inspiration for All-American Grover's Corners in Thornton Wilder's 1938 Pulitzer Prize–winning play, *Our Town*. In modern-day Peterborough, located not far from the MacDowell artist colony where Wilder often summered, choices for worship include three churches with Congregational in their titles, and houses of worship for Baha'ists, Christian Scientists, Catholics, and Lutherans.

My friend Cindy has come along, but once our ninety-mile drive is through, she takes the keys and drives to the town center to browse. Raised Catholic, she stopped attending Mass after being confirmed during her freshman year of high school, one year after we met, and didn't return to organized religion until she recovered from breast cancer at thirty-four. For a couple of years after that, she, her husband, and their three children attended a United Methodist church in their town next to mine. These days, any need Cindy has for spirituality she finds in family, home, garden, and yoga. She will spend the next hour and forty-five minutes browsing a bookstore while I sit in the second chair of the very back row at Trinity Church, a place that pulsed with music even as I walked past the winter-beaten trucks and wagons filling the lot of the sprawling yellow brick building.

In the lobby, a fiftyish white, lanky, balding, and mustachioed man in wire-rimmed glasses had stopped to shake my hand and tell me his name: John Engle. That didn't ring a bell until I entered the sanctuary and read in the program for today's service that John is Pastor John.

My seat in the left-hand section of 3, and just in front of the 25 reserved for families, is one of maybe 200 brown vinyl folding chairs holding 150 worshippers. We face a band of four men and three women playing a flute, guitar, electric keyboard, and drum against a backdrop of four tall and thin windows that show gentle sheets of rain advancing on a pine-treed hill. A simple wooden cross hangs between the two center windows.

I'm happy to spot some large canvases along the wall, but the first is a giant arm, its hand violently nailed to a board. Across the way, a peaceful triptych consists of hills, flowers, ocean, and the words "Resurrection and Life."

Worshippers' wardrobes are more L.L. Bean than Louis Boston, but the same Bibles and binders toted by the suit-and-tie FBS crowd are present, with the added we're-in-it-for-the-long-haul touch of bottled water. The median age is forty-five, and there are maybe fifteen kids in the mix. No people of color. The room is high and wide and could be a basketball court, maybe still is. The band is fully amplified and microphoned, so the music is as clear as the lyrics shown on movie screens at the front and rear of the room.

With an unceremonious start, housekeeping announcements are read by a gray-haired woman wearing the only hat in the church. She informs us of a day of prayer and fasting, and of a special collection for a discretionary fund. When she's through, most of the congregation stands. There is music, and lyrics: *God with us, God so close to us, God with us, Immanuel, Immanuel!*

Some congregants raise their arms. The pianist whispers into the microphone, "We press on to you. You are so good, Lord, so faithful. There is nothing that compares to you." Applause follows.

If I were God, I think I just might be embarrassed by the somewhat pandering lyrics. It's not the first time songs have interrupted my spiritual vibe. Back at New Mount Zion, Reverend Washington had proclaimed, "He's a worthy God," which made me wonder if there were some unworthy ones who also had been in the running. Today's lyrics will include *How marvelous, how wonderful you are.* And *For no-one else in history is like you,* and *For thou, oh Lord, art high above all the earth, thou are exalted far above all gods.* Doesn't God know all that already? How about a number that reminds the mortal rest of us how great we can be, how wonderful the things we might do on this earth?

I flip through my copy of the May/June *TE Connection* and read of the upcoming church picnic ("bring your own meat") and trip to New York to work on a dormitory for missionary students. Then Pastor John stands to talk about evangelization. "Part of my struggle in this area is that I usually spend so much of my time with believers that I don't have many close relationships with non-Christians," he tells us. "But there are also times when I detect in myself what is essentially an attitude of 'I can't do it until I'm a better Christian.' While I want to be growing in my discipleship, I also need an attitude of faith that trusts God is powerful enough to use me in spite of my imperfections."

The choir is silent for the first time in half an hour, and everyone is seated. The woman with the hat steps forward again, saying, "We thank you that you are a faithful God." She stands at a small altar that holds two maybe eighteen-inch-tall wide circular golden columns topped by crosses. She offers prayers for preachers, teachers, the ill, for the spirit of repentance to fall upon this nation.

Policemen, firemen, the youth retreat, and "that children in the community who never heard your name will come to know you."

As in several of the churches I've visited, the relatively few children in this community exit for Sunday school. It's tithing time, and two men with baskets approach the front of the church as some in the seats scribble checks as if they didn't know a collection would be taken.

Pastor John fixes to his ear one of those hands-free rock-star microphones. He wears no pastoral costume, just blue jacket, dark tie, chinos, and takes his place before a music stand that must hold the notes for the sermon he will deliver in not a particularly booming voice, but with conviction.

"We thank God in his presence and want you to hear no matter what your week was like, we welcome you," he tells the congregation. "I don't know there are many places you come to and be told 'We're glad you're here.' If you don't hear me say anything else today, know that: We thank God you're here."

I like that. If I weren't on this quest, the word "conservative" on the sign down by the road might have kept me from ascending the church driveway. But I'm here to experience, it's time to be attentive, and I have to say I am definitely feeling welcome.

Pastor John reminds us that we're in a series about Paul's journey to and ministry in Rome. It's in the Book of Acts, which he pronounces as the Book of X. Before he begins, Pastor John offers another prayer reminding God that he's great. Then he says that "X is more fascinating than my ability to convey it," but he does a pretty good job. It's another example of Protestants knowing their Bible and loving to talk about it. Using either Bibles they brought in or copies of the maroon hardcovers stacked near the door to the sanctuary, people follow along as Pastor John gives the history of the most obscure Roman figures and customs. He even dissects syntax. When Paul says "an angel of the god whose I am and who I serve stood beside me," the pastor points out the order of the words. "It's not that he serves, it's 'My first identity is I belong to him.' Lots of people reverse those two and are trying to find their identity through what they do for God."

When Paul is given a message not to be afraid during a storm at sea, his delivery of that message affected the other 267 (only three of them Christians, Pastor John notes) on board. "You may be the only Christian in your workplace, neighborhood," Pastor John is saying, "Yet God Almighty can use you."

It turns out the golden cylinders hold Communion, which Pastor John says "reminds us of the Lord's great sacrifice on our behalf." Following the sermon, four giant slices of bread from inside are placed on four plates passed through the sanctuary by as many people. The squares look like pound cake, yellow and heavy. Most congregants take a pinch of it. I pass. In a Catholic Church, only members—and only members with clean consciences—are allowed to receive the Eucharist. I'm accustomed to hurdles before one participates in this part. No restrictions have been announced here, yet I still don't feel it's my place. The pianist is singing *Praise the Lord O my soul, who redeems my life from the pit* as the second cylinder is opened to reveal trays of tiny clear cups holding red wine. The cups are passed around. Pastor John is stating, "This is blood shed for you, do this in remembrance of Jesus." And throughout the room, small cups are raised, then swallowed. The same four people who distributed the wine now efficiently circulate trays for the empties.

This part of the service is as plain as Pastor John's wardrobe. In this faith that rejects hierarchy, it's the people who offer the bread, rather than one set of blessed fingers. I like the involvement, the participation, the idea that both pastor and congregation can have vital roles in worship.

New words glow on the screen and the music is marchy. *To God be glory, great things he has done.* Each and every one of the stanzas is sung. Most Catholics dispatch a song after the end of one verse and line of chorus. But these folks hang in, four, six, eight verses, to the end. Which is when Pastor John reads, "To the only wise God"—making me again wonder how many gods are out there, in whatever level of intelligence—"be glory. And all God's children say Amen."

It's over, without even really going near the word on the sign, with only a save-the-sanctity-of-marriage brochure in the lobby doing any of the railing against modern culture I'd anticipated. I felt welcome, and Pastor John taught me something. As did Wilder, whom I read before this trip. Awaiting Cindy's return, I recall a few lines from *Our Town*, the end of the address a minister writes on an envelope. Name, street, town, and then, "The United States of America; Continent of North America; Western Hemisphere; the Earth; the Solar System; the Universe; the Mind of God."

We're all in God's mind. Whatever the license plate. Or the words on the sign at the bottom of the hill.

TRINITY EPISCOPAL CHURCH BY-THE-SEA

KIHEI, MAUI, HAWAII

Betty is on a mission. During my week on Maui, she is determined to show me the "real" Hawaii. I happily submit. It is my first time in this heavenly state, where she has rented us a national park cabin a coconut's throw from the lava-cliffed ocean. I am giddily relaxed and she can take me wherever the heck she wants.

I've known Betty since college, when she and Mary shared an apartment near Boston. Betty's father is from the island of Oahu, and Betty visits the state of Hawaii several times a year, making her more than a casual tourist. Call her ambassador, one fiercely knowledgeable about and supportive of the islands' original culture and inhabitants. Like Mary introducing me to the Greek Orthodox Church she adopted in adulthood, Betty will be my guide here. She picks me up at Maui's Kahului Airport, drapes a sweetly fragrant plumeria lei around my neck, drives us as far east as we can go, and for the rest of our week I smell eucalyptus-lined back roads, gaze at a cloud-hatted volcano, float in clear waterfall-fed pools, walk black-sand beaches, and gorge on homemade feasts of produce purchased for a song at front-yard stands.

We reenter civilization on Sunday, because it's time for Betty to go back to her life as a lawyer north of Boston and for me to go to church. I get the feeling I'm in the new "real" Hawaii here, two hours from that rainforest cabin, this neighborhood of condos, trimmed lawns, and a trailored speedboat at the curb. But I am visiting the church founded by a man who loved the original real Hawaii, who is called the first renowned Hawaiian scholar and philosopher, and who was the second Native Hawaiian ordained in the Christian ministry.

David Malo was born a commoner on Hawaii around 1793, but his father served the court of King Kamehameha I, and that led to David's friendship with a high chief. He soaked up stories about early island life, and went on to marry an older chiefess. After her death, David moved to Maui in the 1820s, to a house near which a school was built. He was thirty-eight when he became a member of the first class of Lahainaluna Seminary, where he ate up books and was a star pupil. He also was encouraged to write all he'd learned about the islands' history. That led to *Hawaiian Antiquities*, one of the most important and earliest books in Hawaiian. David authored other titles and, having accepted Christianity, helped translate into Hawaiian portions of the Bible.

When they arrived on the Hawaiian islands two thousand years ago from Tahiti and the Marquesas, the first settlers brought with them religious faith centering around nature, believing all living things contained divine power. That polytheistic society greeted the first Christian missionaries, fourteen men and women sponsored by a New England Protestant board for foreign missions who arrived from Boston in 1820. Their words were accepted eagerly, and within a quick decade the official religion of Hawaii was Protestant. David Malo was one of the earliest converts, and in 1852 he designed and built Kilolani Church in Kihei. David and Betty would have gotten along. He rued the whites' growing impact on the islands and even requested that his burial be "above the tide of foreign invasion." The church wasn't a year old when he died there on October 3, 1854. In keeping with his wishes, he was buried atop Mount Ball, which overlooks his alma mater.

The ceiling of the former Kilolani Church is now sky, truly one I don't have to worry about. Wall remnants range in height from knee-high to maybe ten feet. Salmon-colored trumpet flowers hang from a bush near the choir space to the right of the simple altar table. Birds sing, and the ubiquitous island roosters crow from greenery in the ancient cemetery behind what remains of the back wall.

The original structure, of coral, rock, and wood, was partially destroyed by fire around 1893, during overthrow of the monarchy. The blaze is believed to have been set in protest of those approving American takeover. A few years later, flooding—the site isn't a full block in from the beach—claimed most of the ruins, which largely went ignored for half a century. In 1976 a small Episcopal congregation began worshipping at the remains of the church that since has become part of the Diocese of Hawaii.

I visit thirty years later, on the day that is both Trinity Sunday and, Hawaii being the only place in America to still honor royalty, the ninetieth anniversary of the annual parade marking King Kamehameha Day. The priest and an altar boy stand at the back entrance as I slip through the opening and take the first seat on the left. Nine hard plastic benches the color Crayola used to call flesh line each side of the aisle. To my left, outside the low church wall, a woman and the blond dog in her lap are the only occupants of six more pews ready to accommodate worshippers numbering more than the one hundred the church proper can fit. Within the wall remnants sit twenty-one adults and one child, and an organist and six choir members are in their place just past the trumpet vine. Everyone is white except for two men of color in the choir, two more in the main church, and the woman with the dog. Dress is casual. The aloha shirts I'd always thought were just a tourist thing are worn by every man here. Some have added leis of black-polished kukui nuts. Women are in summer dresses, some of them with the same bold floral patterns as the men's shirts. The priest, white, in his sixties and with a full head of gray hair receding just a bit, wears wire-rimmed glasses that look like the kind that might turn dark in the sun—probably a smart thing to wear to a church with no roof. He is garbed in a long white robe and beige woven scarf. Chinos and dark brown shoes peek from below the hem. A woman at the back of the church blows a conch shell. The "whooooooo" brings us to our feet. The priest and the altar boy, a tan blond teenager, his white robe ending in bare legs and tennis shoes, walk up the aisle, to the altar covered by a white cloth with a design of three circling yellow fish. The Reverend Robert Nelson introduces himself and says he's filling in today because the regular pastor has gone to the General Convention.

He tells us he's a retired minister from Alaska, living here in town. He then speaks several lines of Hawaiian. Not that I know what correct pronunciation would sound like, but he doesn't seem to trip over any of the words, and probably easily could deliver the name of the street we're on: Kulanihakoi.

The choir members begin to sing an English hymn into microphones that feed sound into big black speakers at the front of the church. The wide open space makes them hard to hear. I reach for the blue hardcover hymnal I was given along with a red hardcover Book of Common Prayer by a man inside the little brown wooden hut just off the parking lot. Tiny ants crawl on the book, on the seat. By the time I find the index, the music has concluded. Pastor Robert is praying and I'm looking through the *Ka Leo O Kahikolu*, the four-page yellow bulletin that offers no translation of its title. In it, Dick Zipf is thanked for electrifying the Book Pavilion and repairing termite damage. Used postage stamps are being collected to benefit Christian education efforts in Africa. And the search for the fifth bishop of Hawaii is on. "Nominations are now open for this position and anyone is eligible to nominate any priest or bishop." I try to imagine a similar notice in Catholic bulletins, parishioners having a say as significant as being able to toss a bishop candidate's name into the hat.

The pages detailing today's service include prompts for when to stand, the first time in my touring that I find such a direction, the first of many other Catholic similarities. The liturgy consists of the same weaving of prayers, hymns, readings, creed, sign of peace. I flash to my uncle's story about wandering into an Anglican church while in England during World War II and thinking it was Catholic. "I didn't realize it wasn't until the Mass was over," he said. I reminded him about the roof-falling-in thing. Had he become afraid once he realized he was in the "wrong" kind of church? My uncle had waved his hand to clear the room of my question. "They only tell you that so you won't find out it's the same thing, only without all the hocus-pocus, confessing, all that."

Far from England, this similar could-be-Catholic church includes a million-dollar view. The dormant volcano Haleakala looms behind Pastor Robert as he begins his sermon, telling us how, in ancient Japan, clocks emitted smells so that if you woke in the night you'd know what time it was. He's on an Anne Graham Lotz kick, talking about awakenings.

Then, like Pastor John in Peterborough, he's on to Paul, who he says "turns our attention to the mission of Jesus, which we sometimes call new birth, or born again." This has been a recurrent theme these past weeks. You must be born again. It's a major issue for non-Catholic Christians, and one not discussed in the church that I know.

Pastor Robert says that Paul reminds us we are not only members of Christ's family, we are heirs. Our inheritance is great, he tells us, putting it in a sentence: "God has more love for you and this world than we will ever have hearts to receive."

Overhead, birds continue to chirp. Wild roosters help with the wakeup theme, even though it's nearly 10:00 a.m. One of the millions of Maui kitties strolls past. This is a laid-back place nearly within earshot of the surf, but Pastor Robert closes with the serious, sharing a Serengeti myth about lion cubs being stillborn, and having to be awakened by a roar.

He recites woes from last night's news. How many kidnappings were reported, how many bombings, how many congressmen brought up on ethics charges, businessmen on influence peddling. Overwhelmed, we tune out the news, Pastor Robert notes. He encourages us to become involved: "We must go where the heart seems least present. To the world where lion cubs are stillborn. Whether Republican, Democrat, Independent, gay, straight, first generation or twentieth generation. We have become accustomed to fear. Passive, immobile compliance."

But we need only remember who we are. Whose we are. "Once in Galilee," Pastor Robert reminds us, "there was a lion who roared to life those who were yet stillborn. They became followers, brothers and sisters of Christ."

The Nicene Creed is recited, a 1,681-year-old expression of faith common in the services of not only Catholics but most Protestant faiths. The woman who blew the conch lists prayer intentions and the bread and wine are carried from the back of the church by two men in aloha shirts. The consecration is one that again could have fooled my uncle, Pastor Robert blessing the bread and wine with nearly the same language used in a Catholic Mass. Communicants step forward to receive, and return to their pews to reflect. In this setting, it's nothing anyone seems to want to rush—I could sit here all day. But Pastor Robert is urging us forward.

"Let us go forth rejoicing in the power of the spirit," he says before walking back to the aisle.

Eight weeks into these visits, I'm mindful of the moment or lesson or image I've been taking with me from each church. Ruby's hugging this stranger at Spartanburg, the ancient sounds from the choir in Newport, that eloquent silence in Philadelphia. Today the piece of gold I carry away might be that detail of the lion, but I'm thinking that it might be this single line: "God has more love for you and this world than we will ever have hearts to receive." As big as that sky that *Dziadziu* pointed to. The same one that is the true roof of this church.

SOUTH ROYALTON WARD MEETINGHOUSE

SOUTH ROYALTON, VERMONT

"You're going alone?"

"Be careful!"

"They're nuts!"

Again and again I heard such comments as I planned my trip to the Mormons. But that only made me look forward to my visit all the more.

Mormon families traditionally are large, a few of their members might show up at your door now and again, and wow do these folks know how to research a genealogy. But certainly, if you're going to pick the top fact most known about this religion, it's the polygamy thing—polygyny, if you want to get all William Safire about the term for one man being married to more than one woman (polygamy is simply having more than one spouse). And if you want to get more technical, it hasn't been a practice promoted by the Latter-day Saints since 1890. That's when, coincidentally and simultaneously, the federal government threatened to seize temples, and God told the LDS Church to change its beliefs. The Great Accommodation, the manifesto that put future plural marriages on hold indefinitely, wasn't embraced by everyone. Some groups joined forces to preserve the practice. Though their members were excommunicated, the groups still exist, the largest being the Fundamentalist Church of Jesus Christ of Latter-day Saints, which is headquartered in Hildale, Utah, and whose members consider themselves to be the original Mormons.

I had pictured myself in Salt Lake City, spending this Father's Day at a religion in which the male rules (though some might comment that this is the case in most). From many a televised concert, I know that city holds an enormous choir-filled Mormon temple, and a service there certainly would have been fitting. I'm just glad I did some research before buying my ticket: the regular Joe or Josephine may enter a Mormon temple only during a special open house held after construction or renovation of the building. After that, one must join the church to gain access. Even then, a visitor won't see much of the interior—temples are used only for sacred ceremonies. And are usually closed on Sunday. That day of the week, Mormons and non-Mormons alike are welcome to worship at a meetinghouse.

The one in Palmyra, New York, is a long way from Salt Lake City, but if it weren't for a few astounding occurrences in this Finger Lakes community known as the Queen of the Canal Towns, there would be no estimated 11.7 million Mormons throughout the world. Certainly no giant Mormon temples.

These Christians consider the word of God to be both the Bible and the Book of Mormon, which they say is additional proof that Jesus Christ actually lived, and was and is God's son. Believed to contain the writing of ancient prophets, the book is named for one of the last ones, Mormon. Another prophet, Lehi, lived in Jerusalem around 600 BC yet is said to have managed to lead a small group of followers to the American continent. In 1820, a fourteen-year-old Palmyran lad named Joseph Smith visited a grove of trees and prayed for insight about which faith to follow. Smith reported that he got his answer, big-time. Both God and Jesus Christ appeared, he said, and spoke, God announcing that all religious denominations were lacking and that Joseph should await further details.

Three years later, a messenger from God arrived to begin sharing four years of teachings with Joseph. In 1827 this messenger gave him a set of gold plates written in a language Joseph did not know yet was able to translate. These were the source for the Book of Mormon, and in 1830 in nearby Fayette, New York, Joseph became the founder of the Mormon Church. Its members include 5.2 million in this country, among them former Massachusetts governor and 2008 presidential hopeful Mitt Romney, *Jeopardy!* million-dollar winner Ken Jennings, Baseball Hall of Famer Harmon Killibrew, music legend Gladys Knight, and Napoleon Dynamite himself, John Heder. All members hold faith in the Holy Trinity, along with Joseph Smith's restoration of the true church, and believe in a modern-day prophet who might bring additional changes to the church. Mormons follow laws prohibiting alcohol, coffee, and drugs. They believe in modest dress, and keep holy the Sabbath, which includes not shopping on the day given to church and family. Most of those families are traditionally large due to church doctrine on something called eternal progression, a belief that all men are the actual children of the Mormon God and one of his wives in heaven, and that every human previously lived in heaven as one of God's "spirit children." In order for those beings to attain both exaltation and godhood, each first has to live on earth, endure trials, and be determined worthy. Early Church leader Brigham Young believed it was members' duty to create earthly bodies for God's children, and that punishment awaited those who failed to do so. But those earthly bodies were to be created only after marriage. According to the church's chastity law, premarital sex is a sin, as are homosexual relations. Gays and lesbians are welcome as members, but are asked to remain celibate, and also to realize that while the church believes some are born homosexual, homosexuality can be controlled.

I'd planned to worship in Palmyra today, but being the athlete she is, my dog Tiny needed surgery to reinvent her torn ACL. I didn't want to be away from her overnight, so luckily I discovered Joseph Smith's New England connection—his birthplace a two-hour-and-forty-minute drive north, in South Royalton, Vermont.

On a hilltop not fifteen minutes from New England–bisecting Route 91 stands both the South Royalton Ward Meetinghouse and a shrine to Smith on the site where he was born and where he lived until the family's 1816 move to Palmyra. He was killed in 1844 in Nauvoo, Illinois, where the Mormons had settled and where Smith both served as mayor and ran for president of the United States. When a former church member printed an exposé of sorts, including details on polygyny among the Mormons, Smith and the city council had the press destroyed. Joseph, the husband of thirty-three—a relatively small wifeship considering successor Brigham Young's fifty-five—was arrested for the crime along with his brother, Hyrum. Both were murdered in their jail cells and both are considered by the church to be martyrs.

After looping around Joseph's thirty-eight-and-a-half-foot-tall granite monument (one foot for every year of his life), I park behind the sprawling white meetinghouse. I am alone, I am being careful—though I don't feel I have to be. Everyone looks nice enough, well-dressed, smiling, ushering gaggles of kids from mini-vans. No one looks nuts. Men and boys, most of them unjacketed in the large heat of the day yet wearing ties, glow in white shirts. Women and girls are dressed sedately in jumpers, more white shirts, and skirts. I haven't seen this much oxford cloth since parochial school.

Inside the meetinghouse I am greeted by another white-shirted man and receive a program for today's Sacrament Service, to be presided over by Bishop Gary Cass and conducted by the wonderfully named Brother Gerald Parrott. Other brothers dot the program, and one female, Sister Katlyn Wrobeleski. I pass a neat bulletin board that includes a wedding announcement and a request to mail a birthday card to Church president Gordon B. Hinckley, whose address in Salt Lake City is given. The choir, of mixed ages and both genders, is perfecting a hymn as I enter the sanctuary bright with white walls and ceiling, and twin rows of eleven pews. Approximately a hundred could fit in this little place, and by the 10:00 a.m. start of the service it is full. Mine is the aisle seat in the last row on the left, where I rest on blue-green upholstered cushions and stretch out in the kneelerless space behind a middle-aged local couple and a man with his own Book of Mormon in a tiny leather cover that closes with a snap.

"Hi, I'm Eric." A dark-haired fortyish man leans from the aisle to shake my hand.

"I like your tie," I say, pointing at the squares. Then I realize the squares have faces, and the faces have bodies.

"They're my kids," he explains. "Two boys and a girl. I get one every year."

I think he means ties. I can't ask because he turns to greet someone else.

The man with the snap Book of Mormon tells a neighbor that he is originally from Minnesota, now working in Boston. A few rows in front of him is a family of six adults, from Utah, we'll learn upon introductions. This service will include the greatest number of children in any of the churches I've attended since Easter. A third, maybe more, are teens or younger. It's another very white congregation—no surprise in a state that is 96.9 percent Caucasian. I later will spot an Asian woman and a black family of five or six, but that will be it for racial diversity.

Brother Gerald, dark suit, dark hair, maybe around forty, takes to the podium at the front of the church, where an organ stands to the left and a white cloth-covered table to the right. "Good morning, brothers and sisters, welcome. Also, welcome, fathers. I just wanted to say... it's great to be a father."

There is another pause and then Brother Gerald does a little housekeeping. The messages are few, mainly because a man he calls to the front to make an important announcement cannot be found.

A woman also in her forties stands next to the podium and motions like a conductor to lead us in song: *High on the mountain top, a banner is unfurled* ... This is another group that seems to know the words without looking in the hymnals, and dispatches each and every stanza energetically, bang bang bang. The hymn is followed by an invocation by Brother Gerald: "Kind, wise father, we're so glad to meet as Latter-day Saints." He asks that we be blessed by the Holy Spirit, that we take what we hear today with us through the week and share it with all whom we meet. The conductor leads us through "In Memory of the Crucified," during which we remain seated. She is our sole focus—again there is no artwork, not a single cross. Only one plain glass window, near the front, next to a side door that remains open for air.

During the hymn, two men at the covered table appear to be shredding pieces of bread. Six boys, ages ten to eighteen, stand in front of them. I consult the program, which tells me it's time for Administration of Sacrament. When the music concludes, one of the men reads aloud, "Bless and sanctify this bread to all the souls that may take part of it." Then the boys are handed flat, rectangular silver trays. They walk from row to row, distributing the pieces. No music, no singing, the only sound a baby fussing. When the boys return the trays to the front they are given others containing little plastic cups of the type I saw in Peterborough. But only after another blessing is asked, this one for the water and all who drink it. All this takes maybe twelve minutes. Four young speakers are next, again maybe ten to eighteen. The three boys and one girl—the aforementioned Sister Katlyn—tell stories about their fathers, Sister tucking in a holy verse and a poem from *Chicken Soup for the Latter-Day Saint Soul.* The oldest, Brother Steven Cass, begins by correcting the spelling of his name—not "Stephen"—in the program. He can say what he likes—as he goes on to point out, he is the son of Bishop Gary, seated a few feet away. "Bishop" is a grand title for the part-time job of leader of this "ward," the term for congregation. The faithful believe that a bishop can receive messages for the ward from the Holy Spirit, but they do not expect a weekly dispatch: Bishop Gary presides but does not always preach, traditionally requesting that service of members, as is the case today.

Brother Gerald thanks the four and points out that fifteen minutes remain in the hour-long service, so anyone else who wishes to speak is welcome. Eric with the baby tie steps up. He tells of being a busy father who took his sons on a campout and how that was worth the time. His talk rambles and ends with him choking up as he recalls his own father. Then, with no other volunteers coming forward to speak, Brother Gerald shyly shares his own recollection of his upbringing as one of six boys in a twelve-child family. He says he hopes to be as good a father and stepfather. None of the speakers have any special oratory gifts, or anything of great interest to impart. We can blame their youth in most cases, but Brother Gerald is no child. He's been leading the service, yet really hasn't been. It's just been happening, the hour ticking by through a filling of slots: hymn, Communion, speakers, and then a check of the clock to see it's finally eleven. I can't wait to tell those who'd been worried about my visit—there was no reason to fear anything but boredom. We've been sitting the entire hour, and continue to through the closing hymn: *Choose the right when a choice is placed before you. In the right the Holy Spirit guides. And its light is forever shining, o'er you when in the right your heart confides.*

Before the congregation exits, packets of cookies are distributed to the fathers by young girls carrying baskets. The man from Minnesota but really Boston asks for a second, for the road. He does not get it. I could use a cookie for the trip home, but not being a father I'm not offered one, and not being a church member I don't feel bold enough to ask. So I leave, still hungry.

ST. SEBASTIAN CATHOLIC CHURCH

BALTIMORE, MARYLAND

A greeting that puts the females first.

A bishop named Sharon.

A priest who's gay and doesn't make you have to guess.

This is not your parents' Catholic Church. But if you're looking for an alternative, it might be yours.

St. Sebastian is one of a small and growing number of churches created for those who desire a Catholic connection but are unwelcome for worship at a traditional Roman Catholic church. It closely mirrors that faith's liturgy and traditions, and draws those who were spiritually and/or physically wounded by what your parents might call the "real" Catholic Church.

But these churches are indeed real to those who feel they've at last found a home for their soul. Whether their signs read "Independent Catholic," "Alternative Catholic," "Old Catholic," "Liberal

Catholic," "American Catholic," "American Orthodox," "United Reform Catholic," or "Continuing Anglican," all are Christian and acknowledge apostolic succession, the belief that the authority given by Jesus Christ to the apostles extends in an unbroken line through ordination to today's bishops. These churches also are diverse and autonomous, formally unrecognized by larger and older faiths. And while they may sound like a newfangled experiment in Catholicism, their histories date as far back as two major splits from the one holy, catholic, and apostolic Church: the Eastern Orthodox Church's exit in 1054, and the Anglicans' in 1534. Worship is held everywhere from living rooms to traditional church buildings. In Baltimore, the location is First United Evangelical United Church of Christ, a 155-year-old red brick building that at 7:00 p.m. on Wednesdays and 4:30 p.m. on Sundays plays host to St. Sebastian Catholic Church.

On the Sunday I visit, the Reverend David B. G. Flaherty stands in the front courtyard on Eastern Avenue in the city's Fell's Point neighborhood, a changing community that had more than its fifteen minutes of fame from 1993 to 1999, when NBC's critically acclaimed series *Homicide: Life on the Streets* was filmed there. Urban renewal has drawn to the nearby waterfront commercial shrines including a Hard Rock Cafe, but has done little for this community just off that bustling tourist area. Though my walk down Edwards Avenue did take me past a ghost-town-creepy section of yet-to-be-renewed urbania where a man lay sprawled in a gutter, it also showed me neatly restored row houses, a wide selection of lively Latino eateries, yuppies jogging behind strollers, and a café devoted to the delights of tea. There, brewer Dell tells me I'll be fascinated by Father David, who welcomed the café by sending flowers. Indeed, floral design is found on Father's résumé, which includes retail sales, restaurant/catering service, and work for an investment firm. He holds a BA in philosophy, an MA in theology, and has completed one of two years toward a PhD in liturgical studies. He worked in Roman Catholic parishes for thirteen years in ministries ranging from youth to adult education and music and was ordained a priest in the United Reform Catholic Church on September 15, 2002. The very next day he founded St. Sebastian and celebrated its first Mass. With a pastoral staff of four, the church now serves a membership of sixty-five, approximately twenty of whom actively worship.

"Hi, I'm David" is the greeting he gives in the courtyard before telling me that music sheets and books are just inside the door. Father David is Caucasian, dark featured, and energetic, and wears a neat short haircut. He dazzles there against the bricks in a white robe decorated with blocks of prism colors from throat to ankles.

I climb the stairs, grab a copy of a definitely newish red hardcover *Gather Comprehensive* liturgy book and hymnal. I also collect a chewing-gum-green program for today's Mass, which I read will be "A Celebration of Pride," which explains Reverend David's color scheme and the multicolored ribbons strung from balcony rail to balcony rail. I sit five rows up on the left in thirteen rows of curved wooden benches that might each hold two dozen people. I find no upholstery or padding, no kneelers or rug on the antique wooden floor beneath them. The center aisle and very skinny side aisles have the same bright red broadloom as back at Sts. Peter and Paul. And, like that church, this one has an altar, this one of wood that's dark like the ceiling. Its three alcoves vacant of statues, the altar is set against a yellowish marble wall that matches the elaborate rails of the balcony curving above. I scan a brochure and read the invitation: "Come and see what it means to reclaim your Catholicism." Today, whatever their religious roots, seven men and seven women have accepted that call. All are white and all are in the casual clothing the program sanctions. Median age is midforties. There are no children present, but there is one growing inside the due-date-nearing woman occupying the seat in front of me. A dark-haired guy in blue raises a guitar at the front of the church. We sing "All Are Welcome," number 741, listed in the bulletin with the italicized stress of "All *Are* Welcome."

"We are an independent Christian community reforming and reclaiming the catholic"—little *c*—"tradition in Baltimore, Maryland," reads the bulletin. "We celebrate liturgy and the sacraments in the catholic tradition and welcome those who have traditionally felt marginalized from their catholic upbringing and heritage. We invite you to come and see the work God is doing in our parish community through the women and men who seek justice and peace in their worship and daily living."

Preceded by a man wearing a red flowered Hawaiian shirt and holding a crucifix, Father David walks up the aisle as we continue to sing all four verses. The acoustics aren't the greatest. People do their best on the uplifting and affirming lyrics: *Here the outcast and the stranger bear the image of God's face; let us bring an end to fear and danger. All are welcome, all are welcome, all are welcome in this place.*

"Happy Sunday," Father begins. "We're happy to see you."

You'd believe him. There's a friendly vibe here. I wonder if I am just feeling more grateful because I've had a long day already—the plane that originally was to have flown me here was delayed several hours due to being hit by lightning en route to the airport—and even though I'm going home tonight I'm feeling a bit homesick. I realize that particular feeling is mainly because of all the Catholicness around me. This service—the order of hymns, prayers, readings, sermon, consecration, Communion, the final See ya next week —is second nature to me. If Episcopalians are Catholics with divorce, as someone recently described them to me, Contemporaries are Catholics without a hoot given to which adult another adult loves. Yes, today is a Celebration of Pride, but we're not getting hit over the head by references to gays, lesbians, bisexuals, or transgendered people. There is a prayer intention to fight against stereotypes, but even gay Father David needs to stop and count on his fingers to see if he missed any specific category among those groups. The sermon concentrates on the Gospel reading about Jesus snoozing in the boat as a storm rages and the apostles are frightened even though Jesus has told them that, with him along, nothing bad will happen.

"What if it's supposed to be that all that we need is already in our boat?" Father David asks. "I promised myself I wouldn't turn this into a Judy Garland sermon, but you don't have to go far beyond your backyard to find what you need. Some of us have gone around the world looking for answers"—here he raises his hand to show he's been that route—"Twice! And here we are, today, in a Catholic church! Look around you. There are answers as close as the person next to you. As close as in your own heart. That's something to celebrate."

Later, when I recounted this day, someone asked me how I felt at this very point. And the answer was that I could have started crying. I fall into none of the categories that Father David listed earlier, and traveled here just as an observer. But now I'm wishing I could sign right up. Unabashed love is as much the structure of St. Sebastian's as the wood and bricks and mortar. And shouldn't that be the first fact in any church that claims to serve God?

Following a very Roman Catholic consecration, Communion is distributed in the traditional walk-up-the-aisle-and-stand-and-receive style. After a meditation period, Father David concludes the Mass with a blessing on the pregnant woman in front of me. Our sister, Eileen, he calls her. Every line that I'm used to hearing preceded by "Brothers and Sisters in Christ" in this church starts with "Sisters and Brothers." Now we pray for our sister. For her baby. For new life, new starts. Father David tells us it's been a joy to celebrate today among us, and asks for blessings on all until we meet again. Something that I indeed hope will happen.

PART TWO: SUMMER

MARANATHA BAPTIST CHURCH

PLAINS, GEORGIA

Any churchgoing experience includes some period of bowed heads and closed eyes as prayers are offered, requests invoked, the holy beseeched. Mine usually remain open, taking in neighboring shirt cuffs, shoes, folded hands. I now can say that my focus once fell on the kneecaps of a former president of the United States.

OK, I admit it: celebrity is what lured me here, down the long flat road off which sits modest Maranatha Baptist Church in Plains, boyhood home of Jimmy Carter and the place to which he and wife Rosalynn returned twenty-five years ago when the thirty-ninth president lost his bid for a second term. But I didn't make this trip just because he was a founding member of this church, continues to worship here, and is so involved that he's been known to mow the lawn. Unless he's off shaming the slothful rest of us—whether we're eighty-two, like he, or twenty-two—by building houses for the poor, teaching college, or preventing blindness, at ten o'clock each Sunday morning, Jimmy Carter can be found here, leading a Sunday school lesson.

For Independence Day weekend, I wondered what it might be like to worship alongside a former president, and I wanted to visit a church in the Deep South. So here I am.

Whether they come for Jimmy's spiritual wisdom or just to ogle, an average of ten thousand tourists annually make this trip, filling both the three-hundred-seat sanctuary and an adjacent function hall equipped with television feed. No one is turned away, even when only two motor coaches are expected and, as was the case recently, nine arrive, packing the building with nearly nine hundred. With a membership of 130, only 30 active, it's a big joke to ask the full house: "Are there any visitors here today?"

Maranatha is ancient Hebrew-Aramaic for "The Lord is coming soon" or, "Oh, Lord, come soon." It is found only once in the Bible —1 Corinthians 16:22, according to the front of the church's yellow program—but has been adopted by thousands of independent churches. This one was founded in 1976, the result of furor up the road at Plains Baptist when an African American man, the Reverend Clennon King, applied for membership. Both Jimmy and Plains Baptist pastor, Rev. Bruce Edwards, supported the application. But the church deacons protested, citing a 1965 church rule banning "all Negroes and civil rights agitators." Rather than letting King enter, they canceled that week's services and called for Edwards to be fired. Jimmy won the presidency two days after the incident. Pastor Edwards was nationally lauded and led prayers on inauguration day. But in Plains, the deacons continued their campaign to rid the church of him. So Edwards resigned, and he, Jimmy, and Jimmy's wife, Rosalynn, along with twenty-six congregants who wanted to worship at a church open to all, formed Maranatha.

The church contributes to the Cooperative Baptist Fellowship, but its most famous member in 2000 disassociated himself from the Southern Baptist Conference, saying it had adopted policies violating "the basic premises of my Christian faith," among them barring women from becoming pastors, and directing wives to "submit . . . graciously" to their husbands.

At Maranatha this morning, congregant Jan Williams is telling us, "We do not care what color you are, what country you're from, as long as you come to worship."

But they do care what you might be packing. "Arms out, feet apart," the female Secret Service agent had instructed me at the church door as her two male colleagues inspected the few items I took from my pockets: rental car keys, pens, notebook, cash, camera. The camera is key. This is the first worship experience that I know will net me a celebrity shot.

"President and Mrs. Carter nearly always remain long enough after worship time for each visitor or group to have a photo taken with them," informs the Maranatha Web site I'd consulted because, of all the living presidents, Jimmy is the only one that I'd actually want to meet. Many say he's been a better postpresident than president, and count me among them. The day after he gives this lesson, he and Rosalynn will fly to Nicaragua and help monitor an election. It's part of the work they perform through the Carter Center, which the couple founded in 1982 and which in more than sixty-five countries has furthered democracy, conflict resolution, human rights, disease prevention, and agricultural education.

"Don't take it personally if Mrs. Carter chooses not to stay to be in the pictures. She might have something to do. She and the president are just like you and me. They only have twenty-four hours in the day." It's Jan Williams again, now at the front of the church, giving us the basic rules of the morning. She's around sixty, reddish-brown short hair, black slacks, yellow short-sleeve sweater, simple gold pendant around her neck. Jimmy personally selected her as visitor liaison when he returned to live in Plains and his lessons at Maranatha became what Jan calls a circus. Jan was first daughter Amy Carter's fourth-grade teacher, and Jimmy had always admired the way she kept a class in order.

I'd arrived at Maranatha at eight thirty and was directed to the very front row at the far right of the church next to five people from Tennessee. We listen up as Jan tells us we are to refrain from applause and from chatting him up. She tells us she knows nothing about a UFO sighting near the church. "But that killer rabbit? That was true." We learn that Secret Service agents sign on for five-year stints, and live in nearby Albany because there's more to do there. Agents accompany the Carters everywhere, even grocery shopping. The couple are alone just when in their own home, which is the only one they've ever owned, having lived otherwise in rented public housing, governor's quarters, and of course the White House. Sorry, Jan doesn't know Jimmy's favorite dessert, but she can tell you that he adores her deviled eggs at church suppers. Jimmy's father, two sisters, and brother died of pancreatic cancer, and Jimmy gets regular checkups. He will have a new book out later this year, something about the Middle East "and all very true," Jan assures. If anything in the church breaks, Jimmy's the one to call. He will be buried probably at his home, or at the Carter Center at Atlanta's Emory University. "But I don't want to live to see that," Jan says, tearing up. "He's going to live forever."

There are now maybe 250 people here in the three-hundred-seat sanctuary. All are white save for four black visitors and a family of four blacks in the member seats, which are the four benches behind me and another four on the far left section, all eight cordoned. The Web site assures that traveling clothes will be suitable for worship, and that is the choice of most, including the woman in the I FOUND GOD T-shirt. Contrasting the rest of us are the six church members in the cordoned sections, so very well dressed, some of the women's suits sequined.

We fill pews made of wood and upholstered with red rug-like material on backs and seats. There are no kneelers. The walls are painted light green. Below is a green almost-shag rug; above, a white ceiling is lit by a dozen shiny brass-and-glass fixtures. The church here in Plains is, well, plain, and is yet another house of worship without a single cross inside. There is no altar, just a raised carpeted stage, a wooden pulpit, and two high-backed white wooden chairs. Behind them is a waist-high partition and then two rows of seats for the choir. An organ sits to the right of the raised platform, a piano to the left. Just below the pulpit is a small table with white legs. THIS DO IN REMEMBRANCE OF ME is carved into the front edge below the tabletop.

There's a palpable feel of excitement as the Reverend Jeff Summers enters from the door behind the organ. He's white, baby-faced, and maybe thirty, in a fine dark suit and one of those photo ties like Eric the Mormon's, his with a laughing bald infant in each square. I join the congregation in bowing my head in prayer, and notice the door behind the organ open and someone take a seat in the folding chair next to my pew. I raise my eyes for a second. Sitting close enough that we could touch knees is Jimmy Carter.

Without being too obvious, I stare at the dark gray trousers, darker socks, and brown tasseled loafers. The folded tan hands, the still-healing nick on the back of the left one, the plain gold wedding band, the wrist bearing a low-end watch with Velcro-ish band. The blue-and-white pinstripe dress shirt. The gray-and-blue plaid jacket. The black strings of the sterling bolo holding seven turquoise dots encircling an eighth. Then the president rises from his chair. It's time for Sunday school.

Everyone behaves, remaining in their seats, refraining from applause while the president roams the front of the three sections of pews. His voice is the familiar drawl but his features certainly are older. Yet it's the real Jimmy Carter. Visitors' places of origin are called out: Texas, Virginia, South Carolina, New Mexico, Romania. Jimmy asks if there are any ministers or missionaries in the room. A hand is raised, and an Episcopal priest from Columbia, Maryland, is asked to say the opening prayer, requesting the help of God, "whose blessing and peace floats all nations of the world."

This lesson is about Paul and the Corinthians, but it's also about Jimmy. I mean that in a good way. He's a good teacher. And one of the reasons is his use of the personal, which shouldn't be surprising considering his lusting-in-his-heart candor in that infamous 1976 *Playboy* interview, after which his ratings plummeted. On this day, the theme is not that different. Because, as Jimmy notes, "This is about the seck-shu-al."

Boiled down, the fifty-minute lesson is about couples—married couples, he notes—and their duties to one another. "What do we know about Corinth?" Jimmy starts.

"Seaport" is shouted.

"What else do we know?"

"Pagan worship."

"Massive pagan worship," Jimmy acknowledges. "It was a religion based on sex. A thousand professional prostitutes packing the city."

He reminds us that marriage is sacred. "This is a special week for Rosalynn and me," he says. "If we survive five more days, we will have been married sixty years." He says they keep their relationship fresh with new experiences—including learning to ski at age sixty-two—and adds that reading a chapter of the Bible at bedtime for the past thirty years has been a big help. "We try to end each day in the spirit of harmony. We try to heal all wounds before we go to sleep."

And for those who can't—before sleep, or ever?

"Jesus said there should be no divorce, except in the case of infidelity. In modern-day culture, the problem of marriage is on the forefront. It took a whole week for the legislature to discuss gay marriage. I'm not in favor of gay marriage. Jesus never mentioned it. But he did mention very strongly not to divorce."

I jump to thoughts of my friend Janice, who last week told me that her aging father has been after her to return to the Catholic Church. "He's asking me," Janice says, "and I tell him I just don't want to hate people."

I don't either, which is a big part of these trips, finding out what other people believe and who—if anyone—they feel is unworthy to worship next to them. I have to say that I'm let down that civil rights icon Jimmy Carter would prevent any two people from marrying.

"Rosalynn and I have been faithful for sixty years," he's telling us. "Our older son married and had two beautiful children. He had a very unhappy marriage. So that happened—he got divorced.

"When I was a child, it was not the thing to do. I knew nobody in Plains who was divorced. We knew people in Hollywood and New York got divorces. We knew those who were living together. My aunt, Miss Cassie Abrams, was married but living with another man—a doctor—but never thought about divorce."

I try to imagine a priest getting up there and sharing such details of the personal. Other than Father David in Baltimore—heck, he referred to his addiction struggle in the bulletin—I can't.

"How do you think we should integrate this command from Jesus Christ himself?" Jimmy asks. "I don't condemn my son, for instance. It's a grievous thing, very hard for parents to have a child divorce. We loved his wife like a daughter . . . Strict interpretation of anything—this is a temptation. We have the same problem in Christian religion. What Christians should strive to achieve—they should comply with God's word, but those who don't comply, there should not be hatred or condemnation of those who don't comply. Strictly speaking, the Bible is against divorce. But those who are divorced should be loved and forgiven and understood as much as possible. Same with those who are selfish, gossip, hurt or ignore the feelings of others. All of us are guilty of these. Paul says all have sinned deserve what?"

"Death," someone behind me calls out.

"But because of the grace of God, they can be forgiven." Jimmy pauses. "What are the keywords? Peace, forgiveness, and love."

He tells us that while studying the problems of two thousand years ago, we are looking at the problems of today. Then he adds a little commercial. "After the church service, Rosalynn and I will be outside. Enjoy Plains while you're visiting and come back to see us."

Two-thirds of the sanctuary hightail it after Jimmy's lesson. The Tennessee family to my left has also left and, because we've been instructed to use the same seat for worship as we have for the lesson, I am alone and obvious in the front row. Jimmy, with Rosalynn in royal blue suit and large pearl necklace, is walking to a seat three benches behind mine. A Secret Service agent takes Jimmy's previous place. He's so close I can hear the chatter from his earpiece.

Choir members, including Jan Williams, walk to the front. Pastor Jeff follows, as does his enormously pregnant wife, Jessica.

She steps to face the center of the choir, which is eleven members large. *Beautiful Savior, King of Creation, Son of God and Son of Man!* they sing to the accompaniment of a recording.

There's no pocket in front of me, and no hymnal on the seats. I'm suddenly offered a copy by the woman seated next to Rosalynn.

Another hymn, "We Utter Our Cry," asks that those gathering to talk peace be free from bias and guile. After a simple offertory prayer, around come the dark wooden collection plates that Jan earlier told us Jimmy himself turned on a lathe. Following a brief children's sermon, another hymn, a reading by Jessica, and yet another hymn, it's time for the pastor's sermon. This message is about faith. How the Bible's famous hemorrhaging woman believed that if she touched the hem of Jesus's cloak she would be cured. I think back to Newport, and the father helping his small son to touch the vestments of Father Anthony. The hemorrhaging woman had been cured. As was a little girl whose loved ones thought she'd passed away. Jesus had chided them: "Do not fear—only believe." All we need do is have that faith.

"Jesus says by your faith you have been healed," Pastor Jeff reminds, the message strong but his presence at the pulpit on the weaker side. "Strength, courage, persistence, not giving up. What if we never had kids because we saw how terrible they could be at two? What if we never loved again because somebody hurt us? Have faith."

I'm looking at Pastor Jeff and wondering what his job must be like. Remove the resident star church members and he's a young man in a remote town of six hundred, lucky if he's preaching to two dozen each weekend. Toss the stars back in and he's still all that, but he also has the stress of following a man who's world famous, and who beats his delivery by a country mile. But at the end of the day, or at least the service, I do like the pastor's message of faith, and prefer its hope and openness to the tired and outdated fundamentals that his Sunday school teacher brought to class this morning.

After Jan snaps a photo of Jimmy, Rosalynn, and me with Jimmy's right hand grasping my waist, I head from town, stopping at the family graveyard and at Jimmy's boyhood home in Archery, now a National Historic Site complete with guides who seem to have evaporated in the heat.

I have the place almost spookily to myself. I rest on the porch swing. I wander the hallway. Placards tell me the house is filled with replicas. That's not Jimmy's kitchen table but it was his kitchen. That's not his bed but it was his room. That's not his eighty-year-old outhouse, but I take a photo anyway. Because I probably won't be back. The service was nice enough, but it didn't make me lust for a Maranatha Baptist life. Sunday school was what gave this morning significance, but school's not what I came here for, and ultimately I was saddened by the Old Testament conservatism of a man I admire for his open and liberal approach to the world's problems. Beyond the thrill of the celebrity, this service was of no service to me.

PHILADELPHIA DELIVERANCE CHURCH OF CHRIST

COLUMBUS, OHIO

My father was a man of simple tastes. The Father's Day gift he raved the most about was the handful of scratch tickets and five pounds of headcheese I once wrapped up for him. Columbus native Michael Redd knows what his dad likes, so in the summer of 2005, shortly after signing a six-year, $91-million contract with the National Basketball Association's Milwaukee Bucks, he bought his father a church.

Pastor James Redd and his wife, Haji, raised Michael and his sister, Michelle, in this Central Ohio city of 711,000. Sister Redd was a schoolteacher. James worked at a Pepsi plant and began studying ministry shortly before the August 24, 1979, birth of Michael, who was two when his father placed a pink trash can in the hallway of their home and began instructing him in the finer points of shooting, using rolled-up socks or a Wiffle ball.

At Columbus's West High School, James Redd had been an All-American recruited by big-name coaches including Bob Knight, Digger Phelps, and Dick Vitale. But his mother had been ill at the time, so James had opted to attend nearby Capital University, where he became a point guard and Haji's suitor. In 1990 he became a minister, four years later founding Philadelphia Deliverance Church of Christ in a Columbus storefront, his son eventually drumming in the church band.

That son also attended West High, and there declared his goals of making the NBA and purchasing his folks both a house and a church. He was an Ohio State freshman leading the Big Ten in scoring before being selected by the Bucks in the 2000 NBA draft. In August of 2005, the now-twenty-six-year-old all-star guard signed a megamillion-dollar contract and began investigating the purchase of an air-conditioned five-hundred-seat church previously used by

Seventh-Day Adventists. Prior to his father's fiftieth birthday, Michael bid on and purchased the white brick testament of a son's love.

My basketball knowledge being equal to my knowledge of Columbus, I have to ask the name of the six-foot-six young man who this morning walks down the side aisle in tan shirt and slacks to extend a shovel-sized hand and become the twelfth person to go out of his or her way since I entered. This congregant's introduction is "I'm Michael Redd."

"Everybody's so nice here," I tell him.

"That's the love of Christ," he says. "But here at Philadelphia Deliverance, that's what it's all about." The man known on the courts as "Silky" tells me, "God has blessed us," then asks if there's anything he can do for me. He shakes my hand again and leaves.

"How'd you find us?" Introducing herself as Sister Redd, it's Michael's mother, standing in the row in front of me, smiling in a light-green tunic and skirt. When I tell her I'm touring churches, she says warmly, "Well, you just come in and make yourself at home."

But home was never like this.

Church home, I mean. In the Catholic churches I've known, if someone wants to share your pew, you angle your knees so they have to step over you. You never speak, or even whisper, to a stranger. Here I am one of five whites in a gathering that I will find will not top fifty. Columbus's black population is 24.5 percent. In this church, it's nearly 100. Yes, I stick out, but everyone is being greeted with the same exuberance. When I comment on the next member's enthusiastic welcome, she says, "That's just Jesus."

"We all have to give it," a woman my age tells me, taking both my hands in hers. "It's like a cup. You have to pour it out so it can get filled up again."

A young white woman walks over and introduces herself as Sister Vanessa. She's in her midthirties, with frosted brunette bob. In a dark sweater and skirt, she's what you'd call respectably dressed, as is most of the congregation.

"This is not just a fashion show," she says when I comment on the general attire. "Pastor Redd wants it to be more than that."

Sister Vanessa says she was raised Catholic and moved here from

Seattle, finding Philadelphia Deliverance a year ago through friends. She's telling me how much she loves this church when her story is interrupted by a woman at the pulpit who's getting our attention with the help of the band—all male, an organist, pianist, bass player, and, there behind the copper-colored Yamaha drum kit, Michael Redd. This must mean it's eleven thirty, start of worship.

People continue to wander in. Right now there might be twenty-five in the sanctuary, its mauve color scheme repeating on plushly padded seats and seat backs, rug and walls. The usual stage is up front, plain again with blond wood pulpit behind a table on which a large vase of silk flowers rests. Behind the pulpit are several rows of benches over which hangs a large screen glowing with a painting of an older black man praying at a table. The only cross is carved on the top of a wooden placard that informs RECORD ATTENDANCE is forty-nine. Artwork is scant—four purple or maroon banners, two on each side wall, their golden letters announcing KING OF KINGS, HOLINESS UNTO THE LORD, WORSHIP HIM, HALLELUJA.

Separate from the similar-sounding United Church of Christ, the Church of Christ is nondenominational and has no central headquarters or leader "other than Jesus Christ himself," to quote Ephesians. Membership is 2 million, in fifteen thousand churches located in each of the fifty states and approximately eighty other countries. Though the faith is a product of the Restoration Movement that started in the late 1700s, members see the genesis as much earlier—Pentecost in the year 30 AD—and seek to mirror the first-century church in a modern world.

The woman at the pulpit—her gender alone a nod to current day—begins to sing: *Lord you are good and your mercy endures forever.* Clapping is contagious. People move to the beat. In the front row, a woman shakes maracas, another, a tambourine. We're asked to walk to the front of the church for what the bulletin calls Worship & Consecration. Sister Vanessa gives me a smile and I join the flow. The woman at the pulpit tells us to "come up, come up, adore him," and she segues into what I know as a Christmas song, "O Come All Ye Faithful," but with a jazzy beat. *O come let us adore Him,* she sings over and again, and we're joining her. In the semicircle before the pulpit, hands are raised. Heads are bowed. Eyes are closed, or at least downcast. This moment makes my visit. There is no statue to adore, there is no grand altar, there is no thousand-pipe organ, no full house. Only twenty-seven in this semicircle. The expression on the singer's face imploring, rapturous. I'm seven hundred miles from home, I know not a soul, yet I feel I'm here with loved ones. I could stand here the rest of the day.

But as sweet as my experience here is, were I homosexual I'd be considered damned. In the Church of Christ, sexual orientation is considered a choice, being gay a sin. That is what holds me back from buying this place part and parcel. The word "Philadelphia" on the sign outside is Greek for "love" and I'd like to feel there's hope here. But exclusionary doctrine is exclusionary doctrine.

A man stands at the pulpit as we return to our seats. He's listing things for which to be grateful. Church, friends, family, work, transportation, maybe some savings, and "that we can pray without fear of retaliation," which resounds. From the start of this project conceived while our country was at war with religion-fueled forces, I've felt grateful to be able to explore other houses of worship. To live in a culture that doesn't care if I show up on Sunday or stay home in my bunny slippers. On the plane to Plains, I sat next to an Islamic man from Dubai and asked him if many in his culture ever consider other faiths. He looked confused. "Why would we? We were brought up in this." So many in America are brought up in some form of "this." Yet so many are searching. And are free to.

"Preaching and teaching is something I want to do," Michael Redd told *Sports Illustrated* earlier this year, and he's getting some practice. "He's the Lord," he tells us passionately from the pulpit. "Hallelujah!" His right hand is raised, nearly grazing the ceiling. "We glorify you, oh Lord. Hallelujah! Hallelujah! Speak to us! We lift you up, Jesus!" He shouts a final "Hallelujah!" and his father is suddenly to his right, taking the wheel.

"I feel something in this place this morning. Let's tap into the spirit!"

Pastor James invites three church members onto the stage. Sister Vanessa, a woman named Chris, and a man named Peter. "Your pastor isn't a liar," he tells us, and he wants to show proof. To each of the three, he'd once promised that God would come through. And things have begun to happen. Sister Vanessa announces a raise of seven thousand dollars and purchase of her first house. Chris says she's begun working in a better salon. Peter wanted a job with the city, applied a year and a half ago. He tells us, "Pastor said to have faith and believe. When I go there tomorrow at eighty thirty in the morning, the job is mine."

Pastor says, "You believe in God, you walk upright before the Lord, you can't be scared. Everything you want, lay it before the Lord."

We move up front to lay down some cash, row by row beginning from the back, the last being first, as it were. Then it's Elder Bennie Meeks's time. All the way from Milwaukee, he's a gray-bearded family friend who considers Michael Redd a son, and who writes music, including last year's gospel hit "If Jesus Can't Fix It," recorded by the Mighty Clouds of Joy. He's dressed in tan suit, pink shirt, striped pink tie, and wire-rimmed glasses, and he's got energy enough for everyone.

"All you gotta do is reach up and God will reach down," he tells us. "Waaaaay down. When praises go up, blessings come down. You just heard a few testimonies. Praise the Lord!" He turns to the band and the music begins. *When praises go up, blessings come down,* he sings. *The love of God is all around.*

"People say God is dead," Elder Bennie continues. "People have their doubts. But I know where I'm going. There's a highway to heaven that leads to heaven!"

The screen gives the sermon title: "Going Out of Business. Everything Must Go." Elder Bennie reads from the book of Acts, and invites those who have Bibles to share with those who don't. A young man in dazzling white shirt and dark tie sidles to my right. He points on the page to where God is asking Saul why he's so horrible to the church, and why he's on his way to do more bad things. Elder Bennie is booming into the microphone now. "Even Saul had to do it. He had to go out of business. When are you gonna make up in your mind, 'I'm goin' out of business. I'm tired of going to the devil all the time? I don't live that life anymore. Everything must go. Everything must go.' Have you made up your mind that you will let nothing separate you from the love of God?"

Half an hour later, Pastor James asks us to join hands. "God, there are people here looking for the perfect church," he says, adding a "there is no perfect church" that speaks squarely to the quest I'm on. "But I believe here at Philadelphia Deliverance there is a river. It's black, Puerto Rican, white, it's welcoming."

This indeed is a warm place, I've felt that, have felt moved here among people of color in a church that asks members to go forth and serve.

Yet there is the intolerance of the gay community. It's one issue; would I be willing to ignore it in compromise for the riches I find here? I wonder if anyone's ever brought up the topic of a new way of thinking, whether Philadelphia Deliverance ever has been confronted by a reformer. Would I be up to that task? I'm no Martina Luther. At this stage I'm basically a note-taking tourist. I know there are no perfect churches. But a big plus of joining one in adulthood is having eyes open and a brain full of knowledge. And in adulthood it would be hard for me to join a faith with a doctrine I felt was wrong.

Announcements follow. Volunteers soon will walk the neighborhood to distribute information about the church. "So if you got a wooden leg, screw it on—you got no excuses," Pastor James says.

Michael Redd is back at the drums and the band plays as another tithing session begins. Then, without further fanfare, or closing hymn, we are done.

"Enter to Worship," ends the bulletin. "Depart to Serve."

CALVARY'S LIGHT CHURCH

THREE RIVERS, MASSACHUSETTS

This is the church I stared at as I passed during those childhood car trips to Mass at Sts. Peter and Paul. The small white-steepled building would fit perfectly into any artist's rendering of a New England town center. But in my mind, it is Notre Dame huge—one blazing icon for "the Other." For the non-Catholic. For the damned.

How perfect, how dramatic it would have been to end this year with a visit to this very house of worship. Well, I got the dramatic, but nine months earlier than planned. And the medical kind, rather than the religious.

Five days ago, I was driving back from a swim at Susan's, wearing only a soaking bikini, when my cell phone rang. I never have the thing on when I'm in town, and I never have it on in my car. But there it was, in my car, power on, and there was Tommy, on the line, saying: "Don't worry, but I'm at the hospital."

An hour earlier, his right side had suddenly ceased to work. This happened just as he was sitting down to meditate, which is another clue as to where clean living will get you. The second he entered the emergency room of our town's hospital two miles down the street, the building was struck by lightning, the CAT scan machine disabled. For further tests, Tommy would be transferred to the regional hospital half an hour away, in Springfield. I trailed in my car, frantically trying to keep sight of the pulsing ambulance lights as they zoomed ahead of me on the pike.

Tommy was admitted and kept for four days of tests in a section of the hospital called Neuroscience, which sounds like the setting for all kinds of weird experiments, and looks that way too, wires glued to the skulls of just about anybody who's not working there. Like most of the other patients, Tommy regularly was rolled from his room and fed into an alphabet soup of machines: MRI, MRA, CAT. Like most of the other family members, I smoothed the bed, straightened the newspapers, and wondered what the hell was happening. He was functioning normally by the second day, but due to his age—fifty-one the coming weekend, young for a stroke—and general good health, the doctors wanted to check for signs of any further problems. Each night I drove a mile up the street to my in-laws', where I fell against the side of the guest bed and prayed.

I prayed for myself almost as much as for Tommy. The out-of-the-blue of this draped me in memories of my childhood best friend's death in a highway accident just after grad school and, ten years later, my father's first and last heart attack. You're driving to buy an iron for your first real apartment, or you're watching a game on a Saturday afternoon, or you're sitting down to meditate. And your number's up.

What I had to remember is that Tommy's wasn't. But I was genuinely panicked even so, and begged God for help.

I had intended to do the same at this Sunday's church. Tommy, home now, is instructed to take it easy. A blood thinner is making him too dizzy to do anything but rest on a chaise lounge on the patio, and that's where I make him promise to stay for the next hour. Scrapping my plans to visit the Shakers up in Maine, I opt for the Protestant church closest to home—the one I planned to save for the very end of this year of church visits.

I make the two-mile drive and I'm actually nervous as I climb the half dozen steps to the white front door. A wave of slight panic begins when I see that I'm late, even though my watch says I'm ten minutes early for the 10:30 service posted on the movable-letter sign outside. The pastor already is speaking. And because the worshippers number only six, my tardiness is extremely obvious as I slip into the last seat on the left.

First, I must look around. I must. I've wondered all my life about this interior, and now I'm in it, the reality of it as hard as the dark wood upholstered seats, their ends decorated with a carved clover shape inside a rounded triangle. Bright red carpet splits the two sets of ten rows occupied by the half dozen worshippers who are near or of retirement age, all dressed casually—sweatshirts, pants, even cowboy boots on one guy.

The wooden seat pocket holds red hardcovers, *Hymns for the Living Church*, and black paperback Bibles, the New King James Version. I pull one of each onto my seat next to the light beige walls broken by four tall windows. To the left, I can see part of the building that holds a hair salon. To the right is the parking lot shared by both the church and Belanger's Funeral Home, where most of the village's French-Canadian residents are waked. Up front, backgrounded by a red curtain, stands an altar table holding a golden cross. A pair of candles and two silk floral arrangements are displayed at the top of a few steps in a wide alcove. To the right is a baptismal font, a door to somewhere, a hymn information board, and a set of maybe twenty organ pipes.

Above me, white tiles hang in what, ironically, is known as a drop ceiling. The very one I feared during my childhood would drop on me if I dared to enter. I think how much smaller this space is than that young mind had conjured. How sweet, really. What a throwback, a hidden treasure, much like the second-floor theater down the street, where my mother and her brothers saw films during their childhood, now a vacant space over a vacant furniture store.

Leading the service is Pastor Laura Rollet, a former realtor licensed to preach through the Association of Faith Churches and Ministers. She was vacuuming in 2005 when she heard God tell her to ask for a meeting with the council members of this church, whose eighty-seven-year-old pastor had moved to Maine three years before. Pastor Laura was no stranger to the building, living less than a mile from it, once having taught Sunday school there, and having married husband Richard—the town's building inspector—there. She requested a meeting. The Evangelical Church Council agreed to allow Calvary's Light to use the building and manage its upkeep.

This independent word-of-faith Holy Ghost Church believes the word of God is literal. Members are born again and are known to speak in tongues, something I've never witnessed. Like many conservative Protestants including Fundamentalists, Evangelicals, Pentecostals, and Baptists—as well as independents like these—they also believe in the Rapture, the end-time event when all living Christians will ascend to heaven at the same instant.

Born again during a youth conference at age fifteen and a full-time pastor since 1988, Pastor Laura looks like a Hollywood-casting-call cheerful grandma. She cuts short her blond curly hair, and today wears a blue-and-pink floral button-front dress and pearl earrings. "We know this is just a picture of what you want to do for us," I hear her praying. I write the words on a new page, and the service is over. Ten minutes after the start.

As I sit there, stunned, I hear my name.

It's Pastor Laura, who has a good memory and who has walked back to my row. She recalls that I interviewed her for the local paper fifteen years ago. But she didn't remember to change the information on the movable-letter sign outside.

"It still says ten thirty?" she asks with wide eyes. "Oh, we start at nine thirty in the summer. We've got to change that outside . . . Will you come back?"

The prospect of the future shoots me back to the patio, where Tommy and his thinning blood are resting. How do I even know what I'll do this afternoon? In the back of this church that once loomed so large, I become very small as I quietly tell Pastor Laura. About Tommy. This past week. What the doctors know, and how there's a lot they don't.

She doesn't wait a second before asking. "Let me pray for him. Would you like that?"

I nod.

"Somethin' like that," Pastor Laura says, "somethin' that can be fatal, Satan is waitin'. We'll ask that he won't come near."

I'm not crazy about the inclusion of Satan in a prayer regarding my husband—the week has been scary enough without bringing him into the mix—but I can't get away: Pastor Laura has taken my hands and is closing her eyes. I keep mine open because maybe this is the speaking-in-tongues part. But she uses the language that I know as she invokes the help of Father God, as she calls him.

She asks Father God to "help this man, help his wife," and says something again about Satan and keeping this man from him. Her words are soft in the carpeted space now free of anyone else. She concludes with an amen and a hand squeeze. She says she hopes things will be all right. She gives me a hug.

I say I hope so. I say thank you. For the prayer, the kindness, the remembering, the offer to intercede to a God this woman knows so well that they converse in the same language. And out of the blue, I have a thought that lifts me and my day: in the back of this church of the Other, of the different, of the non-Catholic, of the condemned, there, along with Pastor Laura and me, the God that is mine and the Father God that is hers, stand together in prayer.

UNITED METHODIST CHURCH OF ENFIELD

ENFIELD, CONNECTICUT

I picked this week's church solely for its convenience.

I've yet to hit one in Connecticut, which is not half an hour south of my front door, but I will today, as I still don't want to be far from Tommy.

Today is his birthday. He is fifty-one, which the doctors say is too young to be dealing with strokes of any kind, which is why they put him on that blood thinner, which is why this past Tuesday I had to rush him back to the ER. The side effects were scary, but they didn't turn out to be signs of another stroke, so after seven hours of tests Tommy was allowed to return home. Even so, I'm not taking any chances. This morning I deliver him and his usual nine Sunday newspapers to Springfield, to his parents' kitchen table, where he will be adult-sat while I sit in church.

I drive seven miles south on Route 91 and take the first Connecticut exit. I soon spot the chalet-like peaked brown-shingled roof of United Methodist, a circa 1963 structure that is the third home for the community that began back in 1791, when Francis Asbury preached to the town's first Methodist Society,

The Methodist Church itself dates to 1736, when brothers and Church of England missionaries John and Charles Wesley arrived in America. In 1968 the United Methodist Church sprang from a blending of the Methodist Church and the Evangelical United Brethren Church. It's now the largest Methodist denomination, and the second-largest Protestant denomination in America, trailing only the Southern Baptist Convention. Membership worldwide is 11 million, 8.2 million of those in the U.S.A.

Including those in Enfield, where a man and woman are welcoming me at the door. They direct me to the sanctuary, where a man in shorts hands me a copy of today's bulletin, a picture of the church bell tower on the cover. I am the first to enter the sanctuary. The row of dark wooden benches at the very back are marked as reserved, so I take the one that's second from the back in the right-hand section. The whole place could hold maybe two hundred on the vivid red upholstered seats. The ceiling, in wood the same tone as the seats, is high and boat-shaped. The front is simple, a long Plains-maroon length of cloth hanging down the center of the wall. A wooden cross is set in front of that, over a light-stained wooden altar holding a pair of candles and an arrangement of fresh flowers. To the left is a piano and an American flag. To the right is a pulpit, baptismal font, an organ, and what must be the Methodist flag: black cross, red flame.

An older couple I'd seen in the parking lot now takes seats in front of me. The woman turns and introduces herself as Ethel, and, FBS-Rubylike, wants to know if I would like a tour. She leads me to the lobby, where a man in a light-gray suit is chatting with a group. I see his black shirt and Roman collar and figure this is Pastor John Morgans, who has been at United Methodist a scant thirteen months. The church Web site tells me it's a second career for the man who for twenty-three years worked for the city of Caribou, Maine, and who in 1994 began preaching as a circuit rider, traveling eighty-six miles every Sunday between three small Down East churches. He was assigned to Enfield last summer after serving for five years at a Methodist church in Naples, Maine. And now he's shaking my hand, as will maybe ten more friendly people Ethel introduces me to before and after we snake our way through past the pastor's office, the kitchen, several classrooms, and a plastic bin holding goods donated to The Food Shelf, where Ethel tells me she volunteers.

Ethel also tells me that she has been a member here for three decades. She says the church is small, and has a family feeling. We pass framed photos of the ten or eleven pastors who've served here, including four white women and an Asian man. The remainder are white males.

The congregation today is similarly Caucasian-heavy. It numbers maybe forty-five, including ten children from infants to teens, and, as I'm finding to be the norm each Sunday, is maybe two-thirds female. Attire is on the casual side—jeans, shorts, chinos. Most of the women are dressed similarly to Ethel in her white crocheted sweater and cotton slacks. Other than Pastor John, Ethel's husband is the only man in a suit. In a clear and animated voice, Pastor John gives the announcements, that three new members soon will be joining the church, and that Olan Mills will come in October to photograph members for a new directory. Just in time for Christmas, Pastor John says, each participant will get a free eight-by-ten portrait, and a directory.

We're asked to greet one another. I reshake the hands of several people I've already met, including a twentysomething woman who's now in front of me, white jeans, striped top, Verizon flip phone, and bulky key lanyard. I inventory the seat pocket and its fat blue hardcover Bible, New Revised Standard Version; small red hymnal; miniature golf–type pencil; envelopes for donations; and scrap paper.

A female organist has started playing "We Sing to You, O God," which the woman in front of me turns to show is the first number in the small hymnal. We go through all verses. Pastor John then prays, "Lord, show us the headlines and the fine print; make them clear to us. Our heads are filled with the worries of the day. Help us to rise above the worries of the day and in the fine print to know you are with us and the world. Transcend race and war and generation gaps. Make the stranger like a brother, the widow like a mother, the convict like a son, our enemy like a friend."

On yet another Sunday, here's a prayer that has an eerie written-just-for-me quality. I can't be the only one in this building who's worrying, but I feel acknowledged already, and appreciate the reminder that God is in my world. A pretty basic belief for a believer, but rather easy for me to overlook when I'm spiraling in fret. Beyond that, I'm struck by the compassion of the suggestions to reach out to the other. The concept of making a son of a convict is heavy and daring. I like this place all the more for the way it's already shaking up my mind.

Pastor John follows that with a few moments of silent prayer. I look down at the rug, which is a bland beige tweed untrampled by kneelers. I sink into gratitude that Tommy is around to celebrate this day. A woman breaks the silence with a passage from Ephesians that I'm sure pertains to some specific moment but that could be applied to anything. I'm thinking of the current Israel/Lebanon crisis as she reads how God "has broken down the dividing wall that is the hostility between us ... He came and proclaimed peace to you who were far off and peace to you who were near." Then Pastor John gives the Gospel, from Mark, and I am back at the hospital as he reads about the sick in the marketplace begging to touch even the hem of Jesus's garment. One night after visiting Tommy, I had spotted the sign for the hospital chapel and pushed open the door. Light glowed faintly from a leaded stained glass display at one end, and along rows of seats. On the opposite wall hung a bulletin board to which people had tacked their wishes, hopes, requests for healing. A guest book was open and asked only the first names of the ill. I wrote *Tommy*, and felt the pen becoming my fingertip reaching for the hem.

Jesus taught, healed, and rested, Pastor John is telling us. Then Jesus needed a break. Into the boat he called the disciples. They floated to seclusion, and returned only when refreshed. I especially like Bible stories that show Jesus being the human. Because he was. He was tired at some points. I am tired now. The idea of floating off in a boat sounds pretty good. So I'm even more keen on Pastor's sermon, which focuses on solitude, silence, and the Sabbath.

In the way things can happen in life, I get another personalized gift from this church I picked solely for location. I hear some wisdom that both Tommy and I can use. Because not only is it smart to wind down, for one of us it is now officially doctor-recommended. Go down the list of stroke factors—weight, exercise, smoking, heredity—and Tommy has only one: stress. So I wish all the more that he were next to me hearing Pastor John detail these several *s*'s.

Solitude is first. "In today's age," he points out, "it's something we don't get much of. Solitude is more mental than physical. I believe that in solitude, we meet God. God enters, bringing fresh hope, new hope, into our lives, into our situation . . . That's why Jesus took the disciples to a secluded place. Each one of us needs time for solitude, to get away, to be close to our savior."

Silence is next, allowing us to meet and hear God. "Life is filled with sounds," Pastor doesn't need to remind us. "We don't need music, we don't need TV, we don't need talking or giggling, we need silence. So let's all just bow our head and close our eyes."

It's quiet suddenly. Arch Street quiet. Then Pastor John says amen and adds, "But that's just a small dose of what we need."

The next thing he advises is the Sabbath, as in keeping it. "A day of rest, a day to give God glory, to remember the blessings we have received, and for being grateful."

He quotes Samuel Taylor Coleridge, who said that God, by giving us the Sabbath, gave us fifty-two springs in every year. Pastor John notes that in the Bible, one phrase is often used regarding Jesus: "As was his custom" he went to worship, he rested. "He was restored, restored and right in his relationship with God."

Tithing is next, then the offertory prayer, followed by a hymn that I know and like: *Ask and it shall be given unto you, seek and ye shall find, knock and the door shall be opened unto you, allelu, alleluia.*

We are invited to voice our joys and concerns, and Pastor John prompts. "Joys?" No one answers, so he chirps, "Our new members next week!" Next: "Concerns?" Hands are raised and the worries flow: safe travel for a mission trip to Estonia, all the bombing going on in the Middle East, young people in the war zone. I want to say *Tommy* but I can't. I'm not accustomed to speaking in church, my voice being the only one.

"Let us be in prayer together," Pastor John says. "As the world is just rushing by us, help us to slow down. Help us to find you in everything."

And everywhere. Including in a church that hadn't even been on the list.

UNITY

UNITY VILLAGE, MISSOURI

When Tommy moved into my house, a whole lot of stuff moved into my mailbox. At the time, he was a sportswriter covering the Red Sox for our regional newspaper, and writing a notes column about baseball in general. Back in that Paleolithic pre-Internet era, the second responsibility meant he gleaned facts from fourteen papers he subscribed to from baseball hotbeds nationwide.

And while the sight of the automobile-sized Sunday *Los Angeles Times* filling our industrial-sized mailbox erected specially for the task certainly was memorable, the piece of mail that has stayed with me the longest was the smallest Tommy received.

The wallet-sized *Daily Word* booklet held a page of meditations for each day of the month, feel-good smarts and hope mixed with brief, similarly themed Bible passages on such topics as perseverance, healing, forgiveness, joy, and God's presence. "Unity, Unity Village, MO" was the return address for the source I never thought of as more than a publishing house. Twenty-two years after Tommy and his massive amounts of mail moved in, I've found out it's much more.

Actually, it's "the three *p*'s: prayer, preaching, and publishing." I get that from clerk JoAnn in the Unity bookstore, where I kill time before worship on this blazing hot morning.

Sure, there's a big rectangular sign out front—UNITY SCHOOL OF CHRISTIANITY—and the Italianate architecture, including a fourteen-story tower, provides a campus feel. Beyond the Unity Institute that trains sixty ministerial students in a two-year program, the Unity umbrella covers more than nine hundred Association of Unity churches; the Silent Unity round-the-clock prayer service that receives more than 2 million requests annually; retreat facilities drawing some of the world's top spiritual guides and speakers; and the printing of publications including those millions of copies of *Daily Word*.

It all started in 1887 with a humble healing prayer circle formed fifteen miles away in Kansas City by Unity founders Charles and Mary Caroline "Myrtle" Fillmore. After attending a lecture on Christian Science, Myrtle, who was suffering from tuberculosis, received a spiritual epiphany and physical healing. Charles, burdened by a withered leg, eventually experienced the same. In 1889 the two began publishing a magazine called *Modern Thought*, touting their belief that God is good and dwells in each of us. Those who attend Unity call this "practical Christianity."

"We like to say that we are not so much the religion about Jesus as the religion of Jesus," wrote poet James Dillet Freeman, who served on the board of Unity for more than fifty years. "We believe that he is the Son of God; we believe that everyone is a child of God. We believe this is true, whatever your faith, and we respect your faith."

Unity considers the Bible its "basic textbook for the teaching of Truth and a manual for the unfoldment of the soul." But biblical study for Unity is metaphysical—seeing the spiritual in everything.

In 1903 the movement became known as the Unity School of Practical Christianity, the present-day name having been adopted in 1914. A vegetarian restaurant, radio broadcasts, and *Wee Wisdom*—this country's oldest magazine for children—followed. As did growth. In 1919 the Fillmores purchased fifty-eight acres of farmland, which over the years has been expanded to fourteen hundred, and in 1953 the property became an actual municipality, possessing its own mayor, water system, security force, and zip code.

Association of Unity Churches number 550, with eighty thousand members in America, 2 million globally. Fifty-five congregations are located in fifteen other countries, most of them in Europe. Followers call themselves Unity students or Truth students and live by five simple principles:

1 God is good and active in everything, everywhere.

2. I am naturally good because God's Divinity is in me and in everyone.

3. I create my experiences by what I choose to think and what I feel and believe.

4. Through affirmative prayer and meditation, I connect with God and bring out the good in my life.

5. I do and give my best by living the Truth I know. I make a difference!

Again, I find myself more excited about a faith that tells me I'm good rather than bad, that promotes the positive rather than running on fear.

There certainly seem to be a lot of happy folks entering Unity's Activities Center, the bright wooden circa 1975 1,110-seat amphitheater where worship is held each Sunday at 10:30. In the air-conditioning, so welcome on this day that will reach 106 degrees, more of them greet me and give me a program with the word WILL scrolled on the front.

This will is more of the upbeat, and is fine with me. As is the jazzy music piped in while congregants choose purple upholstered movie-theater-style seats. I sit in the last row of the far-right-hand section and estimate that 250 to 300 are in attendance, a number I'm later told is average, making this among the larger congregations I've visited since Resurrection Sunday. Yet it doesn't feel impersonal, maybe due to the chatting that's going on all around me. The worshippers are white except for maybe a dozen black people and a couple with Asian features. Most are middle-aged and, once again, two-thirds or more are women. Children are absent. Those of us who aren't chatting with our neighbors are gazing at the spare stage flanked by American flag and pulpit, and a baby grand, drums, bass guitar to the right. In the center, a long low altar-type wooden rectangle bears no cross and no design holier than a pair of big brass wings similar to an airline logo.

Above, a giant screen flashes announcements, many of them the same found in the bulletin insert. Starbucks is coming to Unity Village and it'll include a bookstore, café, and Internet access. Live every Sunday, Unity's worship service can be viewed online. A giant smiling face is the next image flashed, a handsome white guy with wire-rimmed glasses, gray hair and beard, and as the band begins to play a theme song not unlike that for a talk show, that same person takes to the stage and sits on one of two wooden chairs behind the pulpit. He is the fiftyish Reverend Robert G. Robinson, senior minister. Ordained in 1988, he served at churches in Minnesota, Florida, and Washington state before arriving here in 2004, and his background includes industrial construction and counseling and chaplaincy in the fields of alcohol and drug addiction. Taking the seat to his right is red-haired, purple-suited Sandy—I didn't catch her last name—who also is white and who looks to be about forty-five. She takes care of some brief housekeeping before Pastor Robert stands to inform us that Chef Gary will be offering peanut butter pie today in the restaurant. He then invites us to join him in reading the Declaration of Faith in our brochures: "There is only One presence and one power active in my Life and in the Universe—God the Good Omnipotent."

I glance around and notice several people holding bunches of pink and white carnations. They move to the front as Reverend Robert says it's time to welcome visitors. He asks newcomers to stand. I'm not going to, but then he announces that Unity welcome gifts include a 10-percent-off bookstore coupon. I've already scoped out a book of essays by Joan Borysenko that I think would be perfect for Tommy. This is my first weekend on the road since his incident, and I'm feeling very very far away. As if to cheer me, a smiling man hands me my carnation, and my envelope.

I tuck it into the wooden seat pocket above the gray-and-white linoleum and next to the *Wings of Song* hymnal published, of course, by the Unity School of Christianity. I grab it as the opening hymn begins, though I already know the words. It's "This Is the Day." The theme of our wedding ceremony twenty-two years ago was "This is the day that the Lord has made—let us rejoice and be glad in it!" Those words from the Bible were read, rather than sung, by Tommy's brother Joey, and were written on a banner my sister made and hung behind the pulpit. At this pulpit, it's Sandy rather than Joey, and she's reading today's page from *Daily Word*: "The love of God is uniting the people of the world in peace."

That first line seems custom-made for this week, when bombs are raining on Israel and Lebanon. "The conditions of the world may seem impossible to resolve at times," she continues. "Realizing a true and lasting peace in the world may seem like a dream, and we may ask ourselves, What am I to do?

"We surrender to God any adverse conditions that we perceive before us. God is the one power at work in the world. As we surrender fear to God, we allow the consciousness of love and peace to take its place."

Pastor Robert invites us to join in the Lord's Prayer. The lights dim as he says, "Let's be together, breathe together. You might have had one heck of a week—I know I did."

I think of how I pushed Tommy back toward the couch when he wanted to return to work. I know I have no control over anything, but I feel that as long as he's in my sight nothing bad will happen. Now I'm half a continent away, hearing the pastor say, "The universe has put you here to do good work."

He switches gears as I find my eyes closed. I'm back at Arch Street in the Quaker silence, back in the little meditation moment offered last week in Enfield. Pastor Robert sends healing to grieving hearts, he assures the confused and the lost that God is there for them. "Step into this experience and into the love of God," he says. "All is well."

He starts his sermon by telling us of his work in a radio shack —the military kind, not the place you go for batteries—in Hawaii during the Vietnam War. It was his job to deliver ticker-tape transmissions to officials, including those who would crack codes and decipher the all-important information.

"I didn't have the code. Have you ever felt like that in your life? Everybody knows what's going on but you?"

He assures us the code exists. "It's implanted within each and every one of us."

Then he encourages us to "focus on the realization that you have been gifted. Step into the abundance right now! If not now, when? . . . How many of you are starting to crack your own code? You have a wonderful opportunity in Unity Village. I invite you to step up to the plate. Why not give it your best shot? On this planet, in this body, in this life?

"I'm committed to jump-starting you, to remind you of the truth of who and what you are."

I will forgive Pastor John his mixing of sports metaphors and liberally coating them in a cheese. Point is, he's reminding us we're good people, can do some fine things on this earth. It's information we could stand to hear more often, so all remains well.

Ushers step to the front and pass maroon velvet bags for our tithing.

A dozen children walk onto the stage, having concluded their Sunday school. *We are happy in the light, in the light, in the light of God*, Pastor Robert sings, leading them and us.

We close with "Peace Song," subtitled "Village Chapel Version," its *Let there be peace on earth* adjusted to include *With God as Creator*—rather than the usual "my brother"—*in Unity are we,* and *With every step I take, Let this be my joyous*—rather than the original's staid "solemn"—*vow.*

I leave the Activities Center with the song in my head, and in my hand a flower from a stranger.

LAKEWOOD CHURCH

HOUSTON, TEXAS

I file in with the masses, up the concrete steps, through the wide glass doors, into the carpeted lobby, past the souvenir stands and the crowd buzzing about the show that's almost ready to start. Sorry—not the show, the service. If I forget I'm here to worship, please understand that Lakewood Church is unlike the sleepy white-steepled structure in the dictionary illustration. Everything's bigger in Texas, so I guess it only makes sense that the Lone Star State is home to America's largest church.

In the enormous concrete structure once known as the Compaq Center, former home of the Houston Rockets, thirty thousand people now worship. Each weekend they sing, pray, swing, and sway before forty-year-old Joel Osteen arrives to offer them and an estimated 7 million television viewers the modern-church feel-good message that's also a refrain in a popular modern hymn: *Our God is an awesome God!*

A mere seven years ago, Joel Osteen was a household name only under his own roof. The son of a Pentecostal preacher who founded Lakewood Church in an abandoned Houston feed store on Mother's Day of 1959, Joel knew something about reaching souls. His father's congregation grew to a far-from-shabby six thousand, and the television program that Joel produced beamed John Osteen's messages to viewers on one local and one national cable channel. John had hoped to span the entire globe with the news of God's love, but his fatal heart attack in 1999 meant his goal would have to be accomplished by someone else. That turned out to be unlikely Joel. No college degree (a mere semester at Oral Roberts U.), no formal Bible training, just interest, personality, and a curl-framed, telegenic face. He became his father's successor with just one sermon—preached a week before his father's death—to his credit.

Joel Osteen now stands cool and confident in custom-tailored pinstriped suit and glossy polished shoes, front and center in the former sports arena purchased in late 2003 and opened thirteen months ago after a $70 million redesign by a team with credentials including the Academy Awards and three Republican National Conventions.

Replacing the eight-thousand-seat auditorium in Northeast Houston is this dramatic sixteen-thousand-seat Disneyland of churches, the mega-est of the megachurches exploding nationwide. Like most of these enormities, Lakewood is nondenominational, and large numbers of members once were searchers. Of the sixteen churches I've visited since Easter, Lakewood is the most varied in race, gender, and age. Worshippers leaving the 11:00 a.m. English-language service will walk right into a wave entering for the 1:30 p.m. Reunión en Español. Joel credits TV for drawing the crowds. Sure, he takes his act on the road, visiting cities across the globe. And he's all over bookstore shelves, smiling from the cover of his first book, *Your Best Life Now: 7 Steps to Living at Your Full Potential*, which nearly two years after its publication continues to be a best seller. But most non-Houstonites know of him via the half-hour *Lakewood Church*, broadcast weekly on four local television stations, thirty-four national network affiliates, ten national networks, and five farther afield, including in the Middle East. I imagine the debauchery this building once must have known. Wild parties in the skyboxes. Maybe the occasional fight. Drug deals and bookmaking and ticket scalping. Now, instead of queuing for a Miller Lite, I'm browsing a rack of Lakewood literature. The four-color four-page bulletin for this week contains no information about the sequence of the worship but plenty about what the church is and does, starting with a picture of Joel with wife Victoria. Resembling a cross between Christie Brinkley and Nicole Kidman, she met Joel when he entered her family's jewelry store in search of a watch battery. The brochure tells me how, Carter style, these parents of two will meet and greet anyone who assembles in the southwest corner of the Lobby Level after the Saturday and Sunday services.

The two inside pages contain a dazzling lineup of dates and descriptions. There's something for everyone, with praying, playing, studying, and recovery programs. A small box at the bottom announces dates for Communion, baby dedications, and baptism. (Bring a towel and a change of clothes.) Despite being unconnected to any traditional church, Lakewood stresses the importance of baptism as a "symbol of the cleansing power of the blood of Christ and a testimony to our faith."

I head to the bookstore that glows Borders-size over the bank of escalators. A quick browse finds inventory ranging from humorous "Get Out of Hell Free" cards to the only crosses you will see in this building. Displays of Joel's books, tapes, CDs, DVDs, in both English and Spanish, fill shelves near a wide-screen TV beaming a video of him at the pulpit. I spot that pulpit in person as I enter the church and look down at the flat oval space the size of an ice rink, four-fifths full of upholstered movie-theater seats facing the stage and a small wooden podium decorated with a golden magic-lantern shape that is the church's logo. A camera on a boom swings over the stage and audience, focusing on the enormous golden globe spinning behind a ten-piece band. Choir members file in. Waterfalls cascade along courses at the far edges, and hundreds of big lights hanging from ceiling beams are theatrically softened by wafting dry ice.

I am welcomed by usher Chastity. I ask how she is and she answers, "I'm blessed, praise Jesus," as she leads me to row G. I'm blessed to be very close to the right-hand side of the stage, seven rows up. I see that the top—the cheap seats, if you will—are empty, the space dark. Next time she passes, I ask Chastity if that section is used. "The bottom of the bowl fills first," she explains. "After the second song, the top will be filled up."

Soft rock with praise-heavy lyrics continues to play, but not loudly enough to interrupt conversation. The man and the woman next to me admire the embroidery on the Bible cover they just purchased in the gift shop. The lights dim. People spring to their feet, whoop and clap. A vitamin-infused happy theme plays as the big screens shine with film of men toiling at construction, teens playing, a joyous bride running in her wedding gown. *All things are possible and every river's crossable!* sings the entire space.

Fittingly for a church in an arena, Joel Osteen received inspiration for his preaching style on a YMCA basketball court, where he realized that if his fellow players couldn't relate to his delivery what was the sense of trying to share testimony? He made a decision to speak in everyday language. So don't expect any Latin, or Bible verses read in the King's English. Lakewood's slogan is that of a running shoe: "Discover the Champion in You!"

The choir stands, claps, sways, as eight singers take the stage, each of them in fashionable black. The music is loud and everywhere. *I have a promise from heaven. It's my season. It's my time. For the family of the Lord.*

The congregation of roughly sixteen thousand takes to its feet for the second English-language service of the weekend. Suddenly Joel Osteen is at center stage, welcoming us, asking God to bless us, saying we've all got some reason to give praise this morning, praying that we'll be participators, not spectators.

Victoria Osteen steps to the pulpit, her Texas-sized tresses filling the big screen as she thanks God, asks him to fill us with goodness, with love. The couple leaves the stage, led to seats front and center, row one, as the eight singers return: *I'm still standing*, they tell us, *but by the grace of God*. I notice the band is now visible, its stage having been raised from its previous point nearly out of view. Colored lights fall on the lead singer, a woman identified on the big screen as Cindy Cruse Ratcliff, another white blonde, who now asks us, "Aren't you grateful for the grace of God?"

The singers pogo as the music blasts. *Lord, we've come to worship, we've come to lay down our lives at your feet*, offers a handsome black guy the screen identifies as Steve Crawford. As with Cindy Cruse Ratcliff, his voice is pop-star quality, his stage presence sharp. The lighting, the sound, the setting, it's ultraprofessional. I'm in Houston but my mind is back in Columbus, wondering how Pastor James and Sister Vanessa and Michael are. This incredibly polished production has blasted me back to those few dozen worshippers standing with me before the pulpit, singing *O come let us adore him*. Everyone has their own idea of what being close to fellow humans, to the creator who made us, feels like. So far, I'm not getting that at Lakewood. I'm seeing a fine show, a finer than fine show, not a hair out of place. But maybe something a little more spontaneous and less perfect is what I'd prefer.

After yet another song, Joel returns to the stage, reminding God that he's just fabulous: "God," he says with a twang that takes one part of a sentence up a hill and the next part down, "you are a great God . . . We believe even right now as we are worshipping here that you are making our crooked places straight." Applause sweeps. "We believe even right now you are restoring sick bodies. Healing marriages . . ." Hands are raised. "I know he has a great plan for our lives—that he holds me in the palm of his hand."

Then Joel plunges his face into his own palms for what seems like a minute. In the meantime, the congregation applauds. The music soothes. Joel uncovers his face, a close-up on the big screen showing damp eyes. He searches the podium for a box of tissues. "Some of you are stuck in a rut, not experiencing the good," he manages to say. He encourages us to let go. "God's got you in the palm of his hand," he reminds, words coming hard against another urge to weep. "I love that scripture—if God is before me, who can be against me? It may look impossible, but with God all things are possible."

It's the lead-in to introducing people known as prayer partners, who have reserved seating in each section and who await your special request. Joel and Victoria now stand on the floor below the pulpit and receive their own lines of worshippers bearing heavy hearts. Tissues are produced throughout the church. Chastity is at the bottom of my row, motioning for those in need of prayers to form a line heading up the stairs. *Now I've found the greatest gift of all,* sings the choir, and I stand to join the line. Susan's husband, Dominick, who had shaved his head just before I sat with the Quakers in Philadelphia, who has been battling cancer for nearly four years, was hospitalized on Friday. As I climb each stair, I debate on whom I'll spend this prayer. It's the same thing I've done lifelong while in line for Holy Communion. Throughout the week, I felt I could ask for everything from world peace down to luck getting a parking space. But it always seemed to me that the prayer made after receiving Communion should be a biggie. For something really important because if God wasn't listening to you after you'd just received his body and blood, when would he?

But who knows the customs here? I decide on fifty-fifty. I step before the prayer partner, a little Asian woman in a yellow suit, and tell her that my friend is sick with cancer and my husband has been sick with who knows what. She takes both my hands. I lean down because she's short and the music is very loud. I hear the word "cancer" and I hear the words "immune system" and the word "husband" and the Pastor Laura term "Father God Father God." I hold her hands tightly. I want this to work. Then the little Asian woman says "Amen." And lets go. The time with my prayer partner felt too brief, but Victoria is at the pulpit now, steaming ahead. "We stand in your presence in amazement," she begins, and tells us that God sees that we are weak. But he is strong and he is with us. She tells a story about a tree that toppled in her yard. It looked good on the outside, but its roots weren't deep enough. She points her hands to the floor as she prays that our roots will be deep enough in the Lord. Worshippers raise their hands in turn. Joel, looking fine and dandy, walks from an opening in the cave beneath the waterfall at stage right.

"I believe with all my heart God doesn't want us to be money minded," he tells us. "He doesn't mind us having finances, he just doesn't want finances to have us."

With this, Chastity and her fellow ushers begin to distribute silver plastic tubs that resemble ice buckets. Alone on the stage, a brunette in a black miniskirt and stilettos is singing strongly about calling Jesus's name. She leans forward, pulls the music along. Again, this could be Broadway, or at least a very classy dinner theater. But I want some rough edges. I want the sweat on the singer's face. I want the somewhat ill-fitting Sunday best. I want, I don't know what, really. Maybe not stilettos.

The red light on one of the two giant television cameras begins to glow as Joel Osteen tells his viewers it is a joy and an honor each week to come into their homes. The televised portion of the service has begun.

They, and us, are asked to hold up our Bibles. "And say it like you mean it," he commands happily before launching into a prayer that is more like a vow, concluding with, "I'll never never never be the same, never never never, I'll never be the same, in Jesus's name.

"We've been talking about staying healthy physically and how important it is that we develop good eating habits," Joel starts. "I'm going to give tips today for how to live at your best weight."

If this were an actual television studio, I would check to see if it weren't Oprah or Dr. Phil up there speaking. "Most of the time we don't need another diet," Joel is saying. "We need a lifestyle change. We need to identify the eating patterns that cause us to gain this weight."

I'm thinking maybe he'll segue into how light we'll feel when we confess our evils. Or that he'll do the weight thing for a bit and then loop back somehow to the Bibles now open on laps in row after row after row. But he doesn't. For the twenty-eight televised minutes of the ninety minutes we're here, Joel Osteen talks about weight loss. The tips he gives aren't any deeper than the basics you'd get on the back of a box of fiber cereal: don't compare yourself to others, be realistic about what you should weigh, don't eat when you're not hungry, or when you're bored, or on impulse, and try soup, it takes longer to eat.

An ounce of the Almighty is mentioned—"God made us all different due to genetics"—but the rest is Weight Watchers 101. With an added perk: Do all these things, Joel says, and "you'll experience that life of victory that God has in store."

There is a final prayer, in which he thanks God for what we've heard, "and that it not be received as condemnation, that we will receive supernatural strength to do what we can't do, to fulfill our destinies in good health with strength, joy, energy. Help us to be the very best we can be, in Jesus's name we pray. Amen."

I scroll back to some criticisms I've read. How Joel Osteen has been poked at by more traditional pastors, who say his is a feel-good religion more about psychology than God, and I wonder, is that his fault or that of his followers, who don't really want to hear heavy stuff about hell? I know I'd rather not. I've read that Joel's messages are responses to what he hears, what worries people the most.

Topics like relationships, finances, health, overconsumption of the Little Debbies he just admitted were a personal downfall. And while I fall into the camp that's heard enough about the fires of hell, I like my contemporary sermons to contain at least a nod to God. To suggest how we might consider him in our daily struggles, ponder how he's working in our lives. I'm all for self-help information, but this was too much about that self when there's a whole world of problems out there to discuss.

I find Lakewood not much like a church at all. But maybe that's just me. Hundreds are waiting in a cordoned area when I exit the bookstore with a five-dollar CD of today's message, *Living At Your Ideal Weight*, and a tin of scripture-themed breath mints. A dark-clothed line of security men pass me with a whoosh of importance, and then Joel and Victoria stride by on their way to meet their fans, the show being over.

THE RIVERSIDE CHURCH

NEW YORK, NEW YORK

For worship, and for counterfeit Louis Vuitton, I have returned to New York City.

I haven't been here since the start of this pilgrimage, back at Easter. My four teen nieces haven't been here since last July, when they, Tommy, and I enjoyed the overnight Manhattan visit that is their annual Christmas gift.

For me, this year's trip will also include church. So while Tommy takes Kristen, Kelly, and Sara to breakfast, Kara accompanies me on the subway to 116th Street, where we walk four blocks north along Broadway, eyes fixed on the 392-foot-tall church steeple-tower ahead. Kara is twenty-five, Tommy's goddaughter and the eldest of the family's next generation. I have had nothing whatsoever to do with the good and kind person she is, yet I have a great pride in her. I root for her at this especially exciting time in her life, full with a big accounting job, high hopes for a house purchase, and a serious boyfriend who magically holds all the requirements (starting with "tall") on the dream-man-requirement list she told me about a couple of NYC trips ago.

Kara regularly attends Mass and also teaches Confraternity of Christian Doctrine classes, religious education for Catholic kids who attend public school during the week. Her church is in Springfield, the same one in which Tommy's parents were married. The faithful there rave how their pastor can polish off a Mass in less than half an hour. But Kara doesn't mention that fact when I ask her why she attends. "Father Farland just does it for me," she explains with a shrug and a smile.

I'm reminded of how saddened the Sts. Peter and Paul family was following the death several years ago of the pastor we'd had since I was ten. Father Bob had done it for us. And for so long. "But you don't go to a church because of the priest," a friend, himself a priest, told me at the time. "You go because of God." I had argued to the contrary. A Mass led by a spiritually blasé person is just that, nothing but a way to check off that week's religious obligation.

So I might do well today, at a church synonymous with a legendary former preacher. The Reverend William Sloane Coffin was senior minister of The Riverside Church from 1977 to 1987 and was anything but boring. He fired up, engaged, even enraged his congregants about hot topics including the environment, war, gay rights, and race. A former athlete, musician, and CIA agent, this internationally known liberal died four months ago, at age eighty-one, having spent his final years protesting the war in Iraq.

"Let us love our country," he preached at Riverside in 2003 after being introduced by Secretary General of the United Nations Kofi Annan, "but pledge allegiance to the earth . . . one planet indivisible, with clean air, soil and water; with liberty, justice and peace for all."

Dieting advice it was not.

Riverside was born of controversy in New York's Christian scene almost a century ago. The question of whether to interpret the Gospel in a modernist or fundamentalist way led some of the faithful, including John D. Rockefeller Jr., to found a new church. The few requirements were based on Pastor Harry Emerson Fosdick's wishes that, to join, members need only to affirm their belief in Jesus Christ; that the church be interdenominational; that it be a large building in a vital part of the city and offer a far-reaching ministry. An existing building—Park Avenue Baptist—fit the bill and, with great help from Rockefeller's deep pockets, was remodeled to resemble the thirteenth-century Chartres Cathedral in France. Doors opened on October 5, 1930.

For a look at what modern Riversiders believe, glance at the literature rack, filled with statements against the death penalty; for peace and justice; on becoming a sustainable community. A stack of postcards advertises the upcoming screenings of *The Ground Truth*, a film on the challenges facing our troops at war and upon their return home, and the upcoming Fosdick Convocation on Preaching is titled "For the Living of These Days," featuring renowned social liberals Bill Moyers and Cornel West.

Kara and I choose a pew halfway down on the left-hand side. The bells of the carillon play as worshippers enter the main floor and the balcony, the sky-high space accommodating nineteen hundred but today filled with maybe a third of that. Before us, a simple rectangular altar holds a pair of candles and a Bible. A large golden cross hangs above. In this church the subjects of the stained glass windows aren't just Jesus and his family. They include physicians, teachers, prophets, missionaries, reformers, and artists, according to the *Riverside At Worship* brochure that Kara and I were given by a black usher in dark suit and dreads.

In front of the altar table stands a pair of pulpits—the one to the right supported by a carved golden eagle, the other being the type you need stairs to mount. An organ sits to the left, and across from that, several pews for the choir.

A woman takes to the eagle pulpit and announces, "Then David slept with his ancestors." She reads a few more lines of Bible verse, then steps down. She wears black pants and a white shirt, no fancy garb, no staff, no headgear. I wonder who she is and what the heck that was all about. I check the seat pocket for a Bible and find blue or black hardcover New Revised Standard Versions next to a maroon hardcover of *Hymns, Psalms and Spiritual Songs*. I glance at my neighbors and see that Riverside rivals only Lakewood in even mix of race, gender, and age. I smell cologne for the first time in all these Sundays, and I recall the church preparation of my youth, my father smelling of something called Brut that was deep and thick and that I'd give whatever might be the cost to lean into his neck and smell again.

We take to our feet to meet the power of the organ. The choir, in blue robes, processes single file down the middle aisle as all sing: *Thus all my gladsome way along I sing aloud thy praises, that all may hear the grateful song my voice unwearied raises.*

Twenty in all, the choir members are deepest black, chalk white, with spiky red hair, scraggly tresses, and a beard appropriately Jesusy. Now in a green robe, the woman who read the thing about the sleeping David follows the choir, as does another white woman, a larger black woman, and a taller white man. The sleeping David woman, who I now read is the Reverend Lynne Mikulak, is back at the pulpit for the call to worship. "The Spirit of the Lord is here ready to do a new thing in us, for us, and through us." I like the idea of a new thing, and there's plenty to be had here. Intentions cover the usual health and hope, then abducted women and girls; victims of sex trafficking and military abuse; and people living in Iraq, Sudan, the Ivory Coast.

It's a promising start. I glance at Kara but she's churchfaced, eyes straight ahead, and I can't get a read on what she thinks. We hear a solo by choir member Tammy Martz, who easily could get a job on Broadway, and a pastoral prayer led by the Reverend Cari Jackson, the black woman from the procession, who says, "We give thanks to you for this day, a day we've never seen before." On cue, the sun brightens and the sanctuary glows.

We place our offerings onto dark wooden plates passed as the organ softly plays, then congregants reach for us in Passing of the Peace, saying, "Christ's peace be with you," or "Good morning, peace of Christ."

Spending the most time at the pulpit in the seventeen years since Coffin left Riverside has been the Reverend James Alexander Forbes Jr., senior pastor here since 1989. *Newsweek* called him one of the twelve greatest English-language public speakers, and *Ebony* has listed him as one of the best black pastors. But today we'll hear the Reverend Dr. R. Scott Colglazier, speaking on "Listening for the Deepest Voices."

Pastor Scott is white, maybe in his fifties, hair gray, face congenial. He moves with every word, gives power to every syllable, but doesn't overdo it as he talks about listening. He tells us of Sam Keen, whose book *Hymns to an Unknown God* is a memoir set in San Francisco postdivorce. "The best of your life has passed, you have made too many mistakes, hurt too many people, it's over," Pastor Scott tells us each road the author walked would chant. One night he stopped walking, went home, and designated one of his pieces of furniture as a prayer chair. "He made himself sit and listen, sit and listen, sit and listen," Pastor Scott says, "for the deepest voices of life.

"Real life happens at the level of the soul and the soul is where God wants to live," he continues. "All that stuff about cars, houses, the world, being the sole arbiter of global values—it's all surface—all that about one religion, even Christian religion being the one religion—it's all surface. It's wrong."

Well this is something very new—sitting in church and being told that it's not the only show in town. I was always told my church was the center, was right, was it. Pastor Scott's volume and urgency increases as he tells us, "It's ego. Nothing wrong with ego, but we only grow a soul when we risk listening to the deepest voices."

We get a homework assignment: This week, we are to sit with our soul. To stay put when we want to rise. To listen at the precise moment we want to talk.

In his book *The Inner Voice of Love,* Henri Nouwen encourages listening to those deepest voices, Pastor Scott tells us. "I have two cell phones and, yes, I need to see a therapist about that, but that's a whole other sermon. I start scrolling. I call my wife, I call my kids, I call my friends. What if I just sit in my prayer chair instead? This leads you to God. The word 'religion' means 'to bind us back'—not only to God, but also to ourselves. Overwhelmed? Anybody feel overwhelmed? Of course! We're in New York City! Try to escape! You can drink, numb with drugs, with shopping, scurry around and fix what's overwhelming. But what if we sat in our prayer chair? We're told, 'Don't just sit there, do something.' Well, don't just do something, sit there, and ask for God's strength and understanding."

I'm back in Massachusetts now, touring my house, selecting a seat for this practice. I know that whichever one I choose, my little dog Tiny will join me in it, her head on my lap, giving me the feeling I'm the most loved being in the world. As I picture her black and gold face, the pastor offers a mantra for the next time we sit: "Breathing in, I am loved. Breathing out, I give love."

I'm getting some love here at Riverside, which despite being large enough to accommodate an ocean liner manages to give the feeling of a much smaller building, and congregation. Again, it's the preacher. And his message.

"Something remarkable will happen," he's telling us now. "A presence will arrive and an embrace will take place and the words of Jesus, 'I am with you always,' will come through inside your depths."

We are dismissed but only two people exit. The rest of us sit here in this morning's prayer chairs and listen. To the music, and something a little deeper.

Outside, Kara and I start to trade impressions, but find nothing to swap as we come away with the same. Both of us like the idea of the prayer chair, and had been imagining which in our respective homes we might designate as such. "The way he made the chair seem so powerful and peaceful was pretty cool," she tells me. And I agree. "I also loved the diversity," Kara adds. "Looking around and seeing black and white people, high-class and middle-class people, gay and straight people, made me feel very comfortable just being me." I agree again. We tick off the plusses: Helpful, imaginative message, and an inclusive, involved congregation. A large space, yet one that didn't daunt or give an isolated feeling. A morning and a service to be thankful for when we eventually land in those chairs back home.

LAGNIAPPE PRESBYTERIAN CHURCH

BAY ST. LOUIS, MISSISSIPPI

Anyone who's logged even a couple Sundays in church has heard their share of references to storms and floods. Powerful metaphors they are, and frequent fuel for sermons. But when the topics are dusted off this particular Sunday morning, for the first time in my life they are palpable. Perhaps it's because they're used to reference an event that happened just a year ago, rather than two or three thousand, and that took place right where I sit, rather than half a world away. One year ago this coming Tuesday a natural disaster literally of biblical proportions made landfall in Waveland, Mississippi, causing unfathomable destruction, killing at least eighteen hundred people and wreaking $81 billion in damages throughout the Gulf Coast. Including in this little town where I'm worshipping this morning.

I chose neighboring Bay St. Louis because I wanted to visit a church in a town largely ignored assistancewise and publicitywise, and that is still suffering. A year later, the barriers where I-90 halts at a no-longer-existent bridge over wide St. Louis Bay hammer home the fact that Katrina's winds and water were higher and stronger here in rural Hancock County than anywhere in the ninety thousand square miles declared as federal disaster areas. More than half the county's nineteen thousand homes were obliterated, commercial areas were destroyed, landscape transformed to postnuclear skeletal. One year later, the $110 billion in revitalization funding promised by the government is as hard to access as the other side of the bay. Many have left the area, seeing no future here. One former resident has returned, seeing into eternity. Jean Larroux III came back to assist family, and stayed to plant a church.

A native of New Orleans who grew up in this town, Larroux was pastor at an Independent Presbyterian church in Memphis when the storm killed his aunt and uncle and destroyed his mother's home. He made the trip south intending to offer only short-term assistance, but soon felt a calling to remain permanently, and to help with rebuilding both physically and spiritually. Pastor Jean concluded his stint in Memphis on the last day of 2005, and having been approved as a church planter by the Presbyterian Church in America's Mission to North America, returned home and started digging.

His is among the newest of the eleven thousand Presbyterian congregations serving 2.4 million members in a faith that began in the sixteenth century, following the Reformation and John Calvin's writings. We're very far from Olde England here on Demontluzin Street and across from the backside of a strip mall, where I parked in an ovenish 90 degrees beneath a sign that proves God has a sense of black humor. WATER FUN declares the blue-on-white square above the words POOLS AND SPAS. Purchased by Reverend Jean in April, Water Fun is now Lagniappe Presbyterian Church.

"LPC exists to participate in the restoration of the Mississippi Gulf Coast through the declaration and demonstration of the love of God shown to us in Christ Jesus," reads this mission's mission statement. Proof is in both the church building and the adjacent cottages and storage units built for the stream of construction volunteers that has arrived since Katrina left.

Lagniappe—say LAN-yap—is regional parlance for something extra, like how you might be given a thirteenth honey-dipped doughnut with the dozen. A cup running over might be the state of this church one day, but right now there's little extra in its eleven thousand square feet, which is unintentional bare-bones chic down to the exposed pipes and insulation, and gray concrete floor speckled with red paint.

I sit in the last row of the right-hand section of the two hundred seats, most of them mismatched folding chairs, FEMA handwritten in black across their backs. To my left is a guy who tells me his name is Warren, which I take as a welcoming sign because that same name is a town bordering mine. Tan, white, fortyish, Warren has been worshipping at Lagniappe for a month. He was Presbyterian to start with, but wasn't so much looking for a church when he came here as he was looking for a home. Warren's was destroyed by "the storm," which I soon learn is the relatively benign term most people use for the Category 4 monster whose winds topped 140 mph and pushed forth a thirty-five-foot storm surge and flooding that reached as far as seven miles inland. Warren is hoping Lagniappe volunteers will one day help him rebuild. But he's not the only one in need. So for now, his name remains on a list, and he remains lodged with relatives. And because he likes the casual feel of Lagniappe, on this Sunday morning he is seated beside me for the 9:30 a.m. service. Together, Warren and I watch the final few folks enter, in all, thirty-one adults, everyone white, twenties to sixties, half of each gender, in basic picnic attire.

Pastor Jean stands at the metal music stand/pulpit set in front of a movie screen, a box of assorted bug spray cans, soda vending machines, and a door marked FUTURE TOILET. I recognize him from the Lagniappe Web site I found via the Googling of "Mississippi Katrina Church." Salt-and-pepper buzz cut and short beard, white shirt with sleeves rolled back in the AC, gray shorts, Docksiders without socks, watch on right hand, wedding ring on traditional finger, he holds a rolled-up *Orlando Sentinel*, a reminder to introduce the reporter and photographer who've come to the service as part of the new storm of media this anniversary week. To them and to all of us, Pastor Jean says, "We're glad you're here this morning. Hear the word of God and be called to worship."

A man in red polo shirt and jeans steps into Pastor Jean's place and begins to play a faster folkish version of the familiar *Holy, Holy, Holy, merciful and mighty, early in the morning, my song shall rise to thee*. There's a second tune, "Come Thou Font." I don't know this one, and consult the light blue *Mission to the World 2005 Song Book* that one of the four children here had earlier distributed. Pastor Jean, whose audience might number only six or seven on a day that's not just prior to the first anniversary of an enormous regional disaster, steps to the front once again and invites us all to contribute our prayer intentions.

"Folks, we're in Ernesto's path," he starts out, voicing what everyone here well knows—that another meteorological menace right now is powering past Cuba, with early but still-chilling maps predicting this latest hurricane's track to the Gulf Coast. Pastor Jean offers prayers for those who'll be affected and notes, "Only you know where that will be." We know that "you" is not we here in the seats.

Next, Clyde, a man seated in front of Warren, says as plainly as you'd state you had toast for breakfast, "My oldest son has just gone into rehab for cocaine." A woman across the way asks for comfort for everyone lost to Katrina. Barb, who'd welcomed me at the door and soon was telling me how she and her husband had decided to uproot their Florida retirement and move to Bay St. Louis to be part of Lagniappe, wants us to pray for help with the amount of paperwork with which the church must contend.

Closing his eyes and speaking into the mike, Reverend Jean prays, "God, who else would we go to with requests like this? They're as small as an individual but as big as a hurricane. Tuesday's a heavy day. We pray for things that cannot be replaced. Lord, we can make roofs, put up Sheetrock, but only you can heal hearts."

Warren's eyes are closed, too. He rocks as he stands.

Holding a small black paperback Bible, Pastor Jean reads from the book of Psalms, 107, verses 23 to 30: "They who sailed the sea in ships, trading on the deep waters, these saw the works of the Lord and his wonders in the abyss. His command raised up a storm wind which tossed its waves on high. They mounted up to heaven; they sank to the depths; their hearts melted away in their plight. They reeled and staggered like drunken men, and all their skill was swallowed up. They cried to the Lord in their distress; from their straits he rescued them. He hushed the storm to a gentle breeze, and the billows of the sea were stilled. They rejoiced that they were calmed, and he brought them to their desired haven."

We sit as Pastor Jean tells us where he found this psalm. "I was driving the lower bay road in the Lakeshore area of Hancock County. I had gone out there to check on a family we were working with. A piece of siding that had been blown off a house was nailed to a tree, and written on it in Magic Marker were the numbers. It wasn't the twenty-third, 'The Lord is my shepherd,' it was an obscure passage. I opened the Bible and looked at it. If there was a psalm written for Hancock County, this is it. The area where that piece of siding was tacked onto the tree, that's these people. Those are the people who go out, as merchants on the sea, crabbing or shrimping. Whether fishing or floundering or sitting on the seawall pulling in the bounty of the ocean, those are the people of this psalm."

Reverend Jean then interprets the psalm, and the God it references. "On so many occasions, the sea, the ocean, has been that for us—we have gone out on the sea in ships almost as merchants on the mighty waters, and we have seen the wondrous works of God in the deep. That is the God we understand. That is the kind of God we pray thanksgiving to after we go out floundering, catch a bunch of softshells, that's the God we understand. The God of sunrises, sunsets, we love him. He gets high marks from us."

Then he mentions the one we aren't as crazy about. "For he spoke and stirred up a tempest . . . in their peril their courage melted and they were at their wit's end. There's a God we don't understand.

"Can you feel our courage melting away, and we're crying 'God, if you loved us you wouldn't allow this to happen.' If there only could be 'I accept your will, oh God, it's easy.' Put on a fake plastic religious smile and that would be it."

But we're human, Reverend Jean graciously acknowledges, so we can more relate to the screaming masses in the psalm nailed to the tree. "Scripture gives us lip-quivering, trembling children, looking up to a God wondering if he knows how bad it hurts. And we wonder if he notices. I tell you, you're in good company. Elijah, Moses, people from Waveland, people from Bay St. Louis, it still hurts. But in verse twenty-eight, they cried out to the Lord in their trouble, and the waves of the seas were hushed."

During Pastor Jean's first church assignment, in northern Alabama, he became friends with a librarian named Nancy Piper. She was in her forties and she had cancer. "The tempest begins to stir," he says. "She quickly knew this was a storm that would take her life. I had no category, no file for that."

But Nancy created a category for herself. She was one of those patients I myself have yet to comprehend, who are grateful for their illnesses. My life has changed in many ways—many of them good—since my experience with cancer, but I've yet to start running around shouting my gratitude for the diagnosis. As for Nancy, Pastor Jean tells us, "She said 'I wouldn't trade it. I realize now what's important. Cancer showed me.' I don't know what that looked like—how to be grateful from cancer. But the verses show us God was on his throne August 29 and he was on his throne August 30. I've heard from people over and over again in Bay St. Louis, that 'the storm has shown us what's important.' There's a pile of debris at the end of their driveways, but they're grateful. I file those statements with Nancy Piper."

Perhaps some residents indeed feel this way. Lucky to be alive, grateful for the literal wave of a reminder that it's not stuff that's important in this life, it's life itself. But wouldn't they, as was my feeling after cancer, rather have come to this realization via a book or weekend seminar? I'm big on being grateful, but maybe it's far too soon to be wrapping all that horror into such a tidy packet. I'm waiting for someone to leap up and spout their side of the story. But the only movement is Clyde's head, nodding in agreement.

"I ask you," Pastor Jean continues, "what is God shouting to us a year later? Better building codes? Restructuring of government? Move north of I-10? Move to California? It's not in Houston or Atlanta. The storms of cancer, the storms of life have a way of clearing the land and we see what's really important. The only thing Katrina can't strip away, that fire, cancer can't take away, is the love of God. Job sits down on ashes, we sit down on slabs. The tempest was sent by him. The tempest was stirred up to clear the slabs. We see only his unfailing love. It's not the clothes on my body, it's his unfailing love."

More folks are nodding and I wonder what they've seen. Before the service, a teacher ahead of me had been showing a book of drawings by her grade school students. Crayons colored giant waves and floating homes and stick figures in trees.

"Deep as the pain still is, real as it is a year later, our God is shouting to us in our pain," Pastor Jeans says. "Perhaps that's the way he's done it and we're just able to see it now. If psalmists over three thousand years ago write that, maybe that's the way God's always been. God indeed is at work. He is shouting to us."

Simple and less than forty-five minutes, the service is over. Worshippers gather at the back of the church for coffee and sweet tea, and queue for Pastor Jean's tour of the adjacent cabins. I think back to Riverside, to the touted benefits of sitting. All around us here on the Gulf Coast, work needs to be done. But it can't hurt to just sit for a while, which, here in the former Water Fun, next to Warren, I take a few extra minutes to do.

MOFFETT ROAD ASSEMBLY OF GOD

MOBILE, ALABAMA

This church was chosen for no reason other than its glitz.

I drove this morning off the interstate and through a thicket of possibilities, most of them Baptist, plus a Church of God, an African Methodist Episcopal, and then before me stood the electronic Assembly of God sign, its crawl not unlike the news ribbon that feeds the latest in Time Square. This one read SPECIAL GUEST CARLEY TOUCHSTONE. Maybe it was the interesting surname as well as the electronics, as well as the fact that I'd yet to explore an Assemblies of God church. I pulled in.

This faith began unofficially at a Topeka, Kansas, prayer meeting in January of 1901, at which the modern Pentecostal revival started. It officially was founded in 1914 and is now the world's largest Pentecostal denomination, consisting of 30 million members. The U.S. portion is a mere drop in the bucket, with only 2.3 million worshipping in eleven thousand churches.

Members believe in salvation through Jesus, divine healing, baptism in the Holy Spirit, and the Second Coming. Moffett Road's two-sided black-on-white bulletin prepares me for worship that may involve "lifting hands (Ps. 63:4), dancing (Ps. 150:4), prophetic words and speaking in tongues (1 Cor. 14:39–40), singing in the spirit (1 Cor. 14:15), or hand clapping and shouting (Ps. 47:1). We believe in worship that is 'done in a fitting and orderly way' according to scripture, under the leadership of the Holy Spirit."

The bulletin states the church's mission as "to introduce people to Jesus Christ and to the transforming life that is available to them through their personal relationship with Him!"

I receive this bulletin from Sharon and Darma, who greet me at the door with big smiles and welcome me to take a look around and have a seat. They apologize that the early service I've come for is not as well attended as the 10:45, and point out that I can come back for that if I'd like. I can hear singing so I know I'm a bit late for this one. I tell Sharon I'll just go in now and she accompanies me, telling me, "Our pastor has a heart for the Lord, and is full of enthusiasm for the lost." Does she mean me? Do I look lost?

She's offering me a seat next to her and a male friend. I nod but take the seat behind them and watch a fiftyish white man in tight black T-shirt and black slacks singing passionately into a handheld microphone. He's at the center of a stage, this being another stage setting, though a rare one for its giant golden cross, which hangs against a green marble tile wall between two pillars. Below stands a shiny grand piano, a set of bongos, a set of congas, an electric piano a woman is playing, and, behind her, a man on drums. An American flag is displayed to the left, another flag to the right, that one white, blue, and red, probably bearing the AOG logo if there is such a thing.

Lyrics flash on a pair of screens to either side of the big cross and pillars. They're something about Jehovah, and people sing plainly enough but without the passion and volume I've seen in some churches. A man in the first row is the most into it. He's white, like everyone else I see save for two black men, and graying, spectacled, in a black polo and charcoal slacks, big-faced watch on left wrist. He grinds his eyes shut and enunciates every word: *Je-ho-vah!* The song concludes, and this man takes the mike.

He's Pastor Jerry Jenkins, the man with the enthusiasm for the lost, telling us, "This is Mobile, but this is God's city!"

He ventures that maybe our mornings have already been hectic, and at only eight thirty maybe even disappointing for some. But there is a chance here to turn things around, he says. I look up to find him standing between two men holding maroon velvet tithing bags in front of them like trick-or-treaters at your front door.

"Bless the giver," Pastor Jenkins is saying as the men move toward us.

As well as cash, the bulletin tells us we can also donate canned goods. I read on, about a men's power lunch, homebound visitations, a trip to Israel in 2007, a request for Ping-Pong and foosball tables in sturdy condition, then a note from a family who'd had a hospitalized loved one: "It is so comforting to know that we have a church family that will fall on their knees and pray until they touch the throne of God, for any need that you or your family has."

I'm impressed by the comment's passion and look anew at my forty-one fellow worshippers—half of either gender—here on the main floor, which holds maybe 250 below a balcony that I don't explore. No children are present. The median age is maybe fifty.

The singer in the black T-shirt is up front again, this time with some wind instrument that sounds clarinetish, like the one that made Kenny G famous. He plays with the same jazziness, delivering "Amazing Grace" with body language and closed eyes while standing near the big piano with the automobile-showroom finish.

From a metal stand in front of a shiny acrylic podium, Pastor Jenkins asks us to read the bulletin, to take special note that the college students soon will be back in town and in church. We're asked to consider assisting the international students who don't have easy access to furniture, desk, chairs, beds. "Many of them are Hindus, Muslims," Pastor Jerry tells us. "They're not believers, but we just want to show them the love of the Lord."

As for us, he wants to introduce an old friend: the Carley mentioned on the sign. I don't come from a place where Carleys are men, but in the South names are wonderfully quirky, and this Carley is a white-haired guy not yet seventy who hails from just up the road though he's only here this weekend while on a visit from his church in upstate New York. Pastor Jerry gives a brief Carley bio, list of churches served in, how he's helped immigrants start a church community. "God has used him in an apostolic way," he says.

Carley, in short-sleeved blue shirt and dark trousers, tells how he grew up poor and attended Bible college starting with two hundred dollars earned from working at a pharmacy in eighth through twelfth grades. As for the rest of his tuition, "God had to make a way for me." And he did.

People down here don't say, "I'll figure it out," or "We'll come up with a plan." For them God will do it. God is in every sentence, on every shirt, sign, radio signal, bumper sticker, the giantest Jesus fish you've ever seen stuck to the backs of some of the giantest trucks you've ever seen. And in the quickest comment comes a tumble: "Praise God praise Jesus thank you Jesus."

Carley had such faith, and finished school courtesy of "love offerings" made by friends. From there, he says, "God has taken care of me the rest of the way." Not unlike how God took care of Daniel, "A very relevant prophet for today," Carley tells us.

"When a person commits life to Christ prior to the age of eighteen, and understands that commitment, God gives them a special opportunity," he says, and calls males under age eighteen the most endangered species. "Whether they're white, black, or Asian, the devil is out to steal our young men."

As for the counterattack, he suggests this very building. "There is no place better to establish purpose than in the presence of God. . . . You gotta go after young people."

He talks about recently meeting with a group of fifteen evangelicals and fifteen Muslims. "They convert by force," he said of the Muslims. "We convert by loving grace. It was an interesting dialogue. I commend you here in Mobile for reaching out to people of different backgrounds." Then he recalls the day he made the choice to serve God, back in eighth grade, back in that pharmacy. "I made a choice and it set the course for the rest of my life." He looks around. "If we had more young people here . . ." He pauses. "Perhaps in the next service?"

For now, there are a few amens from the adults before Carley gets back to the Bible's Daniel.

"Daniel in the lion's den was what age?" he asked. "He served the king for sixty years, was twenty when he started, so was around seventy when in the den. So all the forming God does in us when we are teenagers lasts."

"That's good, that's good," someone in the seats calls out.

"Kids love that story. But Daniel was successful even in his final years. He overcame the lion by faith. He was a faithful servant. The principles we learned as teenagers we practice, what we were taught at our mother's knee and in Sunday school."

Carley says he wants to leave us with four points, but they seem unconnected to what he's just said. "Be a Daniel," he advises, "and say no to a sinful value system.

"Many people are saying we're living in a post-Christian era. Go to New York and you'll find the churches totally against biblical principle. An Episcopal pastor friend does not agree with homosexuality, they tried to take his church away."

"Yes!"

"The militant homosexual community wants to change our church."

"Amen!"

"Yes!"

Googling later will harvest the fact that the Reverend Carley M. Touchstone is both president of the Greater Rochester Association of Evangelicals and leader of a coalition of churches affirming marriage, and that in July he was among those celebrating a New York court ruling denying same-sex marriages. But I don't know that as I sit here. I only know that there is more important stuff to be worrying about than who loves whom. Less than an hour west of here, for instance, so many people still face misery a year after Hurricane Katrina.

Yesterday, I finished some volunteering through Project Hope and Compassion, which I found on the Internet after I got the idea to spend the week between Gulf Coast churches using the carpentry skills my father taught me. So, armed with some of his tools, after Lagniappe I drove north from Gulfport to the tiny village of Lizana, where St. Anne's Catholic Church has given over its parish hall to living quarters for Gulf Coast volunteers. Participants pay fifteen dollars a day for a cot, showers, and three meals a day, the noon one normally carried to the worksite in one of the project's dozens of coolers.

By the time I arrived in Mississippi, more than 350,000 volunteers had toiled on Katrina-related projects in that state over the previous year. Nearly 4,000 of them had been based at Project Hope and Compassion. A group of 75 were supposed to be staying there this past week, but its plans changed so the parish center was vacant except for Jo, a woman from the Chicago area who volunteered with her church group last year then decided to uproot herself and come to Mississippi indefinitely. By the time I met her, she'd been at the camp for half a year and wanted to say she'd seen great progress in the area, but instead was astounded by how much remains to be done. We became two of those trying to do something, each morning heading out to the addresses on the work-request sheets. Jo and I tended to the yard of an elderly woman in Waveland who'd settled into a new mobile home, having lost hers to the storm. In Gulfport we laid flooring in a newly refurbished kitchen and installed bathroom fixtures in the lavatory of a blind woman in her nineties, who with her surly dachshund had been living on her front lawn in a trailer on eighteen-month loan from the Federal Emergency Management Agency. Across the city, we painted the bathroom of a grandmother whose FEMA unit was parked in the backyard. In the town of Pass Christian, we helped another grandmother, this one raising a granddaughter and grandson, move into a new one-bedroom apartment; all had relocated a year ago when the roof of their former apartment building was ripped off in the storm. At each and every site, we were greeted with hugs and kisses and tears and stories of loss. It is not going anywhere near overdoing it to say I have never felt so deeply needed. It's easy to see why Jo is not the only person I learn about who has just dropped everything and come to live here, so seductive is the feeling that your presence is so vital right this moment.

"Commit to biblical principles!" Pastor Carley is imploring, and I'm thinking how those include loving your neighbor. Including the very needy and hurting and forgotten ones sixty miles west.

He's talking about how we should know our limits and recalls a time in his youth when he worked the midnight shift at a hotel. "All my values were tried," he says. "A woman came and propositioned me every night at 2 a.m. Five nights in a row. Fifth night, I went up, had my hand on the knob, and the Lord said, 'You reached your limit.' "

He resigned the next day.

"Amen!" a few people shout.

"Say to God, 'Here I am, help me. Say, 'God, here I am, help me.'

That decision that night has carried me through the rest of my life. I'm no stronger than when I'm at my weakest point."

This is the end of the racy Pastor Carley info, unless we want to hang around. "At the second service," he says with a smile, "I have a real banger for the kids. But I don't think you want me to talk about sex, abstinence, drugs! Keep to convictions, your reward will be blessings for a lifetime. We need to dare to be Daniels!"

He quotes a hymn: "Dare to be a Daniel, dare to stand alone. Dare to have a purpose, dare to make it known.

"Be a Daniel even at seventy," he continues. "Make a stand—there's no turning back. I said to my wife, Barbara, when I hit seventy I'm not gonna take any more medication at all. I don't want to prolong my life. I know there's death waiting. Let's stick with it. Let's lift our hands. To the Lord, to the word that is alive and rich!"

The entire church is yelling, everyone's clapping, calling out "Hallelujah!"

"We just thank you for it," Pastor Carley shouts over the tumult. "Hallelujah! Worship the Lord, hallelujah!"

There's a story behind everything, and this is mine today. Sitting here flabbergasted by the places I've been this week, including yet another church that chooses to focus on Old Testament demons when there are so many enormous problems right now to attend to.

"Father, our brother has challenged us today," Pastor Jerry prays. "Let us receive that challenge. Your Kingdom is not only the young, the older, the white heads, it takes us all. Not to just sit on the sidelines. We take it up again today. Our value system is still the same. When you call us home, we want to be found to have done what you called us to do."

What I feel called to do in the future is spend more time on my knees—though while laying peel-and-stick floor tiles in a blind lady's kitchen rather than while praying in yet another church where ancient fears and prejudices persist.

MEETINGHOUSE OF THE UNITED SOCIETY OF BELIEVERS IN CHRIST'S SECOND APPEARING

SABBATHDAY LAKE SHAKER VILLAGE,
NEW GLOUCESTER, MAINE

Thirty years ago I attended art school in Portland, Maine, and at my local health food store I regularly purchased tins of comfrey tea leaves grown by the Sabbathday Lake Shakers twenty-five miles north. Other than that they grew the comfrey I brewed, all I knew about the Shakers was what most folks know: that they make furniture and don't make love. There is, of course, a whole lot more to the faith, as I'll find out at this morning's service at the community's meetinghouse.

The Shaker movement began with Ann Lee, originally Ann Standerin, who in 1758 was a twenty-two-year-old blacksmith's daughter in Manchester, England, known for her interruption of worship services and disturbing the peace. The deaths of her four children brought her to the conclusion that she was being judged by God, which pushed her from sexual relations and sparked inner turmoil that led to a spiritual awakening. "Mother Ann" led worship in which quivering masses, whose pejorative "Shaking Quakers" gave the faith its best-known name, prophesied and spoke in tongues before listening to her speak. She often decried the joys of the flesh, railing against marriage and churches that sanctioned such unions, and thusly raised the eyebrows of both citizens and officials, who occasionally saw fit to incarcerate Mother Ann.

So it was fortunate that in 1772 she received a vision from God, who said "a place had been prepared" for the Shakers—but all the way over in America. With eight or nine followers at her side, Mother Ann crossed the Atlantic in 1774 and worked to set up the United Society of Believers in Christ's Second Appearing, which saw peak membership between 1830 and 1840, when six thousand Shakers lived and worked and worshipped in nineteen communities. Celibate pacifists who lived communally, they strove to follow Christian life as it was illustrated in the Gospels and lived in the first Christian settlements. Notable is their veneration of a God who possesses both male and female attributes, which explains the "Father/Mother God," a term used in worship at Sabbathday and echoed by visitors.

Founded in 1783, and traditionally known within the religion as "the least of Mother's children in the east" for both its small bank account and membership rolls, it remains as such: a mere four souls —two men and two women—comprise its membership. Its most important designation might be that it is the world's only remaining Shaker community. My mother has joined me for the trip to this historic village, but will not complete the final seventy-five yards from the dirt parking lot to the meetinghouse. She's a Catholic, not a dabbler, not a seeker, confident in her choice of a spiritual home, and not unlike the Islamic guy I sat next to en route to Plains. She was raised in this faith, what's the reason to look at others? Or even give a peek. Bear in mind that, back in parochial school, some of the nuns who gave my classmates and me the ceiling-falling warning were the very same nuns who had, three decades earlier, handed those very same lines to my mother and her friends. My mother has just turned seventy-nine and that threat hasn't lost its power. So in her car she stays.

Her enduring commitment is something to envy; I'd never given a thought to the possibility I'd look at any other faith, but all that changed with the sex-abuse scandals and my illness. I'm in what seems to be a generation of seekers and peekers. It no longer seems a sin to spend a Sunday in another church, or to hop around. When I recently visited a book club and mentioned this project, the hostess handing me my cup of chamomile said, "Oh I'd read that—I'm on my fifth religion."

I'm on my twenty-first of the year as I walk toward the one-story white meetinghouse this morning, passing several of the eighteen buildings set on the community's eighteen hundred acres, perfect as the property of a living history museum. But this is holy ground. Those four remaining Shakers live here, work here, worship here, and, with the assistance of a group of volunteers, keep this community afloat. I follow two women in modern-day dress through the right-hand door of the meetinghouse. Men use the door at the left, and occupy that side of the building, choosing seats on the ten rows of dark teal wooden benches. Across the room, ten benches are set aside for females. The genders face one another like spiritual football teams.

Kickoff comes with the ringing of a bell. Three double clangs plus a single one tell us worship is about to begin. This is the only church I've visited where the visitors so greatly outnumber actual members—there are twenty-three non-Shakers attending worship this morning.

The Sabbathday Lake community formally began when this meetinghouse was constructed in 1794. Other than an antique clock stuck at 11:25, modernity has not encroached. Light streams through sets of five windows along the front and back of the building, plus a pair at each far end. Along the wall, a double row of pegs stationed every foot or so awaits your shawl or hat. On the seats are copies of blue *Shaker Music* hardcovers. "The Common People heard them gladly," I read in this book copyrighted in 1884.

I try not to stare when an older woman enters and takes a seat in the front row. I guess from her dress (a pink *Little House on the Prairie* number with shawl collar) that she's a Shaker. Indeed, she's sixty-seven-year-old Sister June Carpenter, once a librarian in the Boston suburb of Brookline, and a Shaker since age forty-nine. She's started the brief parade, with bearded Brother Arnold Hadd, a native of none other than Springfield, Massachusetts, walking in next, carrying a Bible and dressed in dark vest and pants, and shirt as white as the clapboards on the building's exterior. Back in his teens, Brother Arnold wrote a letter to the community, sparking a pre-e-mail-era string of letters that led to his spending the summer of 1977 in the village, and discovering at summer's end that he did not want to leave. He's now forty-nine, one of the middle children in this family—the Shaker term—whose eldest is the next to enter. Sister Frances Carr came to the community at age ten, along with her biological siblings, the lot of them sent by their widowed mother, herself soon deceased. The baby of the family is last inside. Former South Portlander Brother Wayne Smith, forty-three and with movie-star good looks, has been a Shaker since eighteen, joining half a year after high school graduation.

You can be a Shaker, too, if you're unmarried and have no dependents or debts. Eighteen novices have logged at least a year at the village since Hadd's arrival, and approximately seventy queries arrive in the mail annually. If you last a year, the community decides your further acceptance, but it will take five before true membership is granted. Get ready for structure: formal prayer is daily at 8:00 and 11:30 a.m., and 5:00 p.m. on Wednesday. But the community is as much about physical rigor as spiritual. As has been the case for centuries, members tend a forest, apple orchard, vegetable gardens, herb gardens, hay fields, and livestock. For extra cash they craft "fancy goods" including baskets, weavings, and, of course, wooden items.

On this day of rest, the fancy goods shop is locked and all activity is in this building, where Brother Arnold stands at the pulpit. "Unless the Lord builds the house," he reads, "those who build it labor in vain."

From her seat three rows up, Sister June invites us to sing hymn 152, "Forgiving Love." The ceiling is low, the building is not large, there are no instruments, yet the singing is loud: *O forgive thy brother as forgiven thou art, pour the oil of healing in the contrite heart. Charity's fair mantle beautiful and white, hide the little frailties of erring from sight.*

Brother Arnold is back at the podium. He reads clearly from Genesis about Joseph making himself known to his brothers. Brother Wayne stands next, to read from Ephesians, praying that Christ may dwell in our hearts. Sister June stands and reads, "For everyone who asks receives; he who seeks finds; and to him who knocks, the door will be opened." She tells us the next hymn is "Infinite Love," which sounds like a Diana Ross hit but is about God not forgetting his children.

The popping up continues. Brother Arnold next, welcoming us with a Mother Ann quote: "A strange gift never came from God, so please don't feel strange, or a stranger." Then Brother Wayne rises to tell us, "Over the years, I have realized I hold unforgiveness in my heart. It's just going to make me into a hard, dried-up old person."

Sister June stands at the wall now, using it as support. She's got a great hat of thick short gray hair and I can see the hearing aid in her left ear now that she's turned. She plays with the knock-on-the-door theme as she tells us that years before busy Route 26 up the hill made the road through the village all the more quiet and quaint, "the doorbell would ring, people with car problems would need to use the phone,"—yes, they have one, along with a police scanner and a computer—"with the new road, we don't see that as much. There isn't the chance to give. But sometimes we didn't want to get up when the doorbell rang. Whatever you give isn't important. What is important is when I'm busy and somebody asks for help—spiritual help, spiritual advice, spiritual advancement—I'm tempted to say, 'Don't bother me now, I don't have the time.' It's not easy, not an easy task, but it's very important to answer that door."

Over on the men's side, someone begins to sing. *Oh give me the faith of the fathers, a courage to dare, how happy the voice that greet me in the heavenly home over there.*

Hymn numbers are no longer announced. It's futile to flip pages.

Standing now with hands in his pockets is Brother Wayne. "What really strikes me in the Gospel is the active," he says. "Seek, get up, get going, do it. Make it happen."

Somebody begins what has to be the only Shaker hit, "Simple Gifts." None of us needs to search for the words: *'Tis a gift to be simple* . . . We all bob legs and tap hands and finish it right down to the *Turn, turn 'twill be our delight, 'til by turning, turning, we come 'round right.*

Now the visitors are joining in. A big middle-aged guy in a big fisherman-knit sweater stands and speaks about forgiveness. Immediately after, one of the Shaker women starts with *O Shall I forgive* . . .

Anyone can stand and make a pronouncement, but instead of following up with silence, someone offers a hymn that touches on what's been said.

I'm sort of disappointed; I had imagined the service would be stronger. These four gave up what most of us would consider "normal" life for their God, and I guess I thought that this fact would make the worship all the richer—the centerpiece of a week of hard work. In a realization that takes me back to Plains, where the presence of Jimmy Carter rather than what he had to say made the morning, it's the presence of these four people that is more striking than the worship they're leading.

A bearded guy in the third row offers: "I have always seen that when we don't get what we want, a lot of times a door opens to something unexpected. Perhaps it's a matter of looking for the right thing. So, what are you looking for?" It's another instance where I wonder if this is being said directly to me; I'll take his lines on the rest of my travels. A song erupts: *Joy, joy, let us have joy, an angel of God has come to bring us the blessings of purified love, the fruits of our heavenly home.*

The hymn concludes and Brother Wayne quickly says, "With the work of the meeting apparently over, let us join in prayer."

Thanks are given to those who came before us, some of whom are buried not fifty yards away in a graveyard marked with the simple single stone reading SHAKERS.

We recite the Our Father with the other ending. Someone says amen, and that's it.

The four members briefly hold court on the front lawn following the sixty-minute service. Sister June reaches for me as I approach. Grasps my hands and tells me they're cold. A genuine Shaker is touching me. And then, as they probably all will be before too long, she's gone, joining her sister and her brothers walking through the gate and across the street, this small family, having worshipped, now heading for home.

SAINT JOHN WILL-I-AM COLTRANE AFRICAN ORTHODOX CHURCH

SAN FRANCISCO, CALIFORNIA

Franzo King attended a John Coltrane concert back in 1965 and came home a changed man. A hairdresser whose father and grandfather had been Pentecostal ministers, preaching was in his blood. Seeing Coltrane perform literally struck a chord in his soul, and provided the flame that five years later sparked a church inspired by and featuring the music of the legendary saxophonist and composer who transformed modern jazz.

Thirty-nine years later, from a storefront in San Francisco's music-rich Fillmore District, Franzo King infuses a three-hour Sunday-morning service with Coltrane's finest, the 1964 album *A Love Supreme*. The worship glorifies both God and Coltrane, who, despite an addiction to heroin, and the liver cancer that killed him in 1967 at age forty, spent his final decade using his music to praise his creator. In this religion, he is a bona fide saint. The first on a sheet of five Frequently Asked Questions found in the visitor's packet anticipates your "Why?"

"The definition of a Saint is to be a follower of Jesus Christ and one who is sanctified and or set aside for God's purpose. John Coltrane was canonized and deemed worthy of being a Saint because it was his desire to live his life in full submission and obedience to God. John Coltrane sought to uplift people through his music, to inspire them to live meaningful and productive lives."

In 1981 Coltrane's widow, the pianist Alice Coltrane, attempted to sue the church—then known as One Mind Temple Evolutionary Transitional Church of Christ—for $7.5 million. Mrs. Coltrane said her husband's name was being exploited and copyright laws were being trampled. King responded that the music simply helped and healed, so much so that he wanted to make "A Love Supreme" the new national anthem.

Nothing came of the lawsuit, but from the media attention a new church was born. A representative of the Chicago-based African Orthodox Church visited King to talk about making his community part of a faith founded in 1919 by George Alexander McGuire, an Antiguan immigrant and former Episcopal priest who'd suffered discrimination by the church against black worshippers and pastors. King was wary of affiliation, and of any edicts against putting Coltrane at the forefront of worship. So the faith's top man, Archbishop George Duncan Hinkson, told him Coltrane could remain revered—he just couldn't be regarded as God.

After spending two years studying in Chicago with members of the faith founded to give black Episcopalians a church of their own, Franzo was awarded a Doctor of Divinity degree in 1984. The sheepskin and the affiliation were benchmarks of legitimacy for a group once connected to the Black Panthers. The African Orthodox Church consists of fifteen churches and five thousand members across the world, but as the sheet points out, this is the "first and only one of its kind."

I visit for that reason. I wish I could say I'm here because I'm a huge jazz fan, because jazz fans seem, well, inherently cool. But I know next to nothing about it.

I do know that this is the same weekend that Jazz at Lincoln Center in New York City begins a new season with a three-night Coltrane Festival, including slices of cake during intermission to commemorate what would have been his eightieth birthday, September 23. On this coast, back in the '40s and '50s, this historically black district located northwest of famed hippie hangout Haight-Ashbury was called the Harlem of the West. These days it's one of the new hot neighborhoods, complete with Starbucks. King's church moved here from Divisadero Street, where for three decades before gentrification hit it offered meals, clothing, counseling, computer instruction, and Sunday services. In the new location, look for the COLTRANE LIVES sign leaning against the bottom of the front door and the black-and-white poster of the man two windows to the left, or you could easily pass the church wedged between a community center and a garage.

Inside the small white-walled space, a young man in boldly printed shirt assembles a wood-trimmed Gretsch drum kit. To his right is a wooden icon of "Trane" himself, maybe eight feet tall, garbed in white, flames burning in the sax he holds in his left hand, *Let us sing all songs to God to whom all praise is due* written across the scroll in his right. A saintly circle of gold is his halo. In front of the icon, a wooden stool, a guitar and a pair of Fender speakers on tall stands promise the sounds to come.

I pass by a piano just inside the door and take a seat in the farther of two sections of chairs, second row from the back, behind a thirtyish woman and a similarly aged guy. Along with a guy in the section to my left flipping through his copy of Lonely Planet's *San Francisco*, we are four of the thirteen whites and two blacks awaiting the service. We sit in the four rows of five chairs that make up each of the two sections on the gray rug. Some of the seat pads are maroon, some forest green, all have black metal frames in generic banquet-house style. Seven more stand near the icon, and a final one up there is quite fancy, covered with floral upholstery.

To the right of the icon and the chairs is a wide lally column, and behind that an altar holding a painting of Jesus in dreadlocks. Candles and a chalice sit on a brocade cloth, alongside a painting of a black Jesus holding a book on which is written *I am the bread of life.* A white guy with dreads down to his posterior enters, carrying some type of horn case, then disappears through a door just behind my row. The wall to my right displays the largest and most striking pieces of art I've seen in this entire journey. More icons, maybe five by eight feet, an angel in salmon robe, a Madonna and child, a tree of life, God on his throne. All subjects are dark-skinned. All are magnificent. All are available in T-shirt and note card via the Web site.

We worshippers rise to our feet at the 12:10 procession from the back door: a woman in her fifties, two around twenty, five children, a tall, thin man in white floor-length ecclesiastical gown who resembles the writer Julius Lester. A twentyish woman is on bass, a Miles Davis look-alike on drums, a big twentyish man at the wide electric keyboard up front. All are black except for the man with the extremely long dreadlocks, now in black cassock and holding a sax, and another in an altar boy's white smock over black gown, a white crocheted cap on his head and horn in his hand.

"How do you feel?" one of the younger women asks. "Are you ready to give praise to God to whom all praise is due?"

There's some applause. Some ringings of a tambourine. A guy to my left has brought his own. Others are distributed and we have our choice, tambourines, or clacking sticks, or maracas. I'm furiously writing so I decline. Though I start to do my share of moving to the music. You can't help it, even if you don't know the first thing about what's being played. It's soft now to start, background for the woman at the microphone, informing us clearly, "We are not here to entertain you."

We're told the worshippers are part of this service, and that its success depends on us. Where are we from, she asks. "New Zealand" is called out by a guy in a black T-shirt. "France" comes from the guy with the Lonely Planet book. "Pennsylvania," says the woman behind me. We're asked to stay for the entire service, to let go of stress, and to refrain from photographing or making audio recordings.

"Open our lips," asks the man in white, who I realize is Archbishop Franzo King. The bassist plays now, and three women are singing over the music. It's hard to hear the words but their faces show they're into it. They confess to almighty God that they have sinned. Everyone stands, except the two white horn players, who are on their knees.

"Almighty God have mercy on us, forgive us our sins, and lead us to everlasting light through Jesus Christ our Lord," the women implore, lifting their eyes to the white ceiling crossed by exposed wires and pipes. The tambourine man to my left adds a few shakes.

The older woman, probably Reverend Mother Marina King, the archbishop's wife, stands in black pants and cardigan, white V-neck sweater beneath, hair pulled back with plastic grabber, gold cross hanging from a chain around her neck. She claps, raises her hands, asks, "Are we here to praise God today? Everybody say, 'Thank you Jesus Christ!' I want to hear everybody. This is a participatory service!" Mother Marina begins singing the Lord's Prayer. A teen boy in a gray Adidas jacket and a young woman in a tight red jersey dress form her chorus. A guy who just entered with two young boys is in the middle row now. He opens his sax case, and he stands in dark suit, peach shirt and tie, filling between the lines.

"Hear what our Lord Jesus Christ said," Mother Marina tells us. "Thou shalt love the Lord thy God with all thy soul, with all thy heart, with all thy strength. This is the first and greatest commandment."

The music thumps anew. No words, just a melody that twirls and kneels, hops, closes its eyes, covers the same postures and movements as the worshippers. The service advances in bits and pieces of lines, prayers, tunes, but it's making sense, the way disparate parts of great jazz are supposed to. I want to put down the notebook and plunge in, but I also don't want to miss recording a detail. Sure, this is some fabulous music—and certainly would be well into the entertainment category were this a jazz club. But this is a church, and we are worshippers lucky enough to be praising God in such an unusual manner, loudly, wildly, joyfully. The white guy with the dreads takes a seat in the front row. The newly arrived sax player now parks himself in the empty seat to my left. It's the feeling of having a ballplayer try to make a catch and tumble into your row in the stadium, but then stay there. Beyond that, it's as if the church organist pulled all those rows of keys and pipes right next to you. I steal a look at his Selmer as if it were Jimmy Carter's knee. The instrument is that wonderful golden brass, terrifically aged with nicks and scratches, bearing that unfathomable lineup of keys and buttons and whatever, all of it shining.

We're an hour into the service and the singers continue, the white-capped saxophonist and my own saxophonist continue. Archbishop Franzo takes a seat on a stool in front of the Saint John icon. And as New Zealand folds his hands and lowers his head in prayer, Mother Marina sings the Twenty-third Psalm, *The Lord is my shepherd* over and again morphing into the line *A love supreme,* the title track of the first jazz album to sell fifty thousand copies.

One of the younger women speaks over Mother's repeats: "The testimony of Saint John Coltrane, all praise be to God." She sings what was in the visitor's packet, the story of Coltrane's spiritual awakening. My sax guy, up front now, loosens his tie. The white skullcap closes his eyes and softly sings: *They comfort me, they comfort me. Surely goodness and mercy shall follow me and I will dwell in the house of the Lord forever.*

There is an amen, then another, and another, each louder than the previous. Both the music and the singing slowly grow softer, until it's just a repeating whisper.

A gospel tune begins, with the young woman blazing the lyrics *The devil don't like it 'cause I'm blessed like that! Blessed like that! Blessed like that!* Archbishop Franzo is strutting around the front of the room, whipping off his red skullcap.

"We've scattered some demons today, y'all," announces Mother Marina. "Let us prepare for the hearing of the word!"

We rise and Archbishop Franzo says, "It's good to be in the house of the Lord today. The praise hasn't stopped. Saints, friends, enemies, we are thankful for all." He reads from the book of Luke, about the lepers seeking healing, and only one of the nine remaining to thank and praise.

A music stand is brought to the front of the room as the women sing a long line of hallelujahs. I'm thinking, here, right here, this is the passion that was shown for the dead pope. Twenty-two churches into my year, I am finding what I saw on CNN. The fervor, the love, the attachment so similar to that shown by the pope's millions. A bell goes off in my head. This is it! This is the place! Then falls a dull thud at the realization that I've found this level of intensity at a church located at the opposite end of the country from my home. Even so, I've found it! Those up front aren't here to knock off an obligation or buy some insurance policy against hell. Their enthusiasm is genuine. Their love nothing short of supreme.

And it's being celebrated in one of the world's coolest cities, where Tommy and I are on a family vacation this week. While he and Kara and his sister Mary are holed up at an Irish pub watching Kerry clobber Mayo in a live broadcast of the All-Ireland football final, I am in church listening to Archbishop Franzo ask, "How many love the Lord today? I said how many love the Lord? Raise your hands!" I shoot mine up with the rest of them.

Some sing, with no organization. *Loves Jesus, my soul loves Jesus,* starts the altar boy. *My soul loves Jesus, bless his name,* the women up front chime in.

It's one fifty, almost two hours into the service, and Archbishop Franzo is just starting to preach. His congregation is now only fourteen, but he speaks with the flame he'd use to address fourteen hundred, suggesting, "Look to God for continued guidance and direction, to Jesus Christ for that uncompromising revolutionary who changed the whole face of the world."

He nods. Tells us, "The old folks used to say 'My bed don't turn into a cooling board.' How many on fire today for the Lord?"

Cheers erupt.

"I do feel the prayers of the saints here today," Archbishop says. "We need to know who Jesus is. Here, with harmony and melody of the keyboard, the sound of the trumpet, the witnessing of believers—he's not just passing through—he's dwelling here!"

There are amens and applause as he continues. "Everywhere

Jesus went, there was a need to fulfill, and there was no need he couldn't fulfill. They recognized him as a master. Jesus, master healer. These were some wise lepers, amen?"

We're encouraged to praise God, to thank him for coming through. Some shouts of "Thank you, Jesus" are offered. I stand silent. I might wave and sing, but it still feels odd to speak aloud in a church when I'm not chanting the same line with the rest of the congregation. "Let's lift voices up together," Archbishop Franzo is saying, and the together part sounds better to me. "You need to have a living testimony so you can lift your voice up . . . I get an idea the lepers had heard something about Jesus. About the promise of God. Look out now—some of our hearts and spirits need healing. Here's a chance for us right now. When he saw them healed, he said 'Go, show yourself.'

"You can't keep this thing to yourself. I tell you, when God does something, you gotta be loud about it! That's why we don't care if you can't sing. You're not singing to us, you're singing to God."

A zero-emission bus passes silently, a street person stops, peers into the church, continues on. And the archishop continues on about trials and faith.

He talks of a great bassist who once asked why he wasn't playing with John Coltrane. "He said he was busy. Are you available or are you too busy?" He steps forward, past the music stand holding his notes. "Anyone like to deepen that commitment to God? Raise your hand. The doors of the church are open. Receive the right hand of fellowship."

No one steps forward for this offer to be born again. But I feel how tempting it could be, to become involved on a deeper level in a church where every second of worship is so heartfelt, intimate, in your face, in your soul.

"John Coltrane said, 'I had a spiritual awakening, I ask for the means and privilege to make others happy,' " Archbishop Franzo tells us in closing. "He didn't ask for a top-ten hit song, he asked to be a servant. And the greatest thing of all is to serve. So let us arise from this place and be busy about the things of God."

SADDLEBACK CHURCH

LAKE FOREST, CALIFORNIA

"Do you have *The Purpose Driven Life?*"

I've been asked this again and again, but as a clerk in a bookstore, not as a soul awaiting direction.

"Certainly," I've responded, walking over to Religion and plucking a copy, and noting, as any good retail person would, that we carry the accompanying workbook, too. The titles usually are grabbed as a pair. And "grabbing" is not too over-the-top a verb. *The Purpose Driven Life*, after all, is the country's best-selling hardcover. Of all time. Without a single review in the hugely influential *New York Times*, *Los Angeles Times*, or *Washington Post*.

A quadruple murder and hostage-taking early last year in suburban Atlanta rocketed author and pastor Rick Warren to secular consciousness when the hostage was released after she read her captor chapter 33, "How Real Servants Act."

Attired in the brightly patterned shirts he chooses to be as comfortable as his congregation, Pastor Rick was interviewed by national and international media, talking about the book and telling of his twenty-six-year-old ministry based at Saddleback Church in Lake Forest, California. Like so many of his peers, including Joel Osteen down in Houston and Franzo King up in San Francisco, this is another pastor's son, one who went from preaching to six people in a living room to standing before twenty-two thousand weekly. His evangelical church, which Pastor Rick has written is "doctrinally and financially affiliated with the Southern Baptist Convention," a fact not played up due to many seekers' qualms about that division's fundamentalism, is headquartered on a 120-acre campus in the shadow of Southern California's Saddleback Mountain. There, weekly services are held and more than three hundred ministries are offered, including those for prisoners, businesspeople, single parents, and the mortally ill. Churches in 162 countries comprise Warren's Purpose Driven Network, which has trained more than four hundred thousand clergy. The mailing list for Pastor Rick's weekly minister's newsletter contains 157,000 names.

Warren takes no salary from Saddleback. He and wife Kay "reverse tithe," donating 90 percent of any other income to three foundations that assist those affected by AIDS, train church leaders in developing countries, and fight poverty, illness, and illiteracy. Warren's Web site states his goal as establishing "a second Reformation by restoring *responsibility* in people, *credibility* in churches, and *civility* in culture."

Make that all cultures, worldwide, which is where you often can find this man who travels so often that even a month ago his office couldn't confirm for me that he'd be here preaching this morning. For his work as global strategist, which has included speaking at the United Nations, *Time* magazine called Warren one of fifteen World Leaders Who Mattered Most in 2004, and the following year he was named both one of the twenty-four most influential evangelicals in America and one of the one hundred most influential people in the world. But to quote the congregant in the Hawaiian shirt who sits next to me this morning at the plainly named Worship Center, "He's like a regular Joe Blow."

And I find myself agreeing with this assessment when Pastor Rick takes the stage after a pair of opening numbers by the eight-piece band. Roly-poly in jeans and untucked aloha shirt on which large red and yellow flowers blossom across the hem and up the buttonholes, with cropped brownish-blond hair and matching goatee, and easygoing in manner, he gives a genuine and enthusiastic "Good Morning, Saddleback!" to the three thousand who pack this simple gymnasium-like room with its exposed ceiling and glass sides. The greeting echoes through seven other on-site Saddleback venues receiving a broadcast but bearing their own style of music and worship, with gospel, rock, Latin, and Hawaiian themes. An additional fifteen hundred worshippers pack Saddleback's satellite church seventeen miles south in coastal San Clemente. Lots closer, dozens whom Warren greets as "the coffee addicts up at the café" watch from umbrella-shaded plastic patio chairs just outside.

A simple tall rusted metal cross hangs at the left of a stage otherwise decorated only by a string of paintings of trees, keyholes, hands, and a fingerprint. The plain background must be telegenic, but the cameras capturing Pastor Rick's sermon aren't worried how it will look to the world. The feed goes to the additional worship sites, and is recorded as a teaching tool for the pastors this pastor assists. He's not interested in broadcasting beyond that, preferring not to compete with the clergy he's mentored.

And that's not harmed him a hair. Pastor Rick's is one of the best known of the ever-growing megachurch phenomenon that began gathering millions of evangelicals throughout America three decades ago. Like so many of the megapastors, Pastor Rick preaches the love of a New Testament God, without all that legendary heaven-splitting anger and judgment. One who just wants us to love everyone.

But from my metal-framed beige plastic chair, I don't see everyone. I count a few Asians, but that's about it for minorities. Saddleback's far-flung location might be a reason—Lake Forest is a well-to-do community. Mass transit is not a lifeblood. The bus I'd hoped to catch from my hotel half an hour away doesn't run on the weekends. My taxi fare was fifty-six dollars, and even the folks at the Saddleback information booth were stymied as to how a cab might find this place, and me, for the return trip.

But I can't worry about that now. It's time to listen to Pastor Rick tell me that "God has never made copies of anything. Every plant, tree, original. Original is always more valuable. That's what we are."

A passage from Job 10 illuminates the screen—*God's hands shaped me and formed me*—as Pastor Rick reminds us that God chose us, he chose our parents, and he's also chosen this experience today. We're told this will be "a very different kind of service." Pastor Rick adds, "In a minute, I'll ask you to go out of here and do something."

We later will be walking to the SHAPE Expo, which sounds like a fitness club but will be a workout of another kind. "We're going to see how your abilities can make a difference in the world," Pastor Rick tells us. He quotes a study that found the average human to have between five and eight hundred skills. He proclaims, "There are no no-talent people.

"The key thing to understand is that your abilities are the map to your life." And none are unnecessary. "Carpentry is as important as preaching, masonry is as important as singing."

He asks us to write and pens fly as Pastor Rick states, "My abilities match my call." He pauses and adds, "Sometimes we think only priests or nuns are called. Every human being is called to do something. You can honor God by balancing books, creating a meal, showing somebody a house to sell."

I realize we're going down the talking points on one of the many sheets I was handed upon entering for worship. Inside the four-page four-color bulletin the letter-size sheet of paper is complete with a trio of holes for your notebook. Its title: "Using Your Abilities—Shaped to Make a Difference—Part 4."

The acronym is spelled out: **S**piritual gifts, **H**eart, **A**bilities, **P**ersonality, **E**xperiences. Today we're on Abilities, and Pastor Rick is explaining what they might be used for. We scribble the possibilities he mentions: to honor God, serve others, make a living, be an example, have money to share, help the church.

Pastor Rick's is an easy delivery, Joel Osteen–friendly but mentioning God ten times as much. I have never met Pastor Rick, but he's familiar. He's up on a stage, certainly, but that's the only thing elevating him. He's one of us. And I'm enjoying this message.

It doesn't hurt that I spiritually bought the idea long ago—that each of us is here to do something. The point is to figure out the purpose to which you're called. It might hit you in infancy, or it might come after a career in the Marines, finally tending to that long-tamped-down desire to design the prettiest dresses ever. You can do something, and there's a place where you're needed.

A heavy side dish of disappointment in an otherwise pleasant morning is the reality of the fundamentalist viewpoint. Behind the happy shirt and face, this is still someone who sees gays and Jews as doomed and who believes a woman's right to choose is wrong. But Pastor Rick, in another connection to Pastor Joel, does not stress controversial views in his sermons. "We have eighty-five thousand names on the church rolls," Pastor Rick is saying instead. "There is no need, no ability that cannot be needed in this church family."

And if you don't use these talents? "You lose," we write. Not only our reward in heaven, but we'll also lose the abilities. To quote

Matthew 25, verse 28, "Take the talent from him—who didn't use it—and give to the one who has ten talents."

We're next asked to do an audit—to estimate what we're capable of. "A secret of success in life," Pastor Rick tells us, "is to build on your strengths so that your weaknesses are irrelevant."

When *The Purpose Driven Life* was published, Pastor Rick says, he wondered "What's all this money for? God said 'Read the first sentence of your book: "It's not about you." And when it makes tens of millions of dollars, that's not about you. Give freely. Don't have a stingy heart.'

"You can't learn to be like God if you can't be generous. Let me tell you this from personal experience: the more generous you are, the more God will bless your life."

There's another pause. "My greatest frustration as your pastor," we're told, "is I know there's great untapped talent in this church . . . God has the right to take from you anything you don't use properly. If you don't use muscles in exercise, mind, it goes dull. He's made an enormous investment in your life and he wants a return."

Pastor Rick then thanks God for the abilities he's been given. "I don't even know what they are," he admits, though looking around he really has to have at least a clue. "I want to use them to honor you, serve others, make a living, be an example."

And we're through, in under an hour. Pastor Rick marvels that, at thirty minutes—"it's the shortest sermon I've ever done."

Awaken my heart, a blond woman in a long pink coat sings from the stage as an American Sign Language translator at the front of our section jives to the zippy beat. *Awaken my heart, awaken my soul, awaken your power and take control.* We watch and listen as if taking in another act, the blonde our entertainment and we, the congregants, merely observers rather than participants.

It's an Osteen moment. No stilettos on this woman, but she still bears the slick delivery of the singers in Houston. I know we're quite near Hollywood, so a showbiz feel shouldn't surprise me this morning, but I'd hoped for something better. Yes, Pastor Rick gave me lots more to think about than Joel did in his weight-loss seminar, and, in the homework to venture out and help the world, something concrete to do, but there's a surface feel to the service. And it's not just size: Unity Village back in Missouri held more than one thousand, but in that large hall, and in the richness of the message, I found a warmth similar to that in the cluster of fourteen last week in San Francisco. I guess I don't need a coffee shop. A bookstore. Five styles of worship. I don't care if the pastor tithes 99.9 or wears his pajamas. I just want the experience to hit home intimately. And maybe that's a different thing for everybody. For me, it was not found here.

At the SHAPE Expo courtyard, hundreds mill at information booths as they ponder how to volunteer their abilities in areas including communications, technology, ministry, recovery, the arts. The only volunteering I'm interested in right now is the kind two Saddleback members want to do for me. Nancy and Howard heard my earlier inquiry about a taxi, and they want to provide a lift. So I'm soon seated in their SUV with them and their camouflage-print-covered Bible, en route to the Amtrak station for my train to Seattle.

Nancy was raised Baptist; Howard, Catholic; they brought up their children as Catholics. When they moved across the street from Saddleback in 1991, the couple walked over. Pastor Rick's brother-in-law, Pastor Tom, caught their interest and they joined.

At the station, just as Pastor Rick had from any first-time visitor back at church, Nancy and Howard refuse money I offer them for the fifteen-minute drive. "Make a donation," Nancy says, pushing my bills back at me. Maybe she considers driving strangers to be one of her eight hundred abilities, and who am I to argue? I take the money back and promise her I will.

MARS HILL CHURCH

SEATTLE, WASHINGTON

I've been whining about the lack of art in the churches I'm visiting. This morning, big-time art awaits. But I can't really look at it.

Just inside the doors to Mars Hill Church, a much-larger-than-life trio of paintings, a Coltrane-sized five-by-eight-foot piece book-ended by two five-by-fives, depicts close-ups of the face of Jesus at the height of his Crucifixion. He screams, bulges his eyes, bleeds, and expires darkly in what has to be the most violent illustration of this I've seen. This is no cleaned-up murder, a tiny spot of blood on foot or hand, dreamy-sleepy countenance. This is his agonized face in yours. He is dying. For you.

Welcome to the no-frills urgency of Mars Hill, a nondenominational evangelical church aimed at reaching souls in a city that, along with Portland, Oregon, shares the distinction of being the nation's least churched metropolis. This place, and its pastor, cut right to the chase. Last fall, Mark Driscoll informed his congregation, "You have been told that God is a loving, gracious, merciful, kind, compassionate, wonderful, and good sky fairy who runs a daycare in the sky and has a bucket of suckers for everyone because we're all good people. That is a lie . . . God looks down and says, 'I hate you, you are my enemy, and I will crush you,' and we say that is deserved, right, and just, and then God says 'Because of Jesus I will love you and forgive you.' This is a miracle."

Many who'd prefer a sermon on diet tips or volunteer opportunities might consider the miracle to be that six thousand worshippers pack four Mars Hill locations to hear similar themes. This is yet another church with roots in a couch and coffee table, a dozen people first meeting in a living room a decade ago to study the Bible and worship with Pastors Mark Driscoll, Lief Moi, and Mike Gunn. Today marks the church's tenth anniversary, and the opening of its fourth location.

Things are only getting busier for Mars Hill, which *Outreach* magazine recently named the nation's fifteenth-fastest-growing church. Pastor Mark, a thirty-five-year-old husband and father of three, holds his own titles—one of the twenty-five most influential pastors in America (*Church Report* magazine) and one of the city's twenty-five most powerful people (*Seattle Magazine*). He's also a columnist, writing a "Faith & Values" feature for the *Seattle Times*. What titles does he give himself? He once listed them, in order of importance, as Christian, Evangelical, Missional, and Reformed. He's also used the term "charismatic Calvinist." The casual visitor might add "a big draw."

I attend the Mars Hill's Ballard location, where corrugated steel buildings housing a marine supplier and paint warehouse make up the immediate neighborhood. The area is Sunday-deserted, so you'll understand why I suppose I'm in peril when a trio emerges from the shadow of the Ballard Bridge overpass just beyond the black-painted concrete building that is Mars Hill. They come into the light and I see that the sacks I assumed were liquor bottles are Bibles. The tallest man holds the door for me as we enter.

Other than the Jesuses, the lobby resembles that of a contemporary theater, which is a perfect description of the experience awaiting me inside. This church with the goal of reaching late-teens-to-early-twenties Seattleites might further an old-fashioned fear of hell but it doesn't skimp on modern presentation. Free literature includes the tabloid-size twenty-four-page monthly *Vox Pop* church newspaper; booklets from the Driscoll-penned Mars Hill Theology Series, their titles including *Reforming Male Sexuality—A Frank Discussion on Pornography & Masturbation for God's Men*; a sheet listing Mars Hill kayaking, rock climbing, mountain biking, and skydiving outings. Take your copy of *The Loop* bulletin and enter a room the size of a Costco, but with rows of black-upholstered metal-framed seats rather than aisles of twelve-gallon shampoo bottles. Several dozen golden lampshades hang from the black exposed ceiling, casting a dim orange glow on the space that accommodates 1,759. I focus on the brightly lit stage, watch the rock band tuning up. The centerpiece is a giant cross made of metal squares and reminiscent of a 9/11 memorial. At either side of the stage are movie screens now prompting us to sing *I will arise and go to Jesus.* A young dark-haired white woman in black top, schoolgirl-plaid skirt, and boots leads us: *He will embrace me in his arms. And in the arms of my great savior, there are one hundred thousand charms.*

The lead guitarist sports a short red/blond Rasputin beard and bell-bottom jeans. The full house is mostly young and white and includes the youngest males of any church I've visited so far. Many worshippers have brought coffee, or coffee and a snack. Next to me, a twentyish woman in a T-shirt that reads I'M NOT FAT, I'M PREGNANT sips her Starbucks and nibbles a scone.

Some hands are raised, some eyes are closed. Worshippers sway and jiggle to the music. The screens become a grid of faces. There is no sound and, apparently, there should be. Congregants laugh.

Wearing a leather necklace, two hefty bracelets, a wedding ring, and a brown snap-front shirt hanging outside dark pants, Pastor Mark Driscoll appears onstage. "Well, we will take a $1.2 million offering today," he starts. "Now you know why." That gets more laughs. "Happy Birthday, Happy Anniversary. Do we have the video? Do we have deaf outreach today or what?" Some more laughter.

On the screen now is the first of the many videos that are a large part of this service aimed at the iPod/camera phone generation. A woman says, "I really realized, crap, I am a Christian! My family's Muslim and I am here." Her new life is yet a secret to her family. Even so, she says, oh, "the glory of it."

A young man raised Mormon is shown next, telling us how he was abused at home, molested by a friend, and began believing he was gay. But, "God pursued me. He showed me." And when this man was on a trip to Africa, God also introduced him to his future wife.

Then the screen flashes images of the lead guitarist and the singer, who tell us, "We must open our minds, we must let go of everything we think about God."

Pastor Mark is back onstage, hands in pockets, weeping. "It's wonderful to see Jesus Christ in your life, isn't it?" he asks. "I didn't know Jesus until I was nineteen, and what he has done since then is overwhelming. This has been the best ten years of my life. I don't regret a day of it."

Pastor Mark's weekend has been a rush thus far. He preached in Minnesota yesterday and flew in late so he could be here for the birthday/anniversary. He's delighted there are so many here today, and encourages those with wives to put them in their laps. "Because it's good, and we need the seats."

Then things get serious. "God," Pastor Mark begins, "I don't know how I lived nineteen years without you."

Nor does he know how he's lived the last ten, wildly busy in Seattle. And that's what his tenth-anniversary sermon is about, "Loving the City."

It's only my second visit, and I'm a convert to beautiful, walkable, edible Seattle. But I'd probably be happy to be anywhere today, having just ended a thirty-one-hour Amtrak trip from Southern California. Cindy used a free ticket to join me here, and we'll be tourists for a few days, with no work except shopping for a dress she'll wear next July, when her youngest marries.

Right now Cindy's back at Pike Place Market, reading the Sunday *Seattle Times*, not interested in spending this sunny morning in a church of any form. I'm here in a onetime paint factory, opening *The Loop* to Pastor Mark's main points, starting with "Be a missionary to the city."

I read that "God places his people in cities they may not like (e.g., Babylon or Seattle) because he wants them to be agents of cultural transformation." We're to be missionaries in this place of 1.7 million, the country's most educated city, a fitting location for a church named for the place in Greece where Paul preached the Gospel to pagan leaders and community intellectuals.

Speaking with nary an um or an ah, Pastor Mark stands to the left of the pulpit and lists the city's plusses: strong economy, high literacy rate, range of arts and culture. But . . . "Living as a city within a city, we view things differently," he says. "We will serve the entire city. Yes, that includes homosexuals and atheists. Does that mean we agree with them? Not at all."

Over the next decade, Mars Hill plans to work on issues of gender, sexuality, and serving the common good. Pastor Mark doesn't give details, but he does note his dislike of the term "social justice." "What we believe in," he says, "is mercy."

I'm wondering where's the mercy in a handout rather than a hand up, helping those in need just as an empty act rather than something that might improve this city he's going on about. OK, I know I just finished saying Saddleback wasn't for me, but suddenly I'm missing Pastor Rick and his touchy-feely aloha-shirt invitation to volunteer and better this world. Pastor Mark scares me on some level. And—look out—he wants me to stay. To settle down here—not the most traditional thing in a city where home ownership is 52 percent, lower than most metropoli. But he has his reasons.

We're told that God names marriage, children, and grace as qualities of the Christian city within a city. That Seattle's cohabitation rate is 250 percent higher than the national average. And that in 1973 a citizen's committee published goals for Seattle that favored "discouraging births" to stabilize the population. Pastor Mark says Seattle contains fewer kids than canines (75,000 / 150,000). If you're like me and consider your pups your progeny, you disgust him.

"The baby is an image-bearer," he says. "A dog is a dog." If you want to better the world, have another child, Pastor Mark advises, pointing to the marvels a single man can spark: Irish warlord Niall is responsible for 3 million descendants (perhaps among them this pastor, whose family was O'Driscoll "'til," as he notes, "we dropped the O—a bunch of crazy Micks."). Pastor Mark says two hundred couples are moving through the premarriage process at Mars Hill. Marriage, he starts, then raises a finger, "heterosexual marriage—I need to clarify—is honored here."

Serving the common good is also suggested to those who love the city. Pastor Mark points out that if a town like Seattle, only 8 percent of which is evangelical Christian (again, dogs rule, 150,000 to 136,000), can be won, why not the world?

Ushers rush to the front as Pastor Mark prays. "A bible study has become a city within a city." I thought this was tithing time, but it's Communion. Goblets of wine and baskets of bread are held forth. Lines form as congregants, including a guy in a JESUS IS MY HOMEBOY T-shirt, partake and singers proclaim the glory of God.

I ponder the message through three consecutive hymns. I'm supposed to love these people. They're supposed to love me. Isn't rejection what kills us?

Friends ask what am I getting from these visits, what am I learning? Certainly I'm starting to understand the subtleties that differentiate one church from the next, and I'm reminded of those that make the young scone eater different from me, who is different from the cardiganed middle-aged woman to my left. Yet we are all supposed to be children of God. The whole thing can give me a headache. I haven't been home in three weeks. I am homesick. And sad: this is a new church, a new chance, and look what they're doing—hammering out the same old hate.

"How Great Thou Art" winds up. Pastor Mark dashes off to inaugurate the new campus. "Can we do this for another ten years? Or twenty or thirty?" asks Leif Moi from the stage. Cheers erupt.

"I hope you got a taste of the heart of what Mars Hill is all about," Pastor Leif wishes.

I think I did.

PART THREE: FALL

TRINITY UNITED CHURCH OF CHRIST

CHICAGO, ILLINOIS

During a visit to Chicago a couple of years ago, I asked a friend what she thought of Barack Obama and his then-ongoing bid for a U.S. Senate seat.

"Ba-who?" was the reply of this woman living in the state where Obama had been a senator for eight years.

Two years later, thanks to extremely early and extremely enthusiastic publicity about this wildly charismatic Democrat bearing "a politics of hope," many predict Obama could become the nation's first African American president. And it's safe to say that few in the Prairie State, or the country, are unfamiliar with his name.

Be it through twenty-four-hour-news-channel osmosis or deliberate investigation, more are learning about the man with an intriguing geneaology, both religious and geographic.

Obama's immediate family includes his late black African father, who hailed from a Christian/Muslim household; a white Kansan mother who balked at organized religion but stocked the home bookshelves with the Bible, the Koran, and the Bhagavad Gita; an Indonesian Muslim stepfather who was lukewarm to religion; and nonpracticing Baptist and Methodist grandparents. By age ten, Obama had attended both a Catholic and a Muslim parochial school in Indonesia, then, upon moving to his grandparents' home in his birthplace of Hawaii, was enrolled in a Christian prep. The salad bar of experiences served up appreciation of other faiths but didn't inspire the self-described "reluctant skeptic" to pick a favorite, even when affiliation might have benefited his early political career.

Seventeen years ago Obama made his choice: the United Church of Christ. Created in this country in 1957 via the union of the Evangelical and Reformed Church and most of the Congregational Christian Churches, the UCC is known for the independence of its nearly six thousand congregations, spiritual home to 1.4 million. It's also known for the nontraditional ways it can present the Protestant experience, including through its recent TV ads showing congregants being plucked from the pews of an anonymous church because of their race or sexual orientation, the message being that at UCC services, all are welcome.

Even so, this denomination remains extremely white. An exception is the church in which you can find Obama worshipping. Located in his South Side Chicago neighborhood, Trinity United Church of Christ describes itself as "a congregation which is Unashamedly Black and Unapologetically Christian . . . We are an African people, and remain 'true to our native land,' the mother continent, the cradle of civilization. God has superintended our pilgrimage through the days of slavery, the days of segregation, and the long night of racism. It is God who gives us the strength and courage to continuously address injustice as a people, and as a congregation." In *The Audacity of Hope*, his second memoir, Obama writes that he was intrigued by "the power of the African American religious tradition to spur social change." He credits the realization that, in such a church, "religious commitment did not require me to suspend critical thinking, disengage from the battle for economic and social justice, or otherwise retreat from the world that I knew and loved." Being baptized into Trinity United Church of Christ, he wrote, "came about as a choice and not an epiphany; the questions I had did not magically disappear. But kneeling beneath that cross on the South Side of Chicago, I felt God's spirit beckoning me. I submitted myself to His will, and dedicated myself to discovering His truth."

A man, as well as his church, helped call Obama to that altar in 1988, and he, wife Michelle, and two young daughters are among the eighty-five hundred members of the country's largest UCC congregation, a population pulled together in large part by the presence of the dynamic and sometimes controversial Rev. Dr. Jeremiah A. Wright Jr. As senior pastor since March of 1972, Pastor Jeremiah has overseen growth that has included more than seventy ministries on fine art, literature, financial counseling, men's mentoring, legal advisement, childcare, addiction programs, and college placement, and that necessitated the 1997 opening of a twenty-seven-hundred-seat worship center. Obama was among the many transfixed by Pastor Jeremiah, whose preaching of liberation theology, which sees Jesus as savior of the underprivileged and espouses improving their plights through political action, often blends the biblical with blasts about local and global wrongs.

"Trinity is a church that is committed to social justice," Pastor Jeremiah writes in the four-color "Welcome" flyer I collect in the foyer colorful with stained glass depictions of historical black figures dating back to the pharaohs. "We speak out against injustice wherever it rears its ugly head—whether on the 5th floor of City Hall in the City of Chicago or in the nation's Capitol in Washington, D.C."

I'm looking forward to some of that fire and fury today, but I will see neither the family pastor nor the congregant who nicked the title of that second book from a Wright sermon. All twenty-seven hundred seats are packed for the service to be led by Rev. Michael G. Sykes, whose usual gig is associate pastor for Trinity's Visitation Ministries for the ill. Inside this angular modern-style beige brick structure across from a row of businesses, we follow the service from a thirty-page four-color-cover bulletin that's more like a magazine. I flip through to find both hymns and readings; six entire pages listing those in need of general prayers; full addresses and phone numbers for those hospitalized, living in extended-care facilities, or homebound; plus categories of "Cards Only," "Communion Visits Only" and "Deacon Visits Only."

That section is impressive for its organization alone. More dazzling are the examples of the social justice efforts. In a "Compassion Explosion: Disaster Recovery Blitz," I read that a group of seventy-five volunteers is needed to head to the Gulf Coast, where the church's Back Bay Mission in Biloxi needs help from licensed plumbers, electricians, roofers, and general contractors.

There's a request for hosts to screen the videos of *The Ground Truth*, the documentary on soldiers' lives pre- and postservice in Iraq I'd seen advertised up at The Riverside Church in Manhattan. "We now know that this war was based, at best, on faulty intelligence, and at worst, on outright lies," the church's Rev. Reginald Williams Jr. writes. "And yet, we, as people of faith, cannot stand idly by and say 'I told you so.' We are compelled to act."

We're asked to boycott Wal-Mart and Sam's Club after Wal-Mart Stores, Inc., this week placed caps on wages and added more part-time positions, which the church alleges is an effort to push out higher-paid longer-term employees. Wal-Mart being the world's largest retailer, other chains might adopt the same practices. Pastor Jeremiah writes that Wal-Mart has "shown the lengths to which greed will take an organization and those who profit from that organization's workers. Moreover, those who continue to shop at Wal-Mart clearly support this greed which is literally killing people." Concluding with: "Whenever you place price over principle, you have defined yourself as a prostitute." That's a pretty heavy statement to make to a community in which many might depend on the megaretailer's low low prices. But there it is. Without apology. Being a fan of the Gulf Coast, and no fan of the murderous war or town-killing Wal-Mart, I've found kin in this place where I've not a single blood relative, nor fellow worshipper of comparatively paler skin. This is the first church bulletin I want to leave on my coffee table to show off, marvel at, and spark discussion, and I wonder why all the others I've collected can't have more substance than a pithy saying of the day.

"Stand on your feet and give God some praise this morning! Hug somebody this morning!"

I no sooner hear this edict than I'm enveloped by the woman in front of me, who grants "The Lord's blessings on you," and another in back who just shakes me joyously there in my right-hand row beneath the wide balcony that arcs around two-thirds of the worship center. The benches, wooden with red padded seats and backs that match the color of the carpet, are well serving their purpose, rows and rows of those who'd previously been chatting in the lobby now taking their seats. A trio of video cameras for the locally televised broadcast is at the ready as two lines of men in dashikis, pants, and hats walk to their seven tiers of seats behind the trio of pulpits. The band—two sets of drums, a keyboard, a baby grand, a horn, and a guitar—begins "Adeste Fidelis," and I hear *O come let us adore him* for the second time in both a non-Christmas season and a black church. The sound is three-dimensional enough to touch, the men's deep voices originating in just about the same ancient place as did those back at St. Spyridon's. The congregation stands in awe as the choir delivers the hymn, then speeds up for *Sing to the Lord a new song,* as a saxophone joins in. *Worship the Lord and praise his holy name.*

A young black pastor, bald and in a dark business suit, stands at the front and asks, "Did you come to worship the Lord this morning?"

Applause and shouts are the answer.

"Enter into his gates with thanksgiving. For the Lord is good, his mercy everlasting. Praise be the Lord!"

The hubbub his order creates dies down in time for the unison scripture, which is just that, the entire congregation reading of Psalm 27:7–14, "Hear, O Lord, when I cry aloud, be gracious to me and answer me! . . . 'Come,' my heart says, 'seek his face!' . . ."

Guests are welcomed and we're told we are the greatest. Congregants swarm to my row, Welcome, welcome, praise Jesus, welcome! Behind me, a thirtyish woman who introduces herself as Yvonne is especially electric, nodding and smiling.

A dozen denim-jacketed members of the dance ministry, from late teens to forties, ten of them women, parade to the front and move with enthusiasm. The lights are dimmed and the congregation whoops with joy. From behind, Yvonne grabs me by the shoulders and says, "He woke us up this morning!"

I get what she means. The nuns always told us that if God weren't thinking of you every second, you would just vanish. He thought of us through the night, and upon the ring of our alarm clocks, we opened our eyes, still on his mind.

The man in the suit is back. "I wish for you this second Sunday of October God's peace in your life."

White tithing envelopes appear from pockets and purses, and ushers stand ready to circulate small collection cans decorated with the Trinity emblem. At most churches, I give the perfunctory few dollars for taking up space (though I added nothing to the million-dollar drive at Mars Hill), but today I am moved to contribute more. I get the message that money handed over here will do the kind of good I like to do myself. That is not a certainty I have experienced often in these twenty-five weeks.

I want to see your Kingdom, not my will but yours be done, sings the choir. A young man in a Negro League baseball jersey nods. The arms of the American Sign Language interpreter swoop. "Yaaay, Jesus!" proclaims a nearby two-year-old. The Altar Call is made.

"Leave it at the altar," the reverend invites. "When they say 'What happened in church?' say 'You should have been there when I left it at the altar.' "

He likens leaving our sins here to traveling light, without any contraband. "You have your ticket, but you can't bring it on board."

The choir and a soloist combine: *What do you do when you've done all you can and it feels like you can't make it through? You just stand.*

We've been standing and sitting for a little more than an hour when it's finally Pastor Michael's time to shine. Wearing a brown/gray tunic and wire-rimmed glasses, and looking to be in his early forties, he begins a story about a young man who wants a sports car for his graduation present. "Trust me and be patient," his father had always told him, "and you will get the desires of your heart."

On graduation day, the father offers a gift box containing a leather-bound Bible. The son's "initial disappointment turns to anger," Pastor Michael says. The Bible is tossed, the son severs the relationship.

Years later, the father dies and leaves all his possessions to his son. In the process of his sorting through the accumulation, the Bible surfaces. A passage in Matthew is underlined: "For everyone who asks receives; he who seeks finds; and to him who knocks, the door will be opened. Which of you, if his son asks for bread, will give him a stone? Or if he asks for a fish, will give him a snake? If you, then, though you are evil, know how to give good gifts to your children, how much more will your Father in heaven give good gifts to those who ask him!"

A car key drops from the back of the book, as does a note from a car dealership: "Paid in full."

We're asked if we, like the boy, spend every day waiting for something we feel we deserve, while impetuous, intolerant, or just plain angry. "There's an epidemic of impatience," Pastor Michael says. "Fast food, FedEx, instant grits. We're rushed. During prayer, the dying and death we're OK with—it's life we have the problem with. We have drive-by shootings—you don't even have to wait to get out of your car to get shot. Drive-by funerals . . ."

"Preach! Come on!" calls a woman.

"I hear it all too often," Pastor Michael says. " 'I know what I want, and I want it now.' We're dying to get to high school, to college, to marriage, to a house, to kids. Some of y'all are just dying to get a divorce. Just say ouch if you can't say amen!"

Why do we no longer value a slower pace, he asks. "In our fast-paced world, that has gone the way of the horse and buggy. But all things don't work that way. As Diana Ross says, you can't hurry love. In 2006, rush hour on the Dan Ryan or any of the alternate routes, the best you can do is hurry up and wait. I'm so sick of people giving me the finger, but not telling me which direction to go."

Some laugh. A toddler screams.

"We're waiting for a job, for the right person. Send our kids to the best schools, sacrifice, wait and pray to make better choices and make our way in life. Loved ones are waiting to be delivered from addiction, those who had surgery and radiation, chemotherapy, are waiting for words on remission. What do you do while you're waiting to exhale?"

Reverend Michael invites us to spend that wait time wisely. "Pray. It does not matter when, where, how you pray, fast, with your feet on the ground, it don't matter."

He next wants us to offer our submission—to be ready to meet the Lord's demands. Then we're to seek divine connection. "Give me that holy hookup that will restore my health and help me." After that, "Accept his correction. This might be a difficult pill to swallow. Now God asks me to clean up my act: Ask for direction. Teach me your way, O Lord, and lead me on a level path. I tried to do it on my own. I asked a friend. Now that life has beaten me up and messed me up, I come to you, Lord."

He calls the church "a hospital for sinners, not a museum of saints. When you go to a doctor's office, do you seek the advice of others in the waiting room? If they knew what to do, they wouldn't be there! Wait to get your prescription from the doctor himself."

We're also instructed to expect the Lord's protection. "Haters, baiters, come at me; to quote Bernie Mac, 'I ain't scared of none of y'all.' "

Finally, we are to "show 'em some affection. Simply believe." I think of the five girls murdered by a gunman who last Monday burst into a remote Amish schoolhouse. Of the killer's family, a community member whose three grandnephews had been inside the school said, "I hope they stay around here. They'll have a lot of friends and a lot of support." The week has been a fog of such horrific news, and unfathomable forgiveness from those so brutally affected. How do you hold onto faith at such times? The reverend knows: "If you're struggling with belief, don't hold your breath, just open your mouth and give him some praise. Wait on Jesus! Wait on Jesus! Wait on Jesus! He will strengthen your heart. Amen!"

There are a few more shouts and whoops and then Pastor Michael tells us, "The doors of the church are open" as the choir takes up his cry: *I'm going to wait on Jesus.*

Yvonne doesn't wait to remind me again that he's already here. "He woke us up today," she is shouting into my left ear. "He woke us up!"

He did. Just in time for me to make this visit to another church on my short list. One that rang true for me in mission, inclusion, and enthusiasm. And one I admit I had visited because of a celebrity, whose presence I then found I didn't need to make this morning meaningful and memorable.

GENESIS CHURCH OF THE BRETHREN

PUTNEY, VERMONT

See TUNKERS.

That's the direction from the *Oxford Concise Dictionary of the Christian Church* when I go looking for information on the Church of the Brethren.

As the media continues to follow both the Amish schoolhouse shootings and the unusual intricacies that make up the victims' religion, I go in search of a church with similar roots. I would have loved to have attended an Amish church, but there aren't any. The Amish worship in their homes, and in High German, which is even more foreign to me than Greek. So instead I'll head up Route 91, toward Joseph Smith's birthplace, stopping in Putney, at a Church of the Brethren.

Like the Amish, Brethren are pacifists, and also Anabaptists, believing an individual must be baptized as an adult—like Barack O—when he or she is able to make a choice consciously. They operate without a set creed. "And always," the church's Web site explains, "we look to Jesus as our source and example. Without dispensing doctrine, Jesus fed multitudes. And in our experience, he still does."

Call them Tunkers ("to dip" in German), Dunkers, Dunkards, or other German-based words for German Baptists, they are members of the Church of the Brethren, which began in Germany in 1708. Persecution by both Catholics and Protestants forced members to emigrate to America between 1719 and 1729. In the 1880s, three sects evolved, including the German Baptist Brethren, which became Church of the Brethren.

Although there are 1,095 Church of the Brethren churches in the U.S., serving 191,000 worshippers, this is the only one in Vermont, and one of only four in New England. So I'm all the more nervous when I arrive and my pick for the day appears to be closed. No one around. Not a vehicle in the parking lot, and the eye hooks where a sign might hang from the post outside are empty. No sign is not a good sign.

After making a quick tour of this town of 2,634 and noting a UCC and a Quaker meetinghouse, I return to spot signs of life: Brethren and Sistren (if they call them that) making their way toward the door of the simple white clapboard structure with MAY PEACE PREVAIL written vertically on a post to the left of the entrance. I feel a heck of a lot more peaceful simply knowing I'll be following them inside.

And inside, I am greeted by a guy named Karl, bespectacled, dark hair bushy, wearing jeans and sweater and black casual lace-ups. I browse the bookshelf titles on peace and pacifism. I scan the sheet where members are invited to sign up as worship leader (Karl's name is in today's space). There's a poster for a bluegrass gospel choir, information on the AIDS Project of Southern Vermont, and on affordable housing. Another poster handily outlines the church's mission: loving God and all people; growing in relationship to God and all people; sharing the good news of Jesus the Christ; serving each other and the needs of the world; living a full and joyful life in the knowledge that God loves us.

The sanctuary is wide, spare and bright beneath a white ceiling crossed with wooden beams. A lavender rug covers the floor wall to wall. Metal chairs in a similar shade are arranged in two semicircular rows of fifteen. They barely fill a third of the space, facing the back wall and its six high windows showing bare tree branches, nature's artwork the only type on display. In the center of that far wall, an altar table holds two small pillar candles, a cross, and a basket with handles.

I take a seat in the second row and pick up the navy-clad *Hymnal* and the light blue *A Worship Book*. My reading is interrupted by Karl's announcement of "This is Suzanne from Massachusetts," and five or six congregants approaching me. It's always awkward to be a newcomer, but here the feeling is magnified—it's such a small group, seven men, fourteen women, and three teen girls who comprise the youth. All wear cozy fleece and jeans and boots, dressed more for yard work than for the work of the Lord. An old-hippie air is given by the mostly forties and fifties adults with their makeup-free faces and au naturel gray hair, the shoeless guy over to the left fooling with his acoustic guitar. Karl offers a quiet "Good morning!" from the wooden pulpit. "We'll start with announcements."

A woman named Ann stands to announce the death of her Uncle Ralph, whom some of the members knew. Her visiting family members, Charlene and Don, are introduced. A man stands and says, "We're glad to have our family here, complete with Emily from Switzerland." He points to a very blond and very pale teen in jeans and Nikes.

For what I figure must be my benefit Karl says, "Generally, it's been our tradition the last year or so, for one person to lead worship." Adding, "I'm the volunteer for the day. I'd like us to . . . we're gonna sing, have some scripture reading, sharing, finish with a song."

He turns pages and begins to read from Isaiah 55:1–2, which tells of an offer of free mercy: "Ho! Every one who thirsts, come to the waters; and you who have no money, come, buy and eat. Come, buy wine and milk without money and without cost. Why do you spend money for what is not bread, and your wages for what does not satisfy? Listen carefully to me, and eat what is good, and delight yourself in abundance."

"Let's sing together," Karl invites optimistically as he slips beneath the strap of his guitar and begins with *Praise to the Lord, the Almighty, the King of Creation* . . . For a small gathering, the voices are impressively loud. Loud enough that I can join in on this familiar hymn without feeling self-conscious. We end and hear the second reading, from Ephesians 6:14–17: "Stand therefore, having your loins girt about with truth, and having on the breastplate of righteousness, and your feet shod with the preparation of the gospel of peace; above all, taking the shield of faith, wherewith ye shall be able to quench all the fiery darts of the wicked. And take the helmet of salvation, and the sword of the Spirit, which is the word of God."

For a pacifist community, the warrior image seems odd, but this won't be the last time it's evoked.

Next comes the tithing, and Karl offers another Isaiah, this chapter 40:3–5 passage having to be one of the biblical top ten: "A voice of one calling: In the desert prepare the way for the Lord, make straight in the wilderness a highway for our God. Every valley shall be raised up, every mountain and hill made low; the rough ground shall become level, the rugged places a plain. And the glory of the Lord will be revealed, and all mankind together will see it."

"It's come to the time for the sharing prayer," Karl says. "Whatever you feel leads you to share prayers for concerns, joy."

Nobody takes him up on the offer, so Karl prompts, "If you have a Bible, you can read, or if you have a song you'd like to sing, I invite you at this time to share."

"I'd like to sing number 658," says a woman way over on the left, and we shuffle to find it, everyone but a few of the teens singing with heart to Karl's guitar: *Keep me, King of Kings, beneath thine own almighty wings.* A woman stands to announce, "I have a joy. My daughter finally produced a baby girl!" Laughter and applause follows. "Jada Marie Wood, six pounds, eighteen inches, a beautiful baby. I mean really!"

"Praise God!" calls out a woman in a purple sweatshirt, who tells us she's anticipating her eightieth birthday party Saturday night at the Putney Inn. From his seat next to a teen girl checking out her fingernails, Karl has his own two cents to toss, telling us how he recently went back to a book of devotions he once read regularly. The latest wisdom he found in there was, "We do not grow into spiritual relations step by step. Let God's truth sink into you by immersing yourself into it rather than by worrying into it."

Since I'm a worrier, I like that idea. I can imagine sitting in the enormous bathtub Tommy and I treated ourselves to several years ago, imagine it filled with nothing but truth, and me in there, soaking.

There's nothing but silence now, then a woman punctures it with, "I'd like to sing 585—'In Your Sickness.' For my mother, who has health problems. She wants to be fixed right away," the woman adds wistfully, "but when you're ninety-four it doesn't happen that way."

The fine print on the hymn's page says this song was adapted from the Twi language, complete with a Ghanaian melody. A reminder that illness and suffering are everywhere, not just in Putney, or Vermont, or America. I think again of the classic film *It's a Wonder-*

ful Life. All those voices at the beginning speaking their joys and concerns simultaneously, God's ears faced with the challenge of hearing each one. And listening to their songs. "Congregational singing is an essential part of worship in the Church of the Brethren," the hymnal's introduction tells. "Our singing reveals much about where we have been and who we are as Anabaptists and Pietists."

I'm wondering what a Pietist is when a guy invites prayers about the violence in the Middle East. I'll later look up the term to find that Pietists got their start in Germany in the seventeenth century, specifically in the Lutheran Church, and place importance on practice rather than doctrine, are skeptical about theological teaching, and believe that faith is best lived serving others.

The bare feet of the longhaired guy now at the pulpit evidence the fact that trappings aren't a trap here. He threads himself through the tie-dyed strap of his guitar and tells us, "It's really easy for me to get kind of depressed, thinking about so much that's wrong with the world. This is one short example of good. Kris Kristofferson wrote it, inspired by a scene in *The Grapes of Wrath*."

His voice is wavery and a bit flat, yet it's pleasing and it suits the slow tune in which kids ask a sympathetic shopkeeper the price of candy: *We've only a penny between us / Them's two for a penny, she lied.* Karl picks up his guitar for harmony. I'm fine with the less-than-perfect music, a live reminder of the fact that all of us are. It's fitting for this homegrown congregant-led service. The image of the shopkeeper's tiny bit of grace makes you want to applaud when they're done, but we are quiet again.

The silence is broken when a woman in a blue jumper offers, "Pray for the heart of the earth." Karl begins to strum and to turn our thoughts to Amish country.

"Not long after the incident in Lancaster County, I realized that the senseless killing affected me in a way," he says. "The same thing is going on in Iraq ten times over. But it just hit me, how could this happen? Some of this is what I want to share with you. Some thoughts. What you heard about the Amish going to the murderer's widow's home, saying, 'We grieve with you, we mourn with you.' Half the money donated to the Amish they gave to the family. It all struck me. We think of the Amish as peaceful, loving, pacifists. To me, what they did was like being a warrior. What a true warrior would have the courage to do."

Karl's take on their actions is a twist that I hadn't considered, a new take that reminds me of Pastor Brian's twist on the parable of the vineyard workers back at the Cowboy Church. Here, as there, the thought-provoking message grows in a setting far from the traditional cathedral, a refreshing reward for having made the journey.

With Karl's guitar backing, the singing begins again: *Troubles and trials often betray thee, causing the weary body to stray. But we shall walk beside the still waters with the great Shepherd leading the way.*

On this day, it's a volunteer pastor leading us through the come-as-you-are comfortable one-hour service and to its assuring conclusion: "Go in peace and be comforted by knowing that God is present with us always. Amen."

DANBURY-BETHEL SEVENTH-DAY ADVENTIST CHURCH

BETHEL, CONNECTICUT

The Great Disappointment sounds like something your mother might have called you after you took your sizable inheritance from Grandma to Atlantic City and flushed it down a Hoot Loot machine. But when it comes to religion, the term is used for a letdown of far more biblical proportions.

Members of Adventist religions expected Christ's Second Coming in 1844. October 22, to be specific.

Half a million followers of the so-called Millerite movement had awaited the return their leader interpreted from scripture. It didn't happen.

In the 1840s, New York Baptist preacher William Miller was leading a revivalist movement known as the Second Great Awakening. When the date failed to be anything more than another autumn day, the majority of his followers returned to their previous churches. Seventh-Day Adventists had been among the groups who'd been anticipating October 22. Their church had been founded that same year in Washington, New Hampshire, making it one of the nation's indigenous faiths. After the Great Disappointment, however, this group continued in the belief that the return—or advent—of Jesus could happen at any minute; members just no longer set a date.

What the world's 14 million Seventh-Day Adventists (including 1 million in the U.S., where the church is multicultural and growing) indeed do is observe the Sabbath, from sunset Friday to sunset Saturday. They also practice temperance, work to proclaim the Gospel, and ready souls for that imminent advent.

I visit this particular church on the day before the 162nd anniversary of the Great Disappointment, in the same town my great-aunt, Sister Benicia, served a decade of her seventy years as a Franciscan nun.

"Happy Sabbath Day" is the greeting that kicks off the 11:00 a.m. service in this church, down a side road in this town of eighteen thousand, fifty-five miles northeast of New York City. Resembling a white-sided contemporary home, the church holds a six-sided sanctuary beneath a wooden ceiling from which fans and brass chandeliers hang. Fourteen long wooden benches are lined up in three angled sections facing an altar area with a podium and a table with white cloth, and without a cross. The tall clear windows are equipped with miniblinds opened to display a fall wood beneath cloud-threaded blue sky. Eighty or so worshippers sit inside on this bright Saturday morning that would find most Christians raking leaves or attending Junior's soccer game. The dress is proper, suits for men, dresses or skirts for the women. True to the church's p.r., the mix is a third Caucasian, a third black, another third Asian, split between the genders. Three men take seats up front as the organist begins number 407, "Let Us Break Bread Together," and we follow along via the black SDA hymnal.

The three men up front kneel during the music, then stand as the call to worship is given by a white man the bulletin identifies as Ray Smith. A brief reading from Isaiah ("Is anyone thirsty? Come and drink."), a few more hymns, and it's Praise and Thanksgiving time.

"Praise the Lord," calls a middle-aged Asian man at the altar who's listed in the program as Rey Magboo. As others share their stories, he alternately shouts with joy and jots on a notepad.

A woman tells of the birth of her fourteenth great-grandchild. Another announces her parents' forty-fifth wedding anniversary, adding, "I thank God that I have two parents who took on the challenge of marriage and stayed together so many years."

"Praise the Lord for a very nice family," Rey says.

We hear about a grandson sent to Iraq, marital problems, and a child attending public school for the first time.

Rey steps to the front. "Praise the Lord," he begins again. "You have shown your love to us in so many ways." Now he consults his jottings. "We're asking for healing guidance, that a soldier in Iraq be shielded from bullets, that the war may end soon and peace and happiness once again will reign in that country."

The organ begins again, background music for tithing. Everyone sits as the church's treasurer tells us this place has never been in the red. But, "we have a $1,276-a-month mortgage," he states. "It's soon to be more than doubled."

We're invited to sing yet another familiar hymn, "Praise God from Whom All Blessings Flow," and I look out the window. It usually kills me to be inside on a nice day, and this is a nice day. I look around. These people have to have spent all the Saturday mornings of their lives indoors. But might they feel sorry for people shut inside a church on a lovely Sunday morning?

An older woman in prim turquoise suit and gray helmet of hair walks to the front and asks the children to "come up nicely for Aunty Olga." She reads a story about a farm and, unless the metaphors have flown right over my head, I don't see the spiritual connection. At the story's conclusion, the kids pick up small baskets and gleefully hit up the congregants for another donation.

Continuing the youth theme, three Asian teens in sparkly lavender dresses stand at the pulpit. They're the Rosalita sisters, a first name I haven't heard since Bruce Springsteen used it in a song.

Against loud recorded piano music, they sing, *Crucified, laid behind a stone, left to die, dejected and alone. Like a rose trampled on the ground, you took the fall, above all, and thought of me.* Their proud mother stands nearby, videotaping.

Olga now reads from 1 Corinthians 11:28–31: "Let a man examine himself and let him eat of the bread and drink of the cup . . ." That makes sense, as this is the day for receiving Communion.

This typically takes place only four times a year in Seventh-Day Adventist churches. And it—no pun—kicks off with foot washing, which in this House of God is called Ordinance of Humility, a ritual that reenacts Jesus washing the feet of his disciples prior to the Last Supper.

So it'll be a round of humility, then Communion, which is represented by unleavened bread and unfermented grape juice. Alcohol, tobacco, and caffeine are *verboten* in this religion, which stresses health. A vegetarian diet is encouraged, and biblically "unclean" items including pork and shellfish are eschewed.

"Communion is an awesome time and I'm so glad to see you here for Communion," Pastor David Berthiaume tells the congregation. I love the word "awesome" coming from a silver-haired guy in his sixties, a white carnation on the lapel of his dark suit. He reminds us that modern custom is to greet a person with a handshake or hug, while "in those days," meaning Jesus's time, "the first thing was to get your feet washed. They wore sandals. It was unheard of not to wash your feet when you came to someone's house."

He jumps to the topic of tragedy. "I've been through some very sad things in the last two months—a young woman killed in a car accident. I just prayed with her mother, she prayed to go be with her daughter. I stand before you saying many times I stand before God saying, 'I don't understand you at all.' And who am I to talk about God like that?"

I'm not sure of the answer, but I like his questioning. He's being human. "God doesn't need pastors who have all the answers," he says. "God sees the big picture. I am able to say, 'Lord, just hold onto me when I don't believe in everything. Lord, I gotta trust you. I gotta know you know the end of the picture, that if we didn't know any of this pain we'd never get it.' This thing about having perfect people at Communion, would anybody be left? Would I be here to wash your feet?"

Then he adds quickly, "The gentlemen will go downstairs and ladies will stay up here."

The men head for a door behind the altar area. The women walk to the exit behind my row. I stay in my seat. This custom is not something I care to try. I attempt to look meditative so the few women still filing out won't hook me. I'm not successful. A skinny blond woman who'd been seated far to my right scoots over and asks, "May I wash your feet?"

So there I am in the circle of folding chairs, my seatmate kneeling before me, removing my vegan Mary Janes and black knee-highs. It's very uncomfortable, even though the water, ladled into the yellow plastic bowl between us, is warm. She sets one foot into the bowl and uses both hands to cascade it several times. The thick towel she uses to dry my foot actually feels quite nice, but not so nice that I don't have at the front of my consciousness that I'm sitting awkwardly in a strange church, in a circle of women I don't know, everyone getting their feet washed. And I mean everyone. As in the washers become the washees. While I push my damp feet back into the knee-highs and shoes, my seatmate goes to dump the used water into a basin, and to request a fresh supply. So I can return the favor.

Her stockings are not knee-highs, they're pantyhose, as in the kind that start up at her waist. What does she want me to do? "Just wash over the nylons, it's OK," she says, mind reading.

I pick up one of her small feet and scoop the water over the top. The nylons make the water run in several rivers. I push the foot underwater, the only way anything is going to sink in. I wrap the second foot in a towel and, thankfully, she puts her own shoes back on. To the accustomed, I'm sure foot washing is quite profound—really a lesson in being humble and serving others, without prissy regard for your own comfort. Perhaps there should be a holy feeling to this, but my only one is that I wish I were somewhere else other than handling a stranger's foot, even a nice stranger's foot. I look up and smile nervously, and she returns a smile. It's a regular one, nothing special or beatific. By the time I think to check how the others appeared during this ritual, they're done, bringing their basins back to the table.

"I've been coming here eleven years," my washer tells me as we wait for everyone to join a circle for a prayer. "I grew up Seventh-Day Adventist. This is my Saturday."

And this is my Saturday. Holding hands with my seatmate and a small Asian girl to my left, each of us is given a moment in the prayer circle to state a blessing or a concern. I listen to the hopes for a grandmother's recovery, a new job working out, a marriage getting a second chance, a husband recovering from addiction, some compassion (though the teen speaker doesn't put it that way) from the mean girls at her new school.

Then we return to the sanctuary, where newcomers are welcomed while two women up front uncover plates of what look like wheat crackers.

"I'm always amazed at how valuable God thinks we are," Pastor David says. "The real First Communion, they were just having supper together. At the end, Jesus took the bread. 'I have received of the Lord what I have delivered unto you.' "

Two men distribute the crackers, two and a half hours into our time together.

"He looked at the table," Pastor David continues. "At the pure grape juice—it could not have been wine because anything of a fermented nature represents sin. Drink in remembrance of what he did for us."

The organ plays softly as the pastor says, echoing a sentiment I first heard this year from Billy Graham's daughter, "The most important part of Communion service is that we don't leave the way we came."

He's referring to a whole lot more than your damp feet, of course. I think about the way this service might have changed me and know already that it knocked off another of my prejudgments. I'd anticipated blazing fire and brimming brimstone from a faith in which the Second Coming is seen as long overdue and ready to take place any minute. As an outsider, perhaps seen as doomed for not being an Adventist, I nevertheless felt included in the service, and indeed was included maybe a bit more than I would have liked. But would I return? The Saturday morning commitment aside, the service seemed a bit too staid. Not technically a great disappointment, but enough of one to make me continue wandering.

CALVARY'S LIGHT CHURCH

THREE RIVERS, MASSACHUSETTS

I'm early, only the fourth person here this morning. Because I'm not taking any chances. My last visit to Calvary's Light, nearly three months ago, lasted about ten minutes due to my very late arrival. This time I want to experience the entire service, rather than just the benediction.

Because the Adventists meet on Saturday, I'm able to double my church visits this weekend. I sit where I did last time, three rows from the back, and think about all that's happened since I last entered this building. Tommy's health has continued to be so normal that his episode three months ago seems like some kind of weird dream. He's right now concluding tests to rule out anything else. More fingers are waved to observe the movement of his eyes, more hands are extended to judge the strength of his grip. He again walks heel of right foot to toe of left, as if pulled over for a suspected DWI. His skull is quadranted by red marker and additional multicolored electrodes are thickly glued to the grid. So far, nothing new, and we continue with normal life. Home to work and back again. For me, add church.

This morning, Calvary's Light, where I read the list defining this church's vision:

1. To lead people to the saving power of Jesus Christ (Matthew 28:19–20).

2. To teach the Word of God so people are no longer destroyed for lack of knowledge (Hosea 4:6).

3. To prepare the church to meet the Lord in the air (called The Rapture) (1 Thessalonians 4:15–17).

Short and to the point. Not unlike the service, which will be free of nonsense, and full of hard-line evangelical reminders that we had better get our acts together, and soon, or the consequences will be—no pun again—hell.

But the music introducing the service is sweet: *In moments like these, I sing out a song, I sing out a love song to Jesus,* the CD player leads. *Singing I love you, Lord, I love you, Jesus.*

Up front, Pastor Laura Rollet, in navy skirt suit, lace blouse, golden pin reading BEST GRANDMOTHER, adds her voice. That's important, because she's not only the leader but one of only eight assembled this morning. All are white. Three are men. And all except for yours truly appear to be around sixty years of age.

"Thank you, God, for the privilege of today," Pastor Laura announces upon the song's conclusion, her eyes closed, her two arms waving. "For Jesus Christ, willin' to become that babe, go to the whippin' post. Even went to hell so we didn't have to go there. The Father didn't leave him there, our soon-comin' king."

Pastor Laura calls out, "You are welcome in our lives in this place!" and I'm half thinking she means me, even more obvious a visitor today than I was among the Brethren. But her eyes are closed. She means God.

Housekeeping includes the news that the basement Fellowship Hall finally has clean windows and curtains. Then Pastor Laura asks, "Richard, would you come up and pray?" Richard is Mr. Pastor Laura, gray hair, teal shirt, khakis, the same guy who signed the permit allowing our bathroom reconstruction a few years back.

"It's a beautiful day here," Pastor Laura continues as Richard stands at her side. She pauses and searches for words to invoke blessings on him before beginning with a polite, "Excuse me Lord," then continuing. "Give him direction and guidance that he seeks you each and every day. This is what this church is founded on: In God we do, in God we trust. We trust you, we bless you. Bless our president, our vice president, cabinet, Senate, judiciary, bless our country. Give us a safe and protected country."

I can't transcribe the rest because I don't know how to spell the words spoken in tongues. I know it only as a biblical term, but here it is, happening. God's language, some say, a gift.

Richard faces the altar and his voice rises and falls with a roll of sometimes drawn-out words that sound consonant-heavy and Middle Eastern, not surprising considering Christianity's place of origin. I have to remind myself where I am, in the center of the village where I was raised, in the building I passed with a stare thousands of times, wondering what the heck went on in there. I am finding out. Tongues in the middle of my tiny burg. Amazing.

Pastor Laura speaks—regular English—over her husband. Maybe a translation: "Lift up our military as they are spread throughout the world, especially those in Afghanistan and Iraq. No strife or confusion when they're there just to do a job on patrols. We lift them up to you each and every day." The tongues continue. It's somewhat thrilling to hear, but sparks nothing special in my soul. I haven't any sudden feeling that God is finally speaking to me loud and clear. I'm more fascinated than anything, and glad to finally hear this. My fellow worshippers, their heads bowed, display no grand response. This has to be old hat to them, maybe the portion of the service in which they tune out and make a mental list of the bread and milk they need to pick up when they grab the Sunday paper on the way home. Moments later, though, a rising static-like sound backdrops the Rollets as church members begin to whisper loudly yet indiscernibly, "Praise Jesus, Praise Jesus."

"Pray for Israel," Pastor Laura continues. "Give wisdom and knowledge, that they no longer give up any land because this is the land they have been given by you. We lift up their cabinet and military leaders."

Pastor Laura tells us that she received an e-mail last night requesting prayers for Oklahoma evangelist and faith healer Vicki Jamison-Peterson, whose Christian psychiatrist husband of twenty-three years allegedly fed her mind-control drugs, then stole her savings. "Isn't this unbelievable that a medical doctor would do this to his own wife?" Pastor Laura asks. "We just bind the devil in this situation. In Jesus's name. We pray your angels of protection around Vicki . . . We claim total victory for her from this attack of the devil."

I flash to my previous visit to Calvary's Light, and Pastor Laura's personal prayer for Tommy that included the devil word. It's clear that when it comes down to an incident or challenge or general problem, Pastor Laura sees Satan at its root.

Old things have passed away, man is born again are the lyrics being fed into an overhead projector to the left of the altar. A woman moves the sheets and also tends to the buttons of the small CD player that is our band throughout the seven songs to follow, a sort of Sunday-morning karaoke in which the small and quiet gathering does its best to participate.

"Come on church, raise up your hands, worship the Lord!" encourages Pastor Laura, who then launches into a hymn that begins *God is great!*

"Praise Jesus," calls out a man behind me. "We ask you, Jesus, we ask you, Jesus, we ask you, Jesus, we ask you, Jesus."

The music concludes and Pastor Laura informs us, "We're not waitin' for it. We're in it. We're prayin' your will be done today on your earth as it is bein' done in heaven today. Praise God, we will take offerin' now."

The we-ask-you guy carries around a bronze plate.

"For God, you said if we brought tithes and offerin's we would receive such blessings we would not have room to pour it out," says Pastor Laura, standing before the altar, sounding like she's making a bargain. "We bind this money in Jesus's name, amen."

The plate of tithes is set on the altar and the pastor takes a sip from a Styrofoam cup before starting her sermon.

"Do you know what I'm gonna preach on today?" She gets no answers. "The Kingdom of God. I'm gonna preach on the Kingdom of God. Until it becomes real to you."

She reminds us that it's part of a series she's doing on the Kingdom, which she says has been separated from the Gospel. "But they go hand in hand . . . Because what did Jesus preach?"

A woman offers the answer, which the pastor repeats: "The Kingdom of God. The Kingdom of God. The Kingdom of God. Repent and become part of the Kingdom of God."

Pastor Laura quotes Luke 12:29: "And seek not what you shall eat or what you shall drink: and be not lifted up on high." Then she interprets: "Don't have an anxious mind about what to eat or drink. Your father knows you need these things. We're to seek first the Kingdom of God and his righteousness, and all these things will be added to us. Everythin' you seek will come."

If anyone is wondering "Like what?" Pastor Laura says, "People have given us stuff. And we don't know why. Richard worked in a union. You don't get no bonuses. One Christmas we prayed, and he got a bonus of five hundred dollars. Don't tell me prayer don't work. I got too much experience with it workin'. Don't worry about anythin'. You know, when you worry, it's a sin."

I take that last line. Whether or not it's true, I'm going to carry it.

"But what is the Kingdom of God?" she asks. "It's God's Kingdom, but it's made up of people. Remember, this Kingdom is an everlastin' Kingdom, an eternal Kingdom. When you die, your spirit and soul go to heaven. The Kingdom is also on earth, for those who have received Jesus as their personal savior. You need to ask yourself what are you goin' to do in a situation. Is this good for the Kingdom of God? Will this add to the Kingdom? If it will, then do it. But if not, you need to not do it. Praise God."

That Kingdom of heaven, Pastor Laura says, is a real place without sin, sickness, or disease. Then: "If you preach the Gospel, always be careful to love the people who come in. Be patient. They will love God and all their sin will fall away—praise God."

And what if the newcomers don't come back?

"Don't you think Jesus ever gets angry because people reject him?" Pastor Laura asks. "He gave us his son, went through that for you and me, and some people walk out the door and never come back? God gets angry!"

She's in full gear now—not loud, but intense as she says, "Those who reject Christ, they're not worthy and, I'm sorry, but they're gonna burn in hell. But they have free will. So what we gotta do is go down the streets of Three Rivers, of Palmer, and tell people the feast is ready and you're invited. Many are called but few are chosen. No wedding garment? When you receive Jesus Christ as your savior, you receive a robe of righteousness. If not, you'll be thrown into utter darkness."

"Amen," somebody says.

"Remember," she continues. "We're comin' back to rule and reign, to set up God's government on the earth. It's not fake. It's real, praise God . . . That's what we're goin' to understand now, because this church is the Kingdom of God. It doesn't mean he strikes you dead, hits you over the head with a big stick. He will convict you of what you didn't do. He won't condemn you. The devil will condemn you."

Pastor raises her hands in an invitation: "Let's pray for discernment to do for the Kingdom of God. Sometimes we get tired: 'Ugh, I do everythin'!' Hello! You do it for the Lord. He'll reward you."

Her eyes close now, seventy-five minutes into the service. Her head bows, leading the other nine in here to do the same. "Anytime you called and I didn't come, I apologize sincerely," she prays. "Father God, I love you and your Kingdom, your people, your word, your spirit. I thank you for havin' every one of us in the palm of your hand and you will not let us go."

She begins the final hymn: *He is Lord! He is Lord! He is risen from the dead and He is Lord.*

I know this one. I learned it long ago, in another church. One just three-quarters of a mile up the street, here in the Kingdom of God. As for what I learned in this church this morning? The theology of fear is the foundation of this church, too. It doesn't scare me, simply scares me away. Which is a shame because the Rollets are nice people. But to me, this type of message, in any tongue, doesn't feel like faith, but like anger and intolerance. And religion furthering negatives, rather than love, is more frightening than the most swiftly falling ceiling.

FIRST SPIRITUAL TEMPLE

BROOKLINE, MASSACHUSETTS

I see a ghost.

I'm not kidding.

Nor am I surprised. After all, I am visiting a church where communication with spirits is believed in, taught, and practiced.

However, the ghost I'm looking at is stitched in bright white yarn onto the back of a black and orange cardigan, and speaks only via the cartoon balloon corralling a long *Boooo!*

I'm calmed rather than frightened. The presence of this ghost on this cardigan on this woman walking in with this man means that I no longer am the only person worshipping this morning at potentially spooky First Spiritual Temple.

For the first half of the 11:00 a.m. service, I had been the one and only person seated on any one of this sanctuary's thirty brown vinyl-upholstered metal-framed chairs. With Halloween / All Soul's Day this week, I wanted to attend a church with one foot firmly in the spirit world, and at 123 years of age, First Spiritual Temple is the world's oldest Christian Spiritualist Church. Founded by businessman Marcellus Seth Ayer to assist those seeking to understand God, the spirit, death and dying, spiritualism, and the Bible, it is an independent and nondenominational entity with the motto "God's Spirit & Truth Revealed through the Ministry and Teachings of Christ."

"God is Spirit, we are Spirit, our departed loved ones are Spirit, our 'enemies' are Spirit," its doctrine states, "and that is how we are all connected."

Its original location was just off Boston's Newbury Street, in a five-story stone building that also housed the city's legendary Exeter Street Theater, which the temple owned and operated. The cornerstone was laid in 1884 but the entire building sold in 1975 because of dwindling membership. A visitor to the church's new home on Monmouth Street, a verdant hidden garden of a neighborhood not far from Fenway Park, finds at number 16 a 1905 two-story black-shuttered brick colonial with white pillars and slate blue door. Rather than a temple, it looks like a private home.

A young man in blue sweater and khakis had opened the door from inside and directed me into a room at the left. There, hymns from an invisible organ played softly and I got a funeral home vibe as I took a seat at the edge of the fourth row and looked to the front of the light blue room, where I almost expected to see a casket. Instead, on a blue-carpeted stage area a single step up from the hardwood floor, I found a table holding a cross, a peace sign, two pumpkins, and a vase of yellow daisies.

The Reverend Stephen R. Fulton entered unceremoniously through a door to the right of the altar. He regarded the sanctuary through his glasses, and if he was shocked or miffed that there were twenty-nine empty chairs, he didn't show it. He simply began the call to worship found in the beige eight-page booklet I received at the door.

"Surely the Presence of God is in this place, as we gather for worship," Pastor Stephen said with confidence.

The doorman and I repeated this as directed on page 3.

Several other lines followed and we segued into the opening hymn, "Come Worship the Lord," the music for which was provided by the new digital sound system mentioned on the first of the four-page bulletin, *The Sower*, which also mentioned Evenings of Spirit Communications held every third Wednesday, bridging "two worlds for an evening of love and communication."

All hail the pow'r of truth to save from error's binding thrall, the three of us sang. Pastor Stephen read the eleven Articles of Faith that make up the booklet's centerfold. The doorman and I responded "Amen" to every two or three of the points, which include belief in one God who's a spirit without gender, form, creed, or color; communication with God's Kingdom of Spirit, "wherein dwell our guardians, loved ones, and sources of inspiration"; and the Bible as scripture, "but not as the absolute Word of God."

Pastor Stephen next read from Psalm 8: "When I consider your heavens, the work of your fingers, the moon and the stars, which you have set in place, what is man that you are mindful of him, the son of man that you care for him?" He might have been pondering just that as he sat for the musical interlude, which was more organ music from the pair of speakers beneath the front windows. Upon its completion, he rose to give announcements. Students of the graduate school of mediumship will meet on Thursday, and *The Sower*'s November issue will be mailed this week. Then it was tithing time and I realized that this was one of those mornings when it would be clear whether or not I placed anything on the plate.

The doorman approaches with his brass tray. I drop my paper money and that's when I see the ghost, moving past me and taking a seat two rows up. The sweater's wearer and her male companion, both white and in their fifties, fish for money. The doorman waits, then delivers our meager tithes.

"I never feel closer to God and creation as when I stand on the shore or look into the night sky," Pastor Stephen begins. I consult the lineup and see we have come to "Sermon or Trance Address." I'm rooting for trance.

"Science and religion are becoming bedfellows," Pastor says. "It's an odd combination. 'Science without religion is lame. Religion without science is blind,' says Albert Einstein. All the more appealing are becoming the laws of the metaphysical world. Einstein, at the end of his life, said were he to do it all over again, he would have looked at spiritualism. Metaphysicians have known for centuries what physicians are just starting to understand: there's a tone, a vibration at the center of everything. We are sounds, vibrations, energy, tonal. The whole of creation are musicians given special instruments to play.

"Jesus said, 'Why are you anxious about your life?' God does hear our prayer. God does know each and every one of us . . . Our question should be not does God hear our prayer, but do we listen? Do we listen when he calls us by name? Do we play our instrument with the great conductor or pluck away just to hear ourselves play?"

He's in a groove now, and I realize that not only is Pastor Stephen's message of our relationship with God compelling, his style is genuine. With the spirit, conviction, and thoughtful delivery he employs, he might as well be up front at Lakewood or Saddleback. Instead he's here in front of three. Four if you count the guy still stationed at the door. I imagine poor Pastor Stephen laboring over his sermon all week. If a little spirit had whispered in his ear, "Why bother, only three—OK, four—are going to show up?" would he still have worked as hard?

Immediately, he's answering the question I've just asked in my head.

"I've come to the realization that there's a reason I'm standing here before four people. I have to keep up the work. It's worth it on some level. We matter to God. Our personal care and concern matters to God. The next time we stare at the sky, listen to a great piece of music, remember that God through every one of his prophets says, God cares for you, God cares for me, God cares for each and every one of us."

Pastor Stephen sits again before introducing the "Healing Service or Communion."

"Let us be mindful of those spirit loved ones that join us here in worship," he's saying, "and let us feel peace. Remove all tumult or craziness of the life around us. As we feel a sense of calm and tranquillity, let us be mindful of the prayer Jesus gave to creation. It offers hope, healing, and forgiveness in many tongues. As we reach to God, let us pray together."

And we do, reciting the Our Father, with its other ending.

Pastor Stephen then encourages us to "listen carefully" to the symphony of creation "reminding that the foundation of each and every one of us is in the simple tone of God's spirit."

I try to do that. Leaves tap the window as they fall. I don't hear anything else, but maybe that right there was the sound. We are silent for a few more minutes before Pastor Stephen says, "For those in need of healing, surround them in this place. If you wish, speak their names aloud."

There is whispering from the couple, from Pastor Stephen, from the doorman. I hear *Joan, Nicholas, Theresa.* I add *Dominick. Tommy.*

"Anyone who wishes healing by laying on of hands," the pastor adds, "it's time to come forward."

The woman with the ghost steps right up. Sits in a Windsor chair. From behind, Pastor Stephen sets his hands on her shoulders. I am filling the seats with those I've loved. The floor too. All my old dogs lie at my feet. My father is to my right. My grandparents behind him. My friend Rosemary sits in back of me and kicks my seat good-naturedly, her code for "Isn't this weird?"

No, I tell her, though not aloud. She's spirit now, she can hear what's in my head. *It's not weird. Aren't you with me all the time?*

My father died before my first book was published. Driving to the readings I found so nerve-racking, I'd place him in my passenger seat. I was not alone. He was there. Today I see Paul Dee, who hired both Tommy and me for our first real newspaper jobs. My *Cioci* Nellie, who never made a fuss whenever I spilled soda on her wall-to-wall. Uncle Louie, who called me Kid and Speed. Cyd, a girl I was just coming to know when she died of meningitis not three weeks into our freshman year of high school. I pass her gravestone nearly every day, and wonder why I am still here and nearly forty-eight and she was stopped in her tracks. Or was she? Haven't she and the others been right next to us all along?

"And all those in need of healing," Pastor adds, "know they're safe in the universe. Amen."

The door of the church is open. Four of us can be seen leaving, our unseen legions all around us.

LIVING WATERS FOURSQUARE GOSPEL CHURCH

SMITHFIELD, RHODE ISLAND

You probably have never met Pastor Elizabeth Janiak, but then again, you probably have. She's the full-of-life auntie whose arrival at your family gathering flicks on the fun switch. The one dressed in a flowing pantsuit, puffily coiffed and manicured from lashes to toes. She grabs the microphone and sends her soprano well past the neighbor's backyard, all the while keeping time to the music with swaying hips and tapping high-heeled sandals.

That's not far from the description of this morning's arrival of Pastor Elizabeth at the Plexiglas pulpit of Living Waters. To begin the 10:00 a.m. service, she ascends three maroon-carpeted stairs and boldly commands, "The Lord just gave me the word, so listen up!"

Pastor Elizabeth's résumé lists her as evangelist, pastor, and nondenominational healer, but most importantly, she's the one who turned on the tap of Living Waters Foursquare Gospel Church back in 1986.

The name Foursquare is divined from biblical verses including the one displayed in all Foursquare churches, proclaiming "Jesus Christ the Same, Yesterday and Today and Forever." It also represents Jesus's mission as savior, baptizer, healer, and "soon-coming" king. The faith's founder, Aimee Semple McPherson, was raised Methodist but at age seventeen proclaimed herself an atheist—then she attended a revival meeting where she met her future husband and experienced a reawakening of faith. She founded the Foursquare Church in Los Angeles in 1923.

Living Waters is one of 1,844 Foursquare congregations in this country, which includes 218,900 of the 3.5 million members worldwide.

One week before my visit, a former male escort in Denver announced that he'd shared a three-year sexual relationship with the Reverend Ted Haggard, the fifty-year-old leader of the 30-million-member National Association of Evangelicals (NAE) and adviser to President George W. Bush. The escort said he went public because Haggard was a hypocrite, publicly supporting a state ballot initiative defining marriage as being between a man and a woman while having a secret affair with him. The day before my visit, an investigation by an independent church board concluded "without a doubt that he [Haggard] has committed sexually immoral conduct," and Haggard subsequently resigned.

But this morning, all's hale and happy here at NAE-member-church Living Waters, a sprawling light gray one-story church in the shadow of the trio of crosses made from telephone poles. At the door

I am greeted by Mo and Preston. Mo hands me a visitor's pack that includes a booklet on Church beliefs and the latest issue of *Prayer Focus*, a magazine including one asking "that the Lord keep unqualified, immoral, dishonest, and ungodly candidates from public office, and that Godly pro-life, pro-family, and pro-marriage candidates find favor with voters in your area and state."

Mo also has given me a Living Waters bulletin with four-color soft-focus photo cover showing an oil lamp glowing in front of a Bible open to the book of Ruth. Inside is information on childcare, scripture, and the service, plus a reminder that prayer is a powerful weapon and "Champions Use It Against Satanic Purposes."

I sit on the left-hand side and take in the light-toned wood, the mauve carpet, and the elevated stage-like area that makes up the front of the church. There's a lot of fake shrubbery up there, an American flag, big speakers, and the guitarist, bassist, and vocalist who make up the band. There is no cross.

There is no artwork either. There are no windows, in the sanctuary at least. Well-dressed worshippers carry stacks of books and swing tote bags as they fill the benches around me. It's a multicultural congregation approximately one-third black, including several women in boldly printed dresses complete with elaborate head wraps. Recorded music plays softly. A trio of wooden ceiling fans rests, retired for the winter.

"Praise the Lord, everybody!" This from the church trio's guitarist, a tall guy who resembles Billy Dee Williams. The congregation rises.

"How many like spiritual aerobics?!" Hands wave.

"Amen? Then just turn to your neighbor and smile." I'm seated to the left of a twentysomething black woman who's dressed to the nines in skirted suit and equipped with a Bible, many of its pages marked by colored tabs. We smile at one another.

The seat pocket in front of us contains a worn red hardcover of *The Hymnal for Worship and Celebration*, but everyone seems to know the words to the songs, even without consulting the screen onstage, where they glow over a picture of the ocean or the Statue of Liberty. *Lift your eyes to heaven, there is freedom*, begins one of the ballads. People leave their seats to stand in front of the stage and sing, the way a

Catholic might kneel before a statue, though there is no statue to be seen. One woman sings to a blank wall, another to one of the many fake bushes. Several adults and a couple of kids kneel at the bottom step and lay their heads on their folded arms.

A man takes to the pulpit. He's graying, balding, and with a mustache and rounded Boston/Rhode Island accent that reminds me of the character Cliff Clavin on the classic TV show *Cheers*. "God told me to tell you something," he informs us. "When I was driving here, the leaves were falling as the sun—S-U-N—began to shine. The Lord, the son, the S-O-N, told me to tell you those dead leaves that have been hanging are gonna fall!"

I count twenty-two people up front now. A woman in a white shawl prostrates herself on the stairs, next to a middle-school boy in shirt and tie. *You are awesome in this place, Abba Father,* sings the crowd. Some in the seats are kneeling, despite there being no kneelers. Pastor Elizabeth is kneeling at her seat in the front row. Even a woman in a leg cast is kneeling.

Pastor Elizabeth grabs the mike and begins singing *I exalt thee, O Lord!* A black woman in black dress and beige beret kneels before the stage, her forehead touching the ground.

"Sing it loud—get that devil outa your life!" Pastor Elizabeth shouts.

She walks to Billy Dee and flips the pages on his music stand. Points to something new. "Alleluia! Come on, shout to the Lord!" Most do as she asks. Pastor Elizabeth is like a warm-up act for herself, lifting the energy of the place. *We're gonna dance in the river, yeah!*

Someone to my left taps my shoulder.

"May I ask what you're doing?" The man, white, sixtyish, light gray suit, points to my trusty notebook.

"I'm writing down what's being said."

"Why?"

"So I'll remember it."

He looks like he's going to ask something else, but leaves. In most of the twenty-eight churches I've visited thus far, paper and pencils in seat pockets have encouraged me to take notes on the services. This is the first time anybody has cared I actually was.

Pastor Elizabeth calls the church's men to the stage. A dozen approach and begin to dance and jump. *Clothed in glory, arrayed in splendor, great and mighty is he!*

There is much carrying on, singing and clapping. "Stop!" Pastor Elizabeth cries suddenly. "We just got a word . . . Paulette just got a word. Paulette doesn't talk much, but she just got a word."

"Victory!" a man on stage shouts. "Victory in Jesus!"

Through the maybe fifty who crowd the front aisle, I see pant legs, horizontal. It's Cliff Clavin, facedown, on one of the stage steps. It's jolting but no one seems concerned. Pastor Elizabeth continues with the Paulette message: "God says there's a growth or a tumor in your body. You need to come forth. Don't let me pull you out. There's a tumor growth, that's the word of the Lord." Suddenly a woman in the front third of the seats begins to scream. I wonder if this is the person with the tumor, or just somebody caught up in this scene.

"You can say what you want to say," Pastor Elizabeth tells us. "We aren't no dead church. You got a problem? Just come up front."

They do, as *Great and mighty is he* continues from the band.

"You're gonna be touched," Pastor tells a man, and he falls backward into the arms of Preston and another man, both of whom lower him to the ground.

Another approaches, sixty-five, balding, wearing a Members Only jacket. "*Shamalagashe malagasha*" is what he seems to be saying while Pastor Elizabeth shouts, "Holy am I, I am holy, King of Kings and Lord of Lords, I am holy!"

The man falls silent, but does not fall down. "You can't hide from me," Pastor continues. She yells at top volume, " 'Do you not see my mighty hand? I am here to set you free and to help those people who are on the very brink of hell,' says the Lord. 'If you only can put your trust in the Lord. There is nothing I can't do!' "

The screamer begins again. Keels as men rush to prevent her head from hitting the floor. A woman covers her, head to toe, with a white cloth.

Pastor Elizabeth continues on, unfazed. "You need to get right with the Lord. Now. Today. Now!"

Beneath her hand, a boy, then a man, collapse backward, into another few pairs of arms, and two more white cloths are unfolded to cover them. Pastor Elizabeth steps around the bodies like it's just another day at the office.

"Say 'I want the Lord to touch me!' " she wails, and her weeping increases to bawling. " 'I want the Lord to use me.' The spirit of the Lord is in this place. I can feel it shaking this place."

In an I-told-you-so tone, she warns a woman, "God says it's gonna be painful." To another she says, "Do you know when I took you, you were in that false religion? We worship not the god of the Mormons, but our God."

To the rest of us she says, "Take your hand and put it on your brain. Like an anvil. Bang out falsity, wrongness, all the things that get pushed into your brain. Watch the people next to you. The spirit of God is moving them." I look to the aisle, where a woman lies writhing and moaning beneath her white sheet. At least forty faithful are up front, awaiting the pastor's healing like bowling pins before the ball of her hand. The church is beginning to look like a triage center, a dozen lying beneath sheets, some weeping loudly, a scream occasionally.

"Some of you were rejected by your mother in your womb," Pastor says. "Come up here." Nine come forward. Nine rejected in utero by their mothers.

"This is D-day," Pastor says. "The devil is getting out today. God will never reject you. God has a plan for your life."

Another nosy white guy in a suit taps my shoulder: "What are you writing?"

"Notes."

"Why?"

"So I'll remember my visit."

He leaves without further questions.

Pastor Elizabeth mops her face and says, "You didn't even want to be born" as a woman before her collapses.

She strides toward the side of the church. "How about abuse of any kind?" she asks, as if reading from a menu of troubles. "There are victims of abuse right here. Mental, spiritual, sexual, physical. 'Now, now, now,' says the Lord."

A dozen soon gather before the pastor, eight of them men. "This day," she tells them, "you will be set free." Her hand touches foreheads. Bodies go limp.

"I need to take my shoes off," Pastor Elizabeth says, and two men assist her. She considers the sixty at the front of the church. Only twenty of us remain seated after an hour and a half.

Standing in her nylons, Pastor tells a congregant, "You will not be an abused woman of God!" Then she regards the rest of us, wanting to leave no problem unaddressed. "Are you grieving? Do you have sexual addiction? Physical problems? Did your mother reject you? This is your day!"

Now Pastor Elizabeth appears tired. She's moving more slowly, taking more time between her words. Yet she rallies.

"You were abused when you were ten years old," she tells a man who had been standing in the aisle for maybe half an hour. He raises his arms in surrender. Pastor Elizabeth grabs one and pumps it as she weeps. "It doesn't matter if it's sixty years later, he's wiping all that away."

A white woman in her midthirties tells Pastor Elizabeth very plainly that she was abused as a child and went on to abuse others. "And if I had a gun I would shoot everybody," she wails. "I'd kill everybody."

I'm looking for the door. But Pastor Elizabeth only nods. "I hate the devil," she answers softly.

From the stage and several pews fly the type of anguished screams I've only heard at very sad funerals.

"Some churches won't touch this," Pastor notes. "They say 'Let's have church as usual.' " It's apparent this isn't church as usual. A hand is laid on the prospective shooter's forehead and she topples.

"I'm exhausted," Pastor Elizabeth breathes. She wanders up the aisle.

"Allah!" comes the scream from beneath one of the white sheets, the one just laid over the shooter. "You can't make me kill anyone! I don't want to shoot anyone! My Lord has set me free!"

She remains covered.

"I believe God wanted everyone set free for tonight," Pastor Elizabeth says. "This was your day."

This was also a two-hour observation of the kind of intense

physical worship to which so many are flocking around the globe. But to which I wouldn't return. Probably no surprise by now, but this place is not for me. I felt more of God's love in Ruby's gentle touch on my wrist, in the hands that grasped mine at New Mount Zion and Philadelphia Deliverance, than I did in this room where scores were toppled amid harsh edicts and agonized cries. I don't enjoy fright, or those who attempt to instill it. As someone is just about to do, to me.

As the last of those under the sheets pick themselves up, Cliff Clavin is at the pulpit, now addressing me. Though he begins coyly.

"If there are any TV reporters here . . ." he scans the seats slowly, waiting for a TV reporter to stand. "If there are any radio reporters." He scans again. "If there are any newspaper reporters . . ." He stops looking around when our eyes meet. He points at me and commands loudly, "You better get your story straight. God knows what you're doing."

I'm in church and being yelled at, something that hasn't happened to me since third grade, when Roseann Gondek and I had a giggling fit during First Communion practice. Lucky for me, there are more people in need than Pastor Elizabeth has already tended, and Cliff moves on with the service, praying for the ill listed in the bulletin.

Then he instructs us to go out and vote this week, and to know what a candidate stands for. "And let me verify and clarify for you: pro-choice is not pro-life."

He reads from Matthew: "And the rain descended, the floods came, and the winds blew, and beat on that house; and it fell. And great was its fall." Pastor Elizabeth is on her feet again, the absence of one gold earring the only sign that she's been through spiritual wear and tear. "A great flood—listen to me—a great flood is coming upon the earth—that's scripture," she says. "Literally. This one will be a flood of evil. Did you hear what I said?"

There are some *Ahas*.

"You need the word," Pastor Elizabeth says. "There is one God. He's not Buddha, he's not Confucius. I get so bent out of shape when people say there are other ways to worship God. Then show me that in the Bible!

"This isn't Pastor Elizabeth speaking, this isn't Foursquare speaking, this isn't the Gospel speaking, this is God."

I join the flow coursing from Living Waters. As I roll through the parking lot, I spot Cliff. I give him a wave to silently assure him I indeed have my story straight.

NORTH REFORMED CHURCH

NEWARK, NEW JERSEY

When it comes to denominational bragging rights, the Reformed Church in America can step to the head of the line. It's the country's oldest Protestant denomination with a continuous ministry, planted in 1628 by the Dutch in New York City—or, as they called it, Nieuw Amsterdam. While Plymouth developed from a quest for religious freedom, the Dutch arrived with the simple goal of working. Like shovel and hammer, religion was just one of the things they'd packed. An estimated three hundred thousand now worship in RCA churches throughout North America, including North Reformed Church, a 147-year-old Gothic masterpiece poking its red-brown stone spire proudly heavenward amid the office buildings on Broad Street in Newark, New Jersey.

Founded by Puritans in 1666, Newark is the third-oldest major city in the country. Originally known for production of beer and leather, Newark held tight to Puritanism, outlasting even New England strongholds. Though home to 273,546, this largest city in the state, the county seat, this major New York Harbor shipping point is nearly deserted when my New Jersey Transit train pulls into the Broad Street station, and I'm the only one walking toward the city center. I spot only a few well-dressed churchgoers at the bus kiosk. The rest look homeless, bunching in doorways, lying on park benches. Loss of manufacturing jobs, traffic diverted to new highways, and the growth of suburbia slammed Newark post World War II, as did the 1967 riots, six days of violence and destruction following a racially motivated crime. Nearly forty years later, only a modest amount of urban renewal is apparent as I move through the downtown. A sign to the left of the church's red main door informs me that Rev. Robert Barrowclough's sermon will be "Jesus is the Lord of Economics." I'm horrible at math, but at least I found the church, so with enthusiasm I enter this building constructed for thirty-two thousand dollars by local scions including beer magnate Peter Ballantine.

"It was built by affluent people who did everything the way they thought was best," says church member Lynn, one of a dozen people who greet me. "It's a lot of upkeep," she adds, raising her eyes toward the ornate wooden buttresses supporting a beige-and-gold ceiling. "But it's worth it."

The church was built to hold 625, but only 39 are official members, most of them elderly or ill. Lynn tells me that a gathering of 50 is considered a very good Sunday morning, but attendance is always high on the last two Sundays of the month, when vouchers for Burger King are distributed.

I'm hit with a feeling I haven't had in a few Sundays—that I'm in a familiar place. It actually looks like a church—the kind I'm used to, that is. Traditional, lots of doodads to look at. Eight chandeliers with electric candles provide atmosphere rather than illumination, candles on the altar drawing your eye forward through the dark sanctuary. Red fabric makes up the back wall below a mosaic of Jesus surrounded by angels. There are no sounds. There is an oldish but not unpleasant smell. I walk the red linoleum and select a pew. These are out of the ordinary, having little wooden gates that you must unlock from a brass catch inside. They're numbered, and I select my lucky 7 from the forty. There, I study the four-page bulletin with cover sketch of the church. On the back page, I learn that worshippers here seek to "follow Christ in mission, in a lost and broken world so loved by God."

I look around. Residents of that lost and broken world, and this broken-but-under-repair city, are opening gates to the pews and resting on the red velvety cushions. They're greeting me, hugging one another, and fussing a few rows up over Elsie, an older woman with white hair. Elsie also has white skin, putting both of us among the minority in this church, and in this city, which is 53 percent black. Of the thirty-three people who'll attend this service, eleven will be white.

In the choir loft, an organ is being skillfully played. Traditional rather than rock. Yesterday was Veterans Day and the bulletin tells me we'll be singing "The Star-Spangled Banner" and "The Battle Hymn of the Republic," found in the 594-song *Pilgrim Hymnal*, one of three hardcovers resting in the wooden seat pocket with *Liturgy and Psalms*, and the Bible, Revised Standard Version.

According to the RCA Web site, being Reformed means agreeing with the Christian beliefs outlined in the Apostles' Creed. Adherents believe that faith is communal, and that a relationship with God always includes responsibility toward others. In keeping with that, the congregation runs the basic outreach projects I believe every church should, at the very least: a food pantry and a clothing barn.

RCA ministers and congregations are overseen by a governing "classis" assigned to eight regional synods, supervised by one general synod that makes the big decisions for the RCA. But the church is open to suggestions. The day after I attend it will receive members' thoughts on homosexuality (since 1978 listed by the RCA as a sin) and the church, "the first step in a program designed to listen to the wider denomination and provide occasions for the denomination to engage in dialogue."

"First listen, then talk" is the motto. Sounds good to me. The idea that this is a faith willing to hear from their members on such a hot-button issue is appealing and gives hope that the RCA might enjoy a more open future.

I'm getting a good vibe from the congregation, too. Everyone seems to know everyone else, women in Sunday best get the latest from the man slouched in his hoodie. It is a real-life version of the pictures on every church's Web site—people of all colors smiling, chatting, hugging. And it is real. "Lookit the baby!" coos one of two older black ladies as she greets elderly Elsie. "How ya doing, baby?" Real again.

Bells chime the Westminster tones so famous from so many church steeple clocks and Big Ben itself. They conclude with ten one-note clangs: ten o'clock. A white man in his seventies takes to the pulpit. His black robe bears two red crosses across the chest, and his gray hair sweeps across the top of his head. "Our help is in the Lord who made heaven and earth," he begins. It's the start of the service, and the start of juggling that for most of the next hour keeps me reaching for hymnal, Bible, and liturgical books. I don't mind—the bulletin gives the page numbers for each song, passage, and prayer. It also gives asterisks for the points at which we're to sit or stand. We go from hymn to invocation, introit and salutation, to summary of the law and general confession. The progression familiar, Old World again, reminiscent of the Catholic Mass, another piece that fits into this familiar setting. After a spring and summer spent worshipping in often sterile modern buildings, I feel a surprising comfort in the old.

A white woman in a blue blazer steps from a chair behind the pulpit and reads the first lesson, from Ephesians, praising God, "For he chose us in him before the creation of the world to be holy and blameless in his sight." We then sing "The Star Spangled Banner" while sitting, which feels odd. The reading of the second lesson, from Revelation, follows, and the Apostles' Creed. "Lord we beseech thee," begins Pastor Robert, as the intercessions begin. He offers prayers for politicians, the congregation, and then for Ruth Thomas's granddaughter Mia in the hospital. A father-in-law. Glen, Oscar, Jerry, and a soldier recovering from injuries suffered in Iraq. For a committee preparing to select a new pastor. Thanks are given. That Amber got a 120 on a math exam due to extra credit. That Pedro has a job. That Aaron will be going to a treatment center on Wednesday (this gets applause).

Pastor Robert runs through some announcements, then asks any veterans to stand and give name, rank, and branch of service.

"Wilson Armstrong," says a black man behind me. "Navy. Rank of corporal."

"John Nelson," says a man in front of me. "Eighth Army, Seventh Division, Rank E1."

Up front, another announces that he was a private first class in the Army. Another, who I cannot see, tells us that he is Joe and that he was a corporal.

They remain standing and receive applause, including my own.

We're months past Memorial Day, but at least someone's acknowledging the sacrifices made in war. And the good news here is that the soldiers we're recognizing are still alive.

Joe from up front who'd been a corporal has become a saxophone player and joins the organist, who has descended from the second floor and is seated at a grand piano to the left of the altar. As the offertory is taken, the two men play a slow jazzy number. Joe wanders down the aisle, pausing at the benches of Elsie and the other older women, offering personal serenades. It's a beautiful little gift to each, and it's the moment that makes this visit worth the journey. There's something extremely touching about the honor he's showing each of these elders, and how the music is received appreciatively. We are not great in number, but we are linked. A few nights before my college graduation, friends held a party and that night it hit me that everyone assembled there probably would never be gathered like that again. I mentioned this to a friend and he found it morose. Maybe, but it's also a good kick in the rear to be in the moment. To appreciate who is around you. I'm having that thought now, in this assembly, and it's absolutely golden, one of those moments that have happened on this quest, the same shining color of Joe's sax as he passes and nods. I feel some level of privilege to be here with these people. I'll probably never worship with them again, but I will carry some part of this morning with me to other churches and services.

A quartet of older ladies, all of them white, proceed to the front with the wooden plates holding our offerings. Pastor Robert blesses them and then says: "Jesus is Lord of Economics."

The sermon turns out to be more interesting than the title led me to anticipate. I get a good lesson in history, how the Slave Trade Act, which abolished Britain's lucrative slave trade in 1807, was sparked by Evangelicals and Quakers led by a Brit named William Wilberforce. He and his group prayed three hours daily, including for this abolishment despite the fact that it would destroy the British economy. "People and ethics matter much more than economics," Reverend Robert quotes Wilberforce.

"He did it all because of Christ. He did it all because he knew

God was the Lord of politics and economics. Now faith only relates to the personal life of the family, and to going to church on Sunday. How could this happen to Christians who believe God is Lord of all?"

I don't know the answer. But I mourn that this is what it's come to. On my checklist of faith qualities, a biggie is one of the many things that turns the stomach of Pastor Mark back in Seattle: social justice. Working for a better world rather than concentrating all efforts and prayers on the self and on saving one's neck, and entire body, from the fires of hell.

Some answer by saying amen. I am one of them.

METROPOLITAN COMMUNITY CHURCH

RICHMOND, VIRGINIA

"You're looking for us, aren't you?"

The loud and cheerfully teasing woman standing on the corner in the calf-length white faux-fur coat is half right. I'm actually looking for the building behind her as I exit my cab, but she and her fellow congregation members are the reason I'm here. They belong to a church that doesn't give a fig that the shes among them may originally have been hes. And because so many faiths do give figs regarding such issues as what you look like under your Sunday best, or whom you choose to love, I want to visit a church where anybody and everybody is welcome.

"Visit them all," advised Walter, the middle-aged cabbie who drove me from the airport to the Metropolitan Community Church. "Episcopal, whatever, they all have a base root." My cabbie happened also to be a pastor working on a master's degree in theology, a pretty amazing piece of luck for a traveler touring religions and on her way to the latest in that quest. As I'd accepted my receipt he leaned to check out my destination through the windshield, saying, "This is a good church. I haven't visited yet but what I hear about this church is they fill a need."

I took my receipt, and Walter's approval, and headed toward the corner and my fellow worshippers.

"Nice church," I say, offering the Sunday-morning equivalent of "Come here often?"

"We can't use it, the ceiling fell in," the woman in faux fur replies.

I'm thinking it's finally happened, and before I even crossed the threshold. Then comes the correction, from her friend in a red chapeau: "Not the ceiling, baby, just one of those scroll things came unglued or whatever after one hundred years."

So we will meet in the basement. The ladies and I head down a few stairs and into a utilitarian space that normally might be used for bingo or daycare. It's long, rectangular, and brightened by mango-colored walls and a trio of pillars supporting the intact tiled ceiling. A sound guy with a computer monitor sits at a table on the left, next to the simple altar table, which is to the left of the choir area, a piano, and a five-piece band.

From the one hundred folding chairs facing all that, I claim my usual spot second from the last row, left-hand side, one chair in, moving *The Hymnal for Worship and Celebration*, a red hardcover copy of which rests on every other chair, alternating with blue hardcovers of the Holy Bible, New Revised Standard Version. Standing to my left, offering a handshake, is a six-foot-tall buzz-cut man in black slacks and jacket and gray shirt that includes a Roman collar. His ears are accented by long teardrop earrings. Their wearer tells me he's Pastor Robin and that he hopes I'll enjoy the service.

Three hundred MCCs exist worldwide, four of them in the ultraconservative Commonwealth of Virginia, including this one a block from an enormous monument to Confederate president Jefferson Davis. Not surprisingly, this religion got its start in more liberal Los Angeles. There, in the early 1960s, Reverend Troy Perry was defrocked by the Pentecostal Church for being gay. He went on to struggle with his need to be true to himself and to honor his spirituality. He endured a failed relationship and a suicide attempt before making a return to God, and in 1968 began the world's first church group with a primary ministry to gay, lesbian, bisexual, and transgendered persons.

Metropolitan Community Churches now claim forty-three thousand members in twenty-two countries. MCC Richmond got its start at a Friends meetinghouse in 1978 and in 1992 purchased a former Holy Spirit Association for the Unification of World Christianity (aka Moonies) church. There, members "share the message of God's all encompassing love within an affirming environment where all are empowered as ministers to serve the community."

I chat with a woman behind me who tells me she's gay and long has wanted to explore this church. "I'm a lifelong member of the United Methodist Church," she says. "But I'm disappointed that they say 'All are welcome,' yet when you go there, they want to pray for you, like it's an illness."

Music begins, a soft piano starting up as the choir enters, neat in khaki trousers and navy polo shirts with a rainbow-winged dove flying over each left breast.

Most of the seats in the sanctuary area are claimed. Walter was right, this church fills a need. With exceptions, including the Contemporary Catholic Church, Christian churches view the souls assembled here as damaged, as sinners. But they look pretty much like everybody else I know in this world. Head, body, arms, legs, teeth, no teeth, hair, no hair, heavy, skinny, dark-skinned, light-skinned, youthful, old, satin suits, fleece and jeans, they are all of us. The majority is white and two-thirds are male, though here it's not a joke to say that's just a guess. These worshippers are no different from those I saw in Spartanburg or Enfield, Houston or Kihei. But somebody thinks they are. So they have come here. To a basement. But it's a basement that this morning is definitely church.

"Good morning and welcome to MCC Richmond!" says a woman at the choir's music stand. She's smiley, short gray hair, pink scarf over her choir polo, British accent. She announces welcome time and I am greeted and hugged by a dozen people. I'm told it's great I'm here. The seventy-five of us settle in.

Announcements are next. We learn that someone's been by to

inspect the building. A 10:45 a.m. worship will be held on Thanksgiving, followed by a potluck. Remember to get your ticket for *Hope Has Come*, the annual Christmas concert.

Pastor Robin Gorsline is front and center—left of center, actually—at the pulpit, as he has been most Sundays since being installed in May of 2003. He greets us, and a community prayer book kept in the entryway is read. "Someone wants help for a lost and confused soul," Pastor Robin reads aloud. "This was written by one person, but it could be the prayer of more than one of us, I'm sure."

There's a prayer requested for Skyler, home with the flu. Another for everyone who's traveling this holiday season. Drivers are sought to give rides to the hospital. The continuing cycle of prayer for the transformation of metropolitan Richmond is mentioned. Other prayers are asked for the homeless, the poor, and note is made of the absence of congregation members Tigger, Forest, Lydia, and of John and Candy, who are over at the Salvation Army, helping feed 150 people. A prayer of thanksgiving is offered for the anniversary of Donna and Janet, a couple celebrating twenty years together in a state where gay marriage is banned and staunchly opposed. "We recoil from the hatred that surrounds us," Pastor Robin prays. "You are our balm in Gilead." The piano plays softly. Heads are bowed. "Help us to stay close to you. Lead us to reach back in love, hear also the yearning of our hearts, for peace."

After a brief children's sermon to three little ones who sit on a quilt, the "Invitation to Give" is made by Loretta Mountcastle, who recalls keeping a gratitude journal while enduring a deep depression. "Sometimes I lose sight of my blessings—until I hear about the tragedies of others," she says. "Sunset, full moon, good health for the most part, a medical test that was good, food to eat, friends, a job that kept me in a comfortable lifestyle. At the end, over time you see how rich you are." She segues to the wealth we have to share, as ushers with wicker baskets move to the front of the room.

Standing below a bare fluorescent light, Pastor Robin literally brightens things as he begins his sermon by recalling the birth of his first child on March 12, 1978, at Pontiac General Hospital in Michigan. In case we didn't know it already, we are told that Pastor Robin once had a very different life, with a female wife.

He then mentions another parent, the biblical Hannah, "who went from being scorned, barren, the first loved but second wife of Elkanah, to becoming the mother of one of the chosen ones, the first judge of Israel, Samuel."

Without Samuel, he adds, there would have been no first and second kings of Israel, that second being the legendary David.

"The writer of 1 Samuel said God caused Hannah's infertility. I know people who think God causes hardship. I don't share that view. God is not the agent of despair. God is as present in that story as he is in every life story—as the agent of hope."

We sing "Bless His Holy Name," recite the Community Peace Prayer and the Lord's Prayer, then it's Communion time. Or, as it's called here, "Sharing the Open Meal of Christ." A fortyish man with a mustache and a golden hoop earring is at the altar removing the covering from two alabaster chalices. The bulletin identifies him as David Wilson.

"I have sometimes felt lonely but I have never been alone," he tells us, "because of my creator, my God, my savior . . . May we be strengthened by every gift, every challenge, every blessing you give to us."

From the side of the altar, Pastor Robin tells us that MCC is "about thanksgiving, the business of creating opportunity, and each and every one of God's people being in communion. Members or visitors, this table is set for you. Come forward and be fed in this glorious thanksgiving."

Glorious it is. The most touching Communion service I've ever witnessed. Pastor Robin dips the bread in a chalice of grape juice before distributing it, and then he wraps his arms around the individual, pair, or family who's come before him, and prays. They form a circle, linked by arms around shoulders.

It's almost too intimate a moment to watch, but it's so beautiful you can't look away. The tenderness being shown is much of the reason, but added to that is the love being given so lavishly to people assembled in this place because they could not be part of another church. Meeting in a basement, a place you throw things you have no use for.

Who wouldn't want these people? Who wouldn't want this

community? I nearly tie myself to a chair leg with my backpack strap, so badly do I want to be standing up there, in a circle of God's children, being told that I am loved and wanted and, above all, OK just the way God made me. Even so, I see Communion as an enormous part of a faith, a liturgy, and I really feel I'd need to have some roots in a religion and a lasting connection to the church community in order to participate in this way. So I stay in my place for the brief remainder of the seventy-minute service. Join in "How Majestic Is Your Name." Receive my blessing. Say goodbye to Pastor Robin and the ladies in their Sunday suits and feel pretty darn good. It's not a cliché when I say I feel blessed to have been in this church this morning.

I find the cab I'd requested in advance, and the cabbie looks familiar. It is indeed Walter. I'm his last fare of the morning. He's off to preach after he drops me off. I ask the subject. It's a theme that could fit perfectly in the place we're just leaving.

"It'll be 'Come as you are,' " Walter says. "Come as you are."

MASHPEE BAPTIST CHURCH

MASHPEE, MASSACHUSETTS

I've been sitting in this church for forty minutes and I'm still checking the bulletin to make sure I'm in the right place.

Yes, it's the one I thought I'd entered—Mashpee Baptist Church, started and attended by Native Americans, namely the Mashpee Wampanoags, the very tribe that welcomed 102 white strangers, the Pilgrims of the *Mayflower*, to North America on November 9, 1620, guided them through their first years, and were paramount in their early survival. This is the same tribe that eventually lost their land and rights to the ancestors of the very same white people to whom they'd extended so many lifesaving hands. Yes, that's them, and this is their church, where, 386 years later, we're being told to beware of all members of another minority.

This makes no sense to me. Wouldn't these people, of all minorities, avoid stereotyping others? And how about the black pastor who's doing the preaching? Has his heritage been without misery due to discrimination? What I'm hearing from the pulpit, the scalding steam of intolerance, is heating this chilly church in which I sit beside a black guy and two rows behind a Native American woman.

I'm not here to judge, but I guess I am. Both here and judging. For Thanksgiving weekend, I'd sought a church connected to the holiday. A few months ago I phoned the Wampanoag Nation to ask the faith of its members and where I might find them on this Sunday. I was told that "many members are Christian," and that most worship at Mashpee Baptist.

In this southwestern Cape Cod town, at 27 Great Neck Road, stands a gray shingled building with green steeple holding a cross, which I don't often see crowning a Protestant church. The sign promises ALL ARE WELCOME, a message I've seen and heard in other churches and was heartened to find here.

Numbering fifteen hundred, the Mashpee Wampanoag are my state's largest native community. Their name translates from the aboriginal *Massippie*—"Land of the Great Cove"—and the region has been their home since well before the Pilgrims' arrival. The tribe's 1684 Old Indian Meeting House, which is the Cape's oldest church and the country's oldest Native American church, has been closed since 1997 due to structural problems, so it's Mashpee Baptist for me and the people known as the Praying Indians, a moniker the tribe's Web site attributes to devotion to religious tolerance.

We assemble at 11:00 a.m. beneath a wooden ceiling from which hang four filigreed light fixtures and two fans. I sit on a forest-green-upholstered bench and set my feet on the forest-green-carpeted floor. I estimate that one hundred could fit in the twenty palomino-hued wooden pews split by a center aisle. My row is at left, three from the back, next to the knotty pine wall and one of the squarish stained glass windows with their center decorations of crown or cross. Above the altar table, where a pair of unlit candles bookend a golden cross, a stained glass Caucasian Jesus spreads his arms beneath two Caucasian angels holding a banner reading COME

UNTO ME. I continue to look over today's bulletin, given to me by the black guy at the door. The church's name floats over a sketch of a Bible, flower, and cross. The back gives me "A Glance at the History of the Mashpee Baptist Church," offered by Deaconess Ellen Hendricks, a fourth-generation member.

"Records indicate that a group of Christian Wampanoag families started the Mashpee Baptist Church at its current location in the late 1800s," the deaconess writes, noting that the founding group was formed at the now-closed Meeting House. The church is affiliated with the American Baptist Churches, described on the denomination's Web site as "a Christ-centered, biblically grounded, ethnically diverse people called to radical personal discipleship in Christ Jesus." Focusing on autonomous Baptist churches in the North since its 1907 founding as the Northern Baptist Convention, American Baptist Churches number 5,780, with 1.5 million members.

"Good morning, church family!" A black woman introduces herself as Sister Matilda. Striking in a dark suit, purple shirt, scarf, and beret, she proceeds with announcements about a display of Christmas crèches, and tells us the thought for the day: "Being with the people of God is an oasis."

She also tells us that her friends from Toronto are here. She nods at a man and a woman of retiree age, two of the seven whites among the thirty-two worshippers, most of them black, a few that I guess are Native American. One of those is Curtis Frye Jr., associate minister, formal in light gray suit, who approaches the altar with Senior Pastor John B. Lopes, a skinny black man of about sixty in a dark suit and tie.

Pastor Curtis's duty is the call to worship and the invocation. "Your Word said to be anxious for nothing," he reminds us. To the music of the Clavinova located to the right of the altar, the congregation sings the Lord's Prayer. A praise hymn, number 214, "I Love You, Lord," follows. The voices are racing or the organ is lagging—it's hard to tell—so upon its conclusion, Pastor John suggests, "Let's try that again." I've been glad for another chance to hear the fiddle played tenderly by an elderly black man seated in the first row of my section. The line *May it be a sweet, sweet sound in your ears* is much more so the second time around.

We sing two more hymns and, as has been the case in every other church I've attended since Easter, no verse is skipped. The organ and the fiddle lend an old-time feeling as we sing. I can't say I feel the great need to cover each and every verse, but the music indeed is lovely. We pray next for church members: for Karen Lovett in the hospital, Vivian, the family of the late Tony Andrews. For those unable to attend today. For those who are saved and who need to be saved.

Visitors are asked to speak up. There's Venita from Malden, bringing greetings from St. Paul's AME Church in Cambridge, Massachusetts. There are the Toronto folks. And there's me. I say my name and my village and, as have all the other visitors, receive nods and smiles.

Two men and two women circulate two brass plates for the church funding and two wooden plates for the missions. And then comes a solo by one of the Toronto contingent, the Reverend Richard Kimball of that city's Centennial-Rouge United Church, who give us all the verses of "Life Is Like a Mountain Railroad": *With an engineer so brave / We must make this run successful, / From the cradle to the grave / Watch the curves, the fills, the tunnels / Never falter, never fail / Keep your hand upon the throttle / And your eye upon the rail . . .*

"We need to know that hymn," Pastor John says enthusiastically at the end. Then he starts his message, "God's Protection."

"There is one God, one mediator," he begins. "If someone asks why you believe in God, I'd hope you'd be able to say, 'Jesus came to this earth, was born in a manger, died on a cross, ascended into heaven, is sitting at the right hand of God, interceding for us.' . . . People come to us with names of other gods, say they're worshipping other gods. Are they really?

"There are no others. We need to stand firm on foundation that God is God. Some families have people who go to other churches. If other churches are not going on the basis of the Father, Son, and Holy Spirit, there should be no compromise. We need to stand on no compromise because there are foes of faith."

This country is in trouble, Pastor John says. "There are those who want to destroy us. Take the ACLU, for example. The liberal movement is trying to undermine our Gospel. We need to understand we have a foe. The foe, his name is Satan. He is really doing his dirt on this earth. Especially in Iraq. Their own people are destroying themselves. Look at Afghanistan, Israel, and you begin to see what's happening in America. Just listen to me very carefully: It is coming to America."

Pastor John says, "Some of us have the idea that we are safe and sound in America," citing a FOX News program reporting that members of al-Qaeda live in forty American states.

Ugh. I wish we had just kept singing. That old-fashioned intimate Sunday-morning feel created by the music has melted before the flamethrower of Pastor John's message.

"They're ready and prepared to harm us," he says. "That's why it's important for this church, for Mashpee Baptist Church, to come together and pray. God is not gonna bless this church if we are divided."

Pastor John knows his FOX, including his FOX reporters. He tells us of the report, by E. D. Hill, titled *Obsession*.

"It was all about Islam. At the end, she asked, 'What's the agenda?' Right up front, they say they want to destroy us."

Pastor John makes no effort to differentiate between all Muslims and those who are terrorists. There is a difference. Just as there are differences between the fine members of any group and the few who do bad things. But this morning, all adherents to Islam, the world's second-largest religion after Christianity, are tossed in the same basket by Pastor John, who's warning, "If we don't wake up, it'll be too late."

As I sit in Mashpee Baptist, Pope Benedict XVI is in Turkey, on a p.r. trip aimed at mending fences with Muslims after his Islamophobic gaffe a few months back, when he quoted a fourteenth-century Christian emperor who called the Prophet Muhammad's teachings "evil and inhuman." Pope Benedict has apologized. Pastor John has yet to. Maybe because he's busy inviting newcomers to the faith. "Anyone here—if you don't have a relationship with Jesus, the altar is open. Feel free to come up."

No one does. The Clavinova comes to life as the congregation sings the closing hymn, "Bind Us Together," a song of unity, which seems to me an odd choice for a church with a pastor who would pick and choose who the "Us" might be.

KOUNTZE MEMORIAL LUTHERAN CHURCH

OMAHA, NEBRASKA

On my childhood Saturday nights, my parents went polka dancing and my sister and I went downstairs to my grandparents and watched *Mutual of Omaha's Wild Kingdom*. I had no idea what a Mutual was, or an Omaha, but I knew that the Wild Kingdom was where I could find Marlin Perkins and trusty sidekick Jim Fowler bringing animals from around the world to the black-and-white screen of my *dziadziu*'s Zenith.

With memories of those cozy Saturday nights, I gaze this frozen morning across the Omaha city skyline to the darkest and tallest building, which is crowned by the words MUTUAL OF OMAHA. My vantage point is the front sidewalk of spired, steepled, and stone Kountze Memorial Lutheran Church. In a windchill factor of ten below, I am wearing all the clothing from my daypack, including last night's pajamas beneath the rest of my layers. I'm forty-five minutes early, thanks to the Happy Cab driver possessing satellite navigation with a voice that flawlessly gave instructions from my hotel, and follow early worshippers, eyes their only unswathed features, through double wooden doors and into a grand, old-fashioned, carved and multicolored-glass sweep of a worship space. I find a seat in the second-to-last row of the left-hand set of a dozen dark-varnished wooden pews made cushy by red seat pad. Ahead, in an alcove crowned by a border of gold, stands a carved wooden altar threaded with blue bunting and holding a pair of candles and a golden cross. Above it floats a wooden carving of Jesus, and above him, a stained glass portrait of an angel. Pulpits stand to either side of the altar table and, as unbelievable as it seems—because wasn't I just at New Mount Zion for Easter service just a few weeks ago?—an Advent wreath is displayed to the right.

Perhaps Miami would have been a smarter choice at this time of year, but Southwest Airlines wasn't having a sale to that city this weekend. And though much of this year's path has been dictated by divine inspiration, and by a checklist of religions and regions I wanted to visit, the rest I left to serendipity—by which I mean the cities to which my local discount carrier was offering budget rates. So this week it was to Omaha.

So here I am admiring the architecture, the dark wooden buttresses that lead the eye up the white ceiling and past the six tall and round hanging lamps to an oval center panel of stained glass. On the right-hand wall, windows hold glass images of an ascending or resurrecting Jesus, then two men. "That's Martin Luther holding the open book," the usher tells me. "The other window . . . that's the guy who wrote down what he said." He searches for the name. "Prylanthin? Mylanthin?"

He shrugs. I shrug. Beyond Martin Luther, I'm without a clue to the Lutheran history roster. Upon later research, I'll learn a whole lot, starting with the fact that Martin was a German Augustinian monk irked by the Roman Catholic Church's practice of selling indulgences, basically paying your way out of punishment for sins, including time in purgatory. So lucrative was this business that the archbishop of Mainz held a special sale in 1517 just to pay the pope for his appointment—another thing apparently with a price tag—and also to raise funds for some of the cost to reconstruct massive St. Peter's in Rome. When the friar who'd been selected by the archbishop to preach the indulgences and run the cash register arrived in Saxony, Luther posted on the door of Wittenberg's All Saints' Church his 95 Theses, titled "Disputation of Martin Luther on the Power and Efficacy of Indulgences." Included was the question, "Why does not the pope, whose wealth today is greater than the wealth of the richest Crassus, build the basilica of St. Peter with his own money rather than with the money of poor believers?"

And that was the start of the split, and the Protestant Reformation.

Martin Luther also is known for translating the Bible into German; for breaking ground in clerical marriage, a practice still prohibited in Roman Catholicism and both Eastern and Oriental Orthodox churches; for the for-better-or-for-worse practice of worshippers joining in on hymns; and for definitely-for-worse writings that called for destroying Jewish homes and synagogues, and for limiting Jews' freedom, ideas that four centuries later were adopted and tragically amplified by the Nazis.

At least a tendril of today's approximately 400 million Protestant Christians' religious roots came from the change he planted.

As for the faith that bears his name, an estimated 70 million people worldwide are members. The 5-million-member Evangelical Lutheran Church in America is this country's biggest Lutheran group. It's also relatively new, created in 1987 through the blending of the Lutheran Church in America, the American Lutheran Church, and the Association of Evangelical Lutheran Churches. An ELCA member, Kountze Memorial was started by missionary Henry Kuhns on December 5, 1858. Consisting of 16 members back when Omaha held only three hundred souls, Kountze Memorial became the first Lutheran congregation west of the Missouri River. Worship has taken place here on Farnam Street since this building was opened in 1904, and 2,018 currently are on the rolls.

In the wooden seat pocket I find a green hardcover Lutheran Book of Worship, a visitors card—We Are Glad You Are Here—and a blue-on-white dollar-shaped envelope on which you can direct your offering to causes including World Hunger, Needy Families, and something simply called TV. "Everybody wants to usher on Christmas Eve," my usher tells his friend as I flip through the blue paperback *With One Voice: A Lutheran Resource for Worship*, 802 hymns in all, starting with "When in Our Music God Is Glorified."

The ushers, like everyone here, are white and adult. I count 98 congregants—approximately 50 of them female—in the main floor seating that I estimate can hold 150. Only ten look below age forty. Fashion wisely considers the temperature. The exceptions are the white robes on the two girls—the only children in view—lighting the candles up front, and the blue-sashed emerald robes on the nine women and seven men in the choir that processes in to fill its seats behind the baby grand to the right of the Advent wreath.

"Advent is the season of waiting and watching for the Lord to come," announces the male pastor now at the front of the church in white robe and embroidered scarf. Caucasian, of medium build, balding and graying, he considers us through wire-rimmed glasses as he continues. "We take four Sundays for waiting and watching."

We're invited to an Advent gathering in the Fellowship Hall after the service. Make wreaths, have some food, browse the book table. But first, worship, led by Senior Pastor Carlos D. Schneider and the blue-robed Associate Pastor Deanne K. Lundahl, according to the beige bulletin. We launch into the "Brief Order of Confession and Forgiveness," answering, "We confess to you, Lord" to a list of infractions that includes "Our indifference toward your coming," "Our desire to control time and seasons," and "Our failure to be alert to signs of your presence in our midst." Next is an opportunity to share handshakes in the sign of peace, which, having no seatmates, I do with the ushers. Only after the opening hymn, number 34, "O Come, O Come, Emmanuel," does the pastor give a greeting.

The first lesson, Jeremiah 33:14–16, is not only given word for word on the bulletin, but also explained. The quote "The Lord is our righteousness," for instance, "serves as a sign that the Lord is even now working salvation for the people."

We progress to the main reading, Luke 21:25–36, with its "People will faint from fear and foreboding of what is coming upon the world, for the powers of the heavens will be shaken" that as a kid I found as scary as the serpents Marlin Perkins might have encountered in a *Wild Kingdom* swamp. Pastor Carlos invites modern-day kids forward for the lighting of the Advent wreath. Surprisingly, six materialize and take a seat on the altar step. *Light one candle to watch for Messiah,* sings the congregation. *Let the light banish darkness.*

The prayers and readings have been just about regular Roman Catholic. The sermon is next. Though this isn't the Spiritual Temple, Pastor Carlos is channeling my thoughts. "It's the week after Thanksgiving, we're busy shopping, putting up lights and decorations, we're well into thinking and doing for Christmas. We come here expecting to hear a Christmaslike story read, then we hear this: 'There will be signs . . .' "

His message doesn't get any cheerier: "All you need to do is watch TV, read the newspaper—do you wonder what's going on, what's happening in this world, what's this world coming to? Jesus says it's coming to an end. Everything you know, everything you see, everything that's brought you to this place and shaped you to this moment in life, this world as you know, will end.

"Words are poetic, symbolic, but they're used to symbolize one fact: we're not going to figure out when the end of the world will come. It's not ours to figure out. We can get distracted by all the signs of end times. But that's not what Jesus is about. Jesus is to play out one thing only: God is coming and we prepare—we watch and wait—we prepare ourselves for the coming of God."

Despite the gloomy subject matter, Pastor Carlos is easy to listen to. Friendly, speaking in plain English, no gobbledygook, he's actually able to turn around the thread and lift our spirits, and present a new way to ponder this annual reading. As I did back at the Cowboy Church, I appreciate a new way to look at a passage I've heard again and again. Especially one that's always struck me as somewhat frightening.

"Before we ask the question 'What's this world coming to?' we need to ask 'Who came to this world?' We've always been living in the end times. Your grandparents, great-great-grandparents, all the people who ever lived here lived in the end times. We need to ask the previous question: Who came to the world? It gives us hope to go on . . . Advent days are given to us so we can indeed face the future with hope. In Bethlehem, in Baby Jesus, God came and claimed this broken-down beat-up world and redeemed it. It's redeemable. I am redeemable. You are redeemable. That's our faith. If that's the God who's coming for us, we have nothing to fear. Unless you have a different God—a god of fear and anger—then you have something to fear. But that's not the God I have."

Pastor Carlos and I share the same God! It's my prize for the journey to this tundra-like city. A minister who wants to spread the idea of a loving God! An assuring God! He's not being dressed up here as a totally don't-worry-be-happy God, but Pastor Carlos is making it clear: the one who's going to return isn't the vindictive, snarling one I've been hearing about in so many churches this year. The fact that this message is given in a church that physically and liturgically so resembles a Catholic one tilts me a bit, makes me wish I could cut and paste into one new church so many of my favorite theologies and pastors and congregants and choirs. I'd snag Pastor Carlos, for starters.

"In that Baby Jesus," he's continuing, "God gave us his word that in the end, God would be there for us. So don't get distracted by signs all over, signs are simply markers along the way . . . Jesus said 'The Kingdom of God is among you.' People would ask 'Where?' He would never point to himself, he'd just say 'It's here.' It's a gift given to each and every one of us. The gift of faith."

Pastor Carlos tells us not to fear. To stand up. Look up. "Your God is coming to you. The whole Advent season is a chance to look up. The end is not about chronology, the end is not about how it will come, the end is about who will come: God."

I'm grateful for his point of view, for this visit, for the pleasant morning that happens to follow a familiar Roman Catholic path of offertory prayer, eucharistic prayer, the Lord's Prayer, and Communion. "Let's live, love, and act on hope until that day our Lord really comes," Pastor Carlos says in blessing before the final hymn, "Fling Wide the Door."

The door of the church is open. Flung open. The cold awaits. As does another Happy Cab, and another voice that magically tells just how to get where I need to be.

BROWN MEMORIAL CHRISTIAN METHODIST EPISCOPAL CHURCH

LOUISVILLE, KENTUCKY

"Come on over here! Come on!"

The woman in the red jacket means me. Because I'm the only person seated where she's pointing, in the vacant middle of the church. "Come on over!"

Beneath this white and bright ceiling, resting on the pink cushion in my dark wooden pew (the last in the section before the final two marked for ushers only), I'd just gotten settled and had been looking at another Advent wreath, with a candle burned markedly lower than those in Omaha at the beginning of the season last weekend.

This morning, thanks to another airfare sale, I'm three states to the east, in Louisville, Kentucky, being invited into the women's Sunday school at Brown Memorial, a Christian Methodist Episcopal church, or CME as it's known. This denomination was high on my short list because of its history. That C in CME once stood for Colored. This is a church founded by forty former slaves just five years after the Civil War. Some having been converted by their masters, they'd worshipped in the whites' Methodist Episcopal Church South. But they soon sought their own, one unconnected to a religion those masters used to justify slavery, and one that would assist their community with education and employment as well as spiritual progress. The result was the Colored Methodist Episcopal Church, formed in Jackson, Tennessee, on December 16, 1870.

By the end of the decade it boasted seventy-eight thousand faithful and today, the church with the C standing for Christian via a 1954 vote claims more than eight hundred thousand members in this country, Africa, and the Caribbean. The approximately three thousand autonomous churches are led by elected male or female bishops who act as superintendents and who serve until age seventy-four. CME churches continue to educate, through their four colleges and a school of theology, and through social activism that has seen members work in the civil rights movement and in efforts to assist the needy in Africa. In this country, the church's twelve-year-old "One Church, One School" effort pairs churches with schools in need of financial assistance.

The school in session this morning is the traditional Sunday one, for which I'm being summoned by the woman in red.

I slide into a seat in back of the gathering but she escorts me to a closer pew, insisting that I sit in the center. The seats face forward, of course, but everyone is turned toward one another. The topic is prophets, prophetesses. "But not like Dionne Warwick on TV," one woman says, "but real ones."

"I never listened to her music after she was arrested in the airport for marijuana," an older lady sniffs.

"We're talking about real prophets," my friend in red reminds her gently. "They are the ones through whom God speaks."

Then my classmates ask how God makes himself known today.

"In the wind," one offers. "Weather," somebody else says. "Wars." My answer would be "Through people like you." I've literally just walked in off the street and not two minutes after I sat down I was plunked in the middle of a flock of very welcoming women. All are black. I am the only white person, not only in the building but, from what I observed on the cab ride from my hotel, maybe for blocks. And I'm a white person wearing her winter-warmest electric-blue floor-length coat and big black Cossack hat. But their invitation and inclusion erase any self-consciousness I might have about my race, or attire, as they do any thoughts of what these women might be wondering about this woman arriving at their church, early and alone. I'm sitting here feeling extremely lucky for the reception, and I decide to tell them all this. How their kindness is a sign that God is right here, probably sitting between me and the woman in the red jacket. Heck, in the God-could-be-anyone theme of the *Joan of Arcadia* television dramas I'm renting on DVD these days, he might even *be* the woman in the red jacket. "We need to remember what she said, and to do this more often," a woman in purple decides, and I wonder how many opportunities they have to usher wandering souls into their circle and make them feel like they've landed somewhere good.

The class ends and the woman in red introduces herself as Ida. I'm invited into her row, four from the front, facing the choir.

An older man in a suit takes the pew in front of us; a younger man in casual clothes pulls into the one behind us. The seats are filling up. Today's dress is a hodgepodge, leaning toward the fancier. Some women wear New Mount Zion–style hats and matching suits. Two women sit up front in the nurse dresses and head doilies I saw on Resurrection Sunday. One of the ushers has arrived in a long-sleeved T-shirt tucked into black nylon jogging pants.

The building's listing on the National Register of Historic Places might call for a bit of added reverence. Of brick and in Greek Revival/Romanesque style, it was constructed in 1863 as a Methodist Episcopal Church South and was the last project of architect Gideon Shryock, whose portfolio includes the Old State Capitol of Kentucky. The first service of what would become Brown Memorial CME was held here in 1907. The church's front is depicted on the cover of the twelve-page bulletin, in which "Enter to Worship: Depart to Serve" is written over the first of five pages guiding us through the service. There's also a calendar of church events ("Breakfast with Santa," a collection of gifts for the needy, work at Elijah's Kitchen), a list of birthdays and anniversaries, names of shut-ins and their addresses, and a directory of church staff.

I love to praise his name, sing the eighteen adults, teens, and children who've assembled in the choir rows without my noticing. The nurses walk to the front table and light the first and second candles set into the Advent wreath.

"Time to shut out the world," announces a pastor in grayish buzz cut listed in the worship guide only as Leader. He's black, as are the rest of the one hundred, with the exception of me and one small girl. He's also around seventy and wearing a gray suit, and he is praising God for being our cover by night. The piano is played softly and skillfully by a woman who doesn't need sheet music.

The choir switches gears and I'm hearing a slow "O Come, All

Ye Faithful" for the third time in this church year, but for the first time in the actual Christmas season.

The pastor offers the Gospel, Luke 3:16, telling of John in the wilderness, "preaching a baptism of repentance for the forgiveness of sins.

"Let's prepare our hearts to rejoice—be exceedingly glad!" he announces. "The Altar Prayer is an opportunity for that, and to pray." Twenty-two adults instantly approach and stand or kneel along the edge of the altar area. To pillows of music, they close their eyes, place faces in their hands. I saw the same postures at Living Waters back in Rhode Island but there felt none of the intensity I do here. This is no holy show. The fervency is rising like heat from August pavement.

"For unto us a child is born, unto us a son is given, and the government will be upon his shoulders." This is the start of the sermon by the Reverend Dr. Raymond F. Williams. He looks to be in his mid-seventies. His short hair is graying and his girth is round. He's dashing in dark suit and purple-striped tie and he speaks powerfully and dramatically as he continues: "And he will be called Wonderful Counselor, the Mighty God, Everlasting Father, Prince of Peace. Of the increase of his government and peace there will be no end."

Pastor Raymond pauses and then gives it to us straight: "Don't dock my pay 'cause I preach short." That gets a few laughs, perhaps some of them relieved. I had no idea what to expect, but I would have bet that I'd be here for at least two hours. Eight months into my church travels, a service of that length no longer seems so long to someone who grew up thinking a forty-minute Mass dragged.

"It does not take all day to tell the story," Pastor Raymond says, "'cause it's the same old story. You just have to hear the Word."

He tells us that next week is the "High Sunday" for Christmas. "Let's look Christmassy. Put on Christmas colors. We'll have soul food, collard greens and fried chicken. Gifts? I wear a 36/19 shirt, size 11 shoes, I'll even take a pair of Fruit of the Loom."

The organ music morphs into some jazz from *A Charlie Brown Christmas*. And Pastor Raymond keeps his word about being short, finishing with a few fast thoughts. In the style of Pastor Carlos last Sunday, Pastor Raymond manages to get through a sermon without using the fear factor or advertising any exclusionary doctrine. For me, whether in a church predominately black or white or green, that's a welcome accomplishment, and message.

"I want you to start telling people about this church. They make us retire at seventy-four, but I don't plan to go anywhere. I want to do something great for God in this church. We're not about pleasing you, we're about pleasing God. 'Methodist' is just a name. The body of Christ has to be pulled out of us to show the world."

I love that idea, of making our faith visible. Which is what's soon to be accomplished by the choir member who up to now has remained seated while the rest of the singers have stood. She's in her fifties, wearing a beige cable zip-front sweater with fake-fur trim, and black pants that become visible as she slowly gets to her feet. She walks a few steps toward the pulpit but stops at a banister edging the choir area.

"This is the first time I have been before you to sing since I couldn't sing," she says slowly. "God restored my vision. I only have one eye but I can see more than ever. Satan—he's attacked my liver, made me bleed, gave me diabetes. Now arthritis in my spine—why I'm not moving. I'm leaning on this right now"—she slaps the banister—"but I'm really leaning on Jesus."

And she's surrendering, as she sings in what swells into a choir-backed testimony about giving it over. *I surrender all, I surrender all, All to Thee, my blessed Savior, I surrender all.*

She's weeping, the congregation is weeping, I'm weeping. I have no idea who she is or the extent of her problems but here is that golden moment I have found in so many services this year. Right here, right now, the heart, the honesty, the faith being shown is worth the price of the flight, the hotel, the dinner, the breakfast, the cab. Just to be present for this moment of genuine faith, of the palpable presence of the Lord.

Tithing begins with a benevolent offering—a dollar a day for those in need, informs Pastor Raymond as brass plates are circulated. "We should be in a giving mood," he says. "Just look at the gifts you have received from God. You are a gift yourself!"

We will praise you the rest of our days, yes, Lord, the rest of our days, sings the choir.

Visitors are welcomed and asked to stand. There are ten, including a man and woman who relocated here from New Orleans after losing their home to Katrina. "We feel at home here," the man says. "It's a real blessing."

A young man who's headed to Iraq is called up front. He wears a green hoodie and dark pants and, already, a new pair of high tan sand boots. "We always put the holy blessings on the folks going to fight," Pastor Raymond says as he places his hands on the soldier's shorn head. "We cover this man with your presence, Holy Spirit, that where he walks will be a blessed place. That you will bless Iraq." I watch the boy walk back to his seat looking a mix of solemn and self-conscious. I cannot imagine what he will face, but I hope the blessings stick. Both on him, and on the Iraq that Pastor Raymond was so good as to remember figures in the equation. Again, inclusion that's unexpected. That has made this frigid morning all the warmer.

All things come of thee, the choir begins, *All things come of thee.* The service ends. The women in white have extinguished the candles. But the sanctuary is left no less bright.

KING'S CHAPEL

BOSTON, MASSACHUSETTS

"You have to do the UUs."

Over and again during my church year came this suggestion. Each time, I'd say thanks for the suggestion but then point out that Unitarian Universalists indeed welcome the study and inspiration of Christian concepts, but also those of every faith, and my year is focusing on non–Roman Catholic Christian churches. Then an actual UU told me some congregations lean Christian, including a very historic one in my very own state.

So I'm back in Boston, home of 320-year-old King's Chapel, which is affiliated with the approximately one-thousand-congregation Unitarian Universalist Association (UUA) headquartered right up Beacon Street. In full disclosure, I must note that the UUA owns

Beacon Press, publisher of this book, and an institution that for 152 years has been dedicated to printing thought-provoking works, including the first publication of the Pentagon Papers. I like the idea of a church that so values the printed word and I'm eager for this morning's visit.

This squat and pillared stone building a few blocks up from Fanueil Hall, and next to the Parker House Hotel famous for its dinner rolls, was founded on June 15, 1686, as an Anglican congregation—the city's first. Sundays weren't always peaceful at this outpost of the Church of England in a land being settled by detractors of that church, and legend has it that Puritans flung rotten vegetables as the mostly Tory congregation entered. The Quincy granite structure I'm entering today opened in 1754, and James Freeman became its first minister in 1783, bringing with him the then-dangerous and heretical Unitarian ideas that he incorporated into the Anglican Book of Common Prayer. The Anglican Church's representatives didn't like what they heard but the congregants listened, and Freeman lit the flame of what would become liberal Christianity.

Born in what is now Transylvania, the Unitarian movement (the Universalists were a separate one, which merged with the Unitarians in 1961) floated across the Atlantic in the late eighteenth century and morphed into a religion in which the Trinity and Divinity of Christ were replaced by the unipersonality of God, and the acceptance of truths found in science and non-Christian religions.

I'm partaking in my own spiritual smorgasbord this year, and this entrée promises to be particularly savory. I find King's Chapel warm, bright, and quietly decorated with a poinsettia, several wreaths, and a line of garland along the balcony. Worshippers in boiled wool jackets, tweeds, bow ties, and tams are greeted by women handing out copies of the ten-page bulletin bearing the church seal—a crowned lion and a unicorn—dated 1686.

The women direct worshippers to six sections, ten pews each. Back in Newark I had a latched door to my pew, but here I have a door to a sort of pew condo, a large U-shaped seat with maroon cushion allowing me a view of the front, side, or back of the church, and room to rest my hymnal on the four wooden corner shelves.

I'm entering the fourth box from the front when an older

woman asks if she can join me. She's Elsie, a forty-year King's Chapel member who's driven up from the Cape, an hour away. She asks where I'm from and I tell her of my church sampling. "This is like Episcopalian, but High Episcopalian," she tells me. Elsie is on the vestry, a sort of church council, and says she has seen many changes in this church over the years, but she likes it still.

"I can attend a service of dignity, with beautiful music, and still have my own beliefs," she says. I'm wondering what those beliefs might be, and I am just about to ask, when she, as if in the Spiritual Temple across town, magically answers my silent question with "That Jesus Christ was born, but not of a virgin."

She turns to greet someone. I take the opportunity to admire the elaborate pulpit that resembles an overturned wine glass accessed by a half door and a small flight of stairs.

To its right is the simple altar, a long and plain dark-wood Communion table that I'll later be told was a gift of King William in memory of Queen Mary. It holds a pair of silver candlesticks placed on either side of a small cross. Worshippers facing the back have a view of the organ and white-robed choir.

Elsie continues to chat with congregants, and I claim one of my box's copies of the ninth edition of the 550-page red hardcover Book of Common Prayer According to the Use in King's Chapel. In it, I learn that the church year at King's Chapel begins with Advent. And the third Sunday of it begins now, with the ushers walking down the center aisle, closing each pew door, and a man and woman in black gowns approaching the no-nonsense pulpit below the ornate one.

Thirty-five people have assembled, all adults and all Caucasians except for a middle-aged African American man with a German shepherd guide dog, and a black woman with a voice that shines as we stand to sing "O Come, O Come, Emmanuel."

"Rejoice and exalt with all your heart," announces the Reverend Rali Weaver, early forties, brunette hair pulled back, oval dark-rimmed glasses: "Gather the outcasts and I will change their shame into praise."

We read the General Confession and Prayer from the Book of Common Prayer. The words are a bit different but it's essentially the same soul-cleaning that has started so many services this year. We admit to a bunch of shortcomings, including following the "devices and desires of our own hearts."

The versicles follow, six lines for the head minister—the Reverend Earl Holt—to read, alternating ones for us to repeat, "O Lord, open thou our lips"; "And our mouths shall show forth they praise." We sing all ten verses of "Cantate Domino" and the music is as joyous as the lyrics: *O sing unto the Lord a new song, for he hath done marvelous things.* Psalm 80 is read, asking in the dark tones of the Old Testament: "O Lord God Almighty, how long will your anger smolder against the prayers of your people?"

A reading from Luke likewise contains no shiny happy message: "John said to the crowds coming out to be baptized by him, 'You brood of vipers! Who warned you to flee from the coming wrath? Produce fruit in keeping with repentance . . . The axe is already at the root of the trees, and every tree that does not produce good fruit will be cut down and thrown into the fire.' "

The people ask how to be spared and John gives them that great answer: You have a couple of tunics? Give one to the person who has none. Same with food. And if you collect taxes for a living, do so fairly. If you're a soldier, stop pushing people around. It's as simple as that, we're reminded. We don't have to go founding megachurches, we don't need to sell all we own, we just have to be good and decent.

We stand for the Te Deum hymn, also from the prayer book, and comprised of no less than eleven verses. The choir is dazzling, and can be heard, I learn, in its own monthly Sunday-afternoon concert series that would tempt me to make the ninety-minute drive just for that. Prayers follow—for all nations, for those in authority, for those in all sorts of conditions of humankind—as does the offertory. The female usher who gave me my bulletin moves from front to back, box to box, opening the door of each to extend the plate rather than just handing it over the wall.

Announcements are next and we learn that the three-decades-old tradition of Milk Punch Sunday will be repeated today. "The punch is hot milk with alcohol," Elsie leans to inform me. We sing "Watchmen, Tell Us of the Night," a Christmas song that's been around since 1825 but that's new to me: *Watchman, tell us of the night / What its signs of promise are. Traveler, o'er yon mountain's height / See that glory beaming star* . . . Then Pastor Earl materializes in the big pulpit. I'm disappointed that I missed him climbing the stairs while I was reading the Watchman lyrics. The title of his sermon is "Love," which he tells us is part of a series that's included hope, faith, and joy.

"There is no way through Advent without John," he tells us. "We're looking forward to a hot toddy Milk Punch Sunday and here he is with his axe. This wild man out there where the wild things are. He welcomes the people by saying 'You brood of vipers.' He'd seen the vipers scurrying from the flames when the dry woods went up. That's what he saw in those coming out to be baptized. The Advent before I retire, I'm gonna start a sermon like that: 'You brood of vipers!' "

Pastor Earl gets laughs. "John the Baptist was a crazy guy. John is a wild man, an early Boy Scout. His word is familiar to every Boy Scout today: be prepared," Pastor Earl says.

"Baptism is a symbol of desire, intent to change, to bear good fruit in our living. How many coats do you have in your closet? Let's ask about our own lives—where have we gone wrong—where shall we turn? To share an extra coat is not going far in the war against poverty, but it is a teensy-weensy step. That is maybe the point: achievable goals. John doesn't say it, but he knows we need to walk before we run. Jesus will say, 'Go and sell all and give to the poor all you have and only after that go and follow me.' Ultimately, he will teach that we will only find our lives by giving it away sacrificially, all for love."

Pastor Earl notes that John never uses the word "love," but that we need to focus on it. "Just start," he tells us, and it's more a kind suggestion than a command put to a brood of vipers. "Turning from self-centered condemnation, from covetousness and envy. When Jesus comes, he won't settle for a spare coat or a few dollars in a Salvation Army kettle. He will demand all we have, all we are. Sacrificial self-giving love is the only path to the life that has no end."

He says John preached what's now known as tough love, adding that people respond to the truth, even when it's harsh.

"Maybe that's why they came out," he suggests, "to be confronted with the truth about themselves."

I'm thinking about that possibility when Pastor Earl begins to recall a film in which a plane is about to crash. A passenger responds by removing both her diamonds and her scar-hiding makeup. When the plane makes a last-minute recovery, she welcomes the opportunity to not hide behind cosmetics. "Honesty was offered to her and she took it gladly," Pastor Earl says. "To love our neighbor as ourselves, we have to love ourselves as we truly are. When it comes to loving our neighbor as ourselves, it seems we have a way to go. It's an ongoing journey of transformation. A journey to a God whose other name is love."

I like Pastor Earl. I like his words. I like his smarts. I like his little white bow tie. I don't know firsthand what goes on in the mainline UU churches, but I could have plunked any member of my Roman Catholic family in this church this morning and afterward heard nary a "What was that about?"

People, look east, we begin as the service closes, *and sing today, Love, the guest, is on the way.*

Its path began at that grand pulpit, from which Pastor Earl spoke of assisting others, rather than of shutting them out. Maybe it's the good will of the Christmas season, but I've just visited three churches in a row in which anyone could feel welcome, and in which the message is helpful and heartening. Again, why these factors are so rare in a house of the Lord is beyond me. But I'm on a roll here, and hoping to make it four in a row.

PART FOUR: WINTER

Central Moravian Church, Bethlehem, Pennsylvania

Times Square Church, New York, New York

The Portland New Church, Portland, Maine

Holy Cross Polish National Catholic Church, Hamtramck, Michigan

Kykotsmovi Mennonite Church, Kykotsmovi Village, Hopi Nation

Kingdom Hall of Jehovah's Witnesses, Milwaukie, Oregon

Northampton Vineyard, Northampton, Massachusetts

Calvary Chapel, Fort Lauderdale, Florida

Harvest Church of the Nazarene, Las Vegas, Nevada

Full Gospel Tabernacle Church, Memphis, Tennessee

All Saints Parish, Brookline, Massachusetts

St. Mary's Convent, Greenwich, New York

Revolution Church, Brooklyn, New York

Interfaith Chapel, Denver International Airport, Denver, Colorado

CENTRAL MORAVIAN CHURCH

BETHLEHEM, PENNSYLVANIA

The last time I entered a church in Bethlehem, soldiers with machine guns watched from the barbwire-edged roofs of adjacent buildings. This morning, the only onlooker is a yawning and apparently unarmed bellman in the doorway of Hotel Bethlehem.

The difference is location, the first being the beleaguered West Bank eleven years ago, for a visit to the Church of the Nativity and the actual site of Jesus's birth. The second, East Pennsylvania this morning, and Central Moravian Church, the oldest such church in North America.

I've come to what's known as Christmas City U.S.A. to spend Christmas Eve Sunday. And I've brought Tanya. More correctly, she's brought me. Despite rental car reservations, no vehicle was awaiting me at the airport in Philadelphia, so Tanya and her Rabbit saved me from having to use a donkey. The journey gave us a chance to catch up in person—I hadn't seen her since Susan and I flew down to Tanya's house for my Arch Street visit seven months ago. Tanya and I arrived after dark in this city ninety minutes from that house, an eighty-one-foot-tall electric star marking our destination.

The state's eighth-largest city was founded on Christmas Eve 1741, by German Nikolaus Ludwig von Zinzendorf and a group of Moravians who named the hilly spot after the biblical village in Judea.

If 1741 sounds eons ago, consider that the Worldwide Moravian

Church was founded 449 years ago, in 1457. That's sixty years before Martin Luther nailed his theses to a door and one hundred before the Anglican Church began. From their start, Moravians flocked to missionary work, often finding themselves in forgotten corners of the world. (The contingent that founded Bethlehem was interested in saving the souls of Native Americans and unchurched colonists.) As a result, more than a quarter of its current six hundred thousand members worldwide live in Tanzania.

The community in Bethlehem, Pennsylvania, meets at Central Moravian on Main Street in a town that six months ago was declared by *Money* magazine to be one of the 100 Best Places to Live. Tanya tells me housing is hot here, commuters snapping up the sturdy brick row houses within walking distance of a quaint downtown. Of course, it was a different story not too long ago. Bethlehem Steel Corporation ruled this city during and after World War II, employing almost half the population at its massive plant along five miles of the Lehigh River, until the industry went bust and "The Steel" was sold in 2003 and now sits silently, awaiting plans to convert the 120-acre brownfield into a $600 million gaming/recreational/residential/historical destination.

On this Christmas Eve morning, the biggest draw for visitors is the large Moravian Book Shop, founded in 1745 and claiming to be "The world's oldest bookseller," now also selling food and gifts including hundreds of the twenty-six-point Moravian stars first made in Germany in 1850.

A disco-ball-sized such star hangs from the ceiling of two-hundred-year-old Central Moravian Church, which bears its own media claim to fame, once chosen by *USA Today* as one of the nation's Ten Greatest Places to Reflect on Christmas Eve. Tanya and I enter the side door, through which a hand-bell choir practices, the black-gloved hands of its seven adult and five child members wielding bells in sizes from fist to Crisco can.

We walk the brown aisle carpet until the sixth row and choose a seat in the middle of the white-painted pews. The wood floor beneath our feet is worn and the kneelers, which I've hardly seen in my travels this year, are positioned up. Settling in, we face an altar area befitting the city's name. A large arch shelters an eight-foot-high painting of a manger in which the Holy Family is being visited by four shepherds. The manger's ceiling is made of actual logs, giving the crèche a 3-D touch, complete with large rocks behind the pulpit. Christmas trees—pleasingly plain in their undecorated state—stand on either side of the painting, which is the only piece of visual art in the sanctuary. The only other nods to the holiday are a pair of poinsettias at the altar and a wreath hanging between each of the ten tall windows.

Tanya is reading the teal blue hardcover Moravian Book of Worship she found in the seat pocket. At 954 pages, it's 954 pages more than she's used to. Tanya is a Quaker. No words, no books. She came to the faith over the summer. She'd long been curious about it and felt something spiritual click when she entered the meetinghouse in her town. Born in largely Catholic Guatemala, Tanya was raised in predominantly Protestant Texas by parents who encouraged their kids to sample religions. Tanya tells me she's tried Episcopal, Methodist, Catholic, Evangelical, and Presbyterian services. "The Quakers say you've found your home when you walk in and you feel 'That's it,' " she says.

Whatever inspired them to come here this morning, I see a crowd of 120 white and middle-age-on-up worshippers with only five children among them. The numbers will swell to three hundred by the end of the 10:00 a.m. service. Two women—one in her forties and in a dark pantsuit, the other about fifty and in a red skirt suit—walk to the pulpit from a side door. Joining them is a man in his early fifties wearing a dark suit and purple striped tie. An older man and woman in the front row walk to the Advent wreath and light the fourth candle. I think back to Omaha, to Louisville, to Boston, the wreaths in each church, the people, and what a pleasant stretch of visits this has been. The service hasn't even begun and it's already a promising morning. Tanya has no idea what she's done for me by accompanying me to this city adjacent to the one in which Rosemary, my first-ever friend, whom I met when both of us were three, was killed in a car accident twenty-four years ago. I'd always intended to visit this area. To look at the street she'd barely spent a month living on when she'd landed her first job after grad school. I thought I might drive the same route she had that last evening. But when I spotted the sign for Allentown last night I went stiff and silent and was glad I wasn't alone. This morning, I am wearing the red, white, and maroon scarf Rosemary sent me when she spent an undergrad semester studying in London. Before I left yesterday, I received the annual Christmas letter from the man who was her boyfriend at the time of her death. He went on to get married, and to have a daughter whose photograph he tucks into the envelope each December. This year he tells me she has her driver's license. It has been that long, and more.

"Blessed be the Lord God," begins the woman in the suit now at the pulpit greeting us with a prayer. This is the Reverend Janel R. Rice, according to the eight-page bulletin that lists, among other news, the visiting hours for the Putz. I always thought that was an insult, but here in the Moravian Church the German word *putzen* means to decorate, and the Putz is a series of miniature scenes illustrating the Nativity story.

That very story is the first reading, Luke 2:1–20, given by Pastor Douglas W. Caldwell, who is right when he prefaces it with, "I don't think there's another passage in Scripture that has created as many images and memories we carry as this passage from Luke." Certainly, just the first line—"In those days Caesar Augustus issued a decree that a census should be taken of the entire Roman world"—rings something in me.

Pastor Douglas reads of the shepherds keeping watch over their flocks, the angel of the Lord appearing, and the line we hear once a year but tend to forget for most of the rest of it: "Do not be afraid."

In this city of 71,329, we sing "O Little Town of Bethlehem," ending with *The hopes and fears of all the years are met in thee tonight*, then sit for "Everywhere, Everywhere, Christmas Tonight," the sermon by the lady in red, Pastor Carol A. Reifinger. The title is the opening line of a poem she learned as a child. Only as an adult did she learn it was written by Phillips Brooks, a pastor in Philadelphia who in 1868 had penned the song we just sang.

Brooks was writing during the Civil War, "a big time for such carols," Pastor Carol says, mentioning "It Came Upon the Midnight Clear" by Edmund Sears and "I Heard the Bells on Christmas Day" by Henry Wadsworth Longfellow. "Apparently, the Civil War sparked conversions to Christianity, and a lot of poetry."

She calls "Everywhere" a powerful commentary on war. "In the winter of 1864, seven thousand of Robert E. Lee's troops became Christians. A flurry of Christmas carols were written in the North."

She reads the poem, the fourth verse of which is, "Then let every heart keep its Christmas within / Christ's pity for sorrow, Christ's hatred for sin. / Christ's care for the weakest, Christ's courage for right, / Christ's dread of the darkness, Christ's love of the light. / Everywhere, everywhere, Christmas to-night."

Pastor Carol talks about how expansive is Christianity, from Labrador to Nicaragua to Tanzania, where Christmas preparations take all year and new shoes for Christmas worship are the big thing. In Tanzania, "they say, 'If we are going to see Jesus, we must look our best.' " Pastor tells us the world over, people are preparing for the arrival of the Christ Child tonight.

"You can't put a fence around Christianity," she says. "What is the Christmas story but the hovering of peace above a dark and conflicted world? It goes beyond Moravian stars and beeswax candles. We try to focus on Christ and his character, who saves us from dark deeds and characters—especially those that dwell within us."

She leaves the pulpit and we enter a moment of silent meditation, which I figure Tanya must be an expert at by now. The church is warm and quiet, not even a sound from the man with special needs who's sitting behind us in a Santa hat and has been saying "God God good good," after each prayer or reading.

"We are not alone in the world. We are connected to something greater," Pastor Douglas now tells us. "We are people, human beings, visited in both spirit and image, we believe, by God."

This morning I feel that spirit sitting next to me in the person of Tanya, whom I met a dozen years ago when she was a reporter who interviewed me when I came to Philadelphia on my very first book tour. I'm lucky enough to have been interviewed by scores of reporters in the dozen years since, but Tanya both wrote about my life and then magically became an important part of it. That was kismet, as was meeting Rosemary when we were tots staring at a pony stabled up my street next to her *dziadziu*'s house. I'm suddenly glad I never made the trip to this region before this weekend, when I happened to visit with a friend I love dearly. Traveling so often, I'm really grateful when anyone decides to accompany me. Today, having Tanya here is not only appreciated, but is fitting, and a blessing.

And on this holiday-eve morning, Tanya's presence provides the family feel I miss due to being away from Tommy, whom I won't see until so late tonight that both Santa and I will be in the air at the same time. If Tanya and I stayed the night, though, we would have our choice of four services here at Central Moravian. As Pastor Douglas is saying, "There is nothing quite like Christmas in Bethlehem, PA."

The brass collection plate is passed, the bell-choir plays, and the man behind us in the Santa hat exclaims "All right!" before the congregation slides into the rolling *Glor-or-ias* of the hymn "Angels We Have Heard on High."

Pastor Carol reminds us that we live in a world that is old, fragile, and tender. "When the Christ Child comes to us, let us embrace him." Bells ring solemnly as the three pastors exit the altar area and disappear through a door to the left that magically opens for them.

"Joy to the World" begins and its second verse paints my favorite images: *While fields and floods, rocks, hills, and plains / Repeat the sounding joy* . . . I like the idea of nature in on the whole celebration. In the fields, in the hills. We are not alone in this world. I am not alone in this town. Or in this pew. And that indeed is a reason for joy.

TIMES SQUARE CHURCH

NEW YORK, NEW YORK

In 1958, an illustration in *Life* magazine changed Pastor David Wilkerson's life. He was ministering in a small Pennsylvania town when he came across the drawing of several New York City teenage gang members on trial for the murder of a fifteen-year-old polio victim. He was reduced to tears, and to action.

Up in Manhattan he started Teen Challenge, a Bible-centered program for troubled youth that now runs 173 residential programs in New York and 241 centers across the globe. The 1963 bestseller *The Cross and the Switchblade* and the 1970 movie on which it was based, starring Pat Boone as Pastor David and Erik Estrada as a punk, detail how Teen Challenge started. But Pastor David's mission had yet to end.

One night in 1986, he was walking down West Forty-second Street near Times Square. This was the pre-family-friendly Disney Store/ESPN Zone Times Square, and the area was lined with porn shops and X-rated movie theaters. Pastor David prayed that God might send a solution for the drugged, abused, and hopeless adults and children he passed. The response he received was that he was the solution.

Then living in Texas, on the verge of retirement after three decades of working with kids, Pastor David had been looking forward to moving farther west to write and visiting eastern Europe to preach. He roamed the city for the next two nights and spent three months in intense prayer before he heard God promise him that if he returned to Times Square, a grand church would await him. So he moved back to Manhattan, preached in a rented auditorium, built a following, and in 1989 bought the stunning building at Fifty-first and Broadway constructed by Warner Brothers as the city's first "talkie" movie house. In 1949 the place had been renamed for Broadway critic and columnist Mark Hellinger, and became a home for live theater. Pastor David changed the name to Times Square Church, which today offers five evangelical interdenominational services a week, three on Sunday. It also hosts a support group for police and firefighters; a fellowship group for lawyers; networking for single mothers; and a ministry for inmates and their families. Here, worshippers hail from all corners of the world, and headsets offer simultaneous translation of Sunday and Tuesday worship in Arabic, Chinese, French, German, Italian, Japanese, Polish, Portuguese, Russian, Spanish, and Tagalog.

It would be heretical for me to suggest that what goes on now is playacting, but as I approach the building I do feel as if I'm headed to a performance. The last Broadway production I saw was on a Popsicle of a night four Januaries ago, celebrating my niece's twenty-first birthday by attending her favorite musical, *Rent*. The exit was what left an impression on me. Written on the back of the theater door was 525,600, the number of minutes in a year, and a key lyric in the production.

What have I seen in the last 525,600? What will I in the next? December 31 is a good day to ponder such things.

I pass the Winter Garden Theater and cross the street toward the TIMES SQUARE CHURCH marquee. Some of the worshippers indeed are dressed for the theater, with their furs and cashmere. I also see puffy snow coats, utilitarian wool, and at least one bomber jacket belonging to a member of the Christian Motorcyclists Association who, according to the lettering on the back, is RIDING FOR THE SON.

Gold shines everywhere in the round multitiered lobby, including all over the cherubs that outglitz even those at St. Peter's. Lines awaiting entry to the sanctuary are Vatican-tourist thick. This is one of the largest theaters on Broadway, seating eighteen hundred, yet I wait a good half hour for one of the gold-blazered ushers to lead me to my place. I imagine that this is the line for heaven, that we are at the mercy of the gold-clad angel who determines how close to God we get to sit. Well, I must have been living right: I am directed to a maroon-upholstered seat three rows from the stage. Sure, my view to the left is obscured, but I'm close enough to count (three) the hair bands on the braided bun of the woman praying at the edge of the stage.

Thirty-two faithful line the stage alongside her, praying silently and deeply, ala Foursquare. Again, there is no altar for the fervent to face. The curtain is up—a disappointment, as I thought I'd get to see the grand raising—and a piano, organ, and drum kit take up the part of the stage I can't see entirely. A dozen plain wooden chairs line the right side, facing the six-sided Plexiglas pulpit planted in the center. I count eighty-three beige choir chairs along the back wall where a large Christmas wreath hangs above a poinsettia plant. There is no cross to be seen, no dove, no smidgen of ecclesiastical symbology.

O, how I love Jesus, sings a smartly suited midthirties white man roaming the stage with a microphone. He's accompanied by a black piano player I can only partially glimpse. The crowd joins in, some of them standing, swaying. The prayerful at the stage stay focused and the woman with the bun faces a giant column where the left side of the stage ends. A man a few feet to her left stands in a corner, as if he's done something bad.

The singer speaks: "You open prison doors and give sight to the spiritually blind . . . You'll never leave your name without a testament to every generation."

Suddenly the quote "God is great" leaps into my mind. Those were supposedly the last words of Saddam Hussein, hanged last night in Baghdad.

"I encourage you to stay in an attitude of worship," the singer says, and that sounds like a good idea so I shove Saddam aside. "We're going to lower the curtain to prepare for worship."

The descent is steady and smooth. Those praying up front continue, like the curtain hadn't just landed feet away.

"Don't go out the same way you came in" is the last thing we hear from the man as the curtain blocks our view. It's one of the first things I heard on this journey, back at First Baptist Spartanburg.

So different is this place from plain FBS. Glitzy wallpaper, wide balcony, a stained glass oval in the ceiling edged with Victorian paintings of young people riding sleighs, skating, and swimming. Seated below those lily-white holidaymakers is the most multicultural congregation I've seen. And another all-adult one, with only four children in view.

Alleluia! Alleluia! Alleluia! You hear them before the curtain begins to rise. We rise as it does, to see every choir seat taken by singers in yellow robes. They sway, they clap: *Our God reigns forever, forever, O God, you reign.* The words appear on a large screen above the stage, and are known by heart by the seven white men, two black men, and one white woman in the chairs set aside for clergy. Everyone moves to the trumpet-heavy calypso music. A sign language interpreter stands before my section, creating the word "soul" by placing his hands together, palms up, and raising them.

"Hallelooooo!" calls out a woman in front of me who'd been reading Peter 2 in her pocket-sized Bible.

The hymns continue. *My God, in him will I trust,* we now sing, and the sign language guy makes "trust," one hand grasped over the other, like climbing a rope. *Jesus you are worthy of all the honor* follows. I think back to the Church of the Brethren. Small and simple. Yesterday, I saw a worn-out man sitting in the subway with a carton labeled BOX OF PRAYERS. Would reaching into that give me more than sitting in this too-grand place listening to hymns performed to showbiz perfection? I'm not won over. But I'll give it time.

I will love you all my days, sings a black baritone in his thirties. The interpreter signs "love" with fisted hands crossed hard and convincingly over his chest.

To my left, a man in his twenties in a dark sweat suit is weeping. The high-energy and packed house reminds me of Mars Hill. The volume, too.

"Good morning to Times Square church on this very last day of 2006! Can you believe how time has flown?" The well-kept middle-aged man asking this after forty minutes of music is white, tall, slim, graying, a bit stodgy, greeting us in an accent that sounds faintly Australian. I'll later learn that this is Senior Pastor Carter Conlon, from Canada, where, along with work in law enforcement, he once shepherded humans (in church) and sheep (on a farm). He wants to know the number of first timers. Maybe three dozen hands raise.

The drummer gives a three count and a gospel tune begins as, without further adieu, blue wax canisters are circulated for our tithing. *Clap your hands with us, stamp your feet with us, lift your voice with us. This is the way we give him praise!*

"Jesus!" "Jesus!" People are whispering.

"Lord hallelooooo" calls out the Peter 2 woman. An hour after the curtain went up, the music ends.

Pastor Carter is at the pulpit now, asking us to look at Exodus, a passage containing rules for keeping a flame burning. Pages turn, a sound both soft and huge here.

"If you are going to say you're Christian today, your husband, your wife, your workplace, the people in your apartment building should see that," he says. "That there's something of God in you. That God is working through human vessels.

"You are a witness of the fact that Jesus Christ is alive. Whatever the reason for us to be here today, all else is stupidity. All is transient. The Kingdom is coming."

"Halleloooo," yells Peter 2.

The hoodie man seated to my right shifts but doesn't raise his head.

Pastor Carter consults notes but speaks easily, gesturing often. "There's no reason for you to be sitting here in spiritual blindness. God says 'I will give you a new heart.' Why in heaven's name would you choose an old way of living?"

"Glory to God!" calls Peter 2.

"It could be where you are is just where God wants you to be. Right in the center of God's work. The devil might come to ask what kind of Christian are you, and everybody hates you. It may be that your testament is the only one that will burn for God.

"We're living in a generation where—at least in New York—many are not gonna read a Bible anymore. The only one might be you, coming in with this oil, a light burning every day."

He pauses, switches gears, says, "Seek in this year with all your heart the other path. Let this be the cry of this church in 2007. God spoke to Pastor David when he founded this church. God said it would be a sending church. I'm not talking about going on a mission trip. Over one hundred nations are represented in this sanctuary."

Pastor Carter charges us to "Go back where no one else can go," be it to our ethnic neighborhoods or even our countries of origin, and speak of our faith there. Then he taps the Bible. "That's the last altar call I will preach for 2006 as we move into 2007. Lead us into the light, help us to honor your name, to stand in the marketplace and say that you are alive."

The congregation rises. The man next to me remains still. The front of the church fills with people. The aisles are jammed with others headed for the stage.

Pastor prays, his face growing red and shiny. "As we move into '07, let us be a testament of God. Let us send eight thousand into this city, from every borough, let your name be lifted up. Thank you, Lord! Thank you, God!"

"Hallelloooo!" I hear a final time as I walk to the back of the church, through a sea of those moving forward. In yet another church, I'm headed in the opposite direction. Toward the door. Though I was heartened by the truly multicultural congregation, I was put off by the glitz and staginess. On the other hand, the truly multicultural congregation is not. They are eating it up, loving the setting and the presentation, getting as much, perhaps, from the service as from the surrounding flash and glamour that doesn't exist in their lives the other six days of the week. As I step out onto Broadway, I realize that the theater district is a good metaphor for a church search. Don't care for one story? Try another. Enjoy the music in this one? Then you might love the show that's two doors down. This production wasn't for me, but there are many others out there, and a seat in each awaits.

THE PORTLAND NEW CHURCH

PORTLAND, MAINE

"This will be an experiential arts service," the minister announces. "We'll do meditation, a drawing from the Kabbalah, we'll sing, we'll dance ..."

I glance at Patricia, wondering if this is more than she bargained for.

Perhaps fearing just such a drawing, singing, meditating experience, few of my friends or family members who've joined me on these weekend trips have actually attended worship. And not because they've been at their own churches—most don't claim one. Most once attended a church but, like so many of our generation, don't any longer. Most consider my yearlong quest interesting, and it has made some think that they might want to browse around the world of religion one day. But that just won't be happening on our Sundays together. So they go off to breakfast or the Sunday papers or bed.

But Patricia wanted to come along. I'm grateful for her being game, and for the time together. I haven't seen her for a year and that's a shame because being in her presence is like pulling up to a spiritual gas pump. A recovering alcoholic sober for nearly six years, she works constantly on her recovery and has accumulated mountains of wisdom. She long ago scaled the second of AA's 12 steps, believing that a power greater than herself could restore her to sanity. Some call that God. Patricia calls it her Higher Power, or simply HP. Her early religious experience was similar to Tanya's, Patricia's parents also encouraging exploration, but she doesn't believe in organized religion.

Despite that, she was willing to enter the Portland New Church, a member of the Swedenborgian Church of North America. As the name suggests, this church began in Sweden. It was named for Emanuel Swedenborg, a scientist at the Swedish Board of Mines who in the early 1740s began to have visions, including that of a New Church, a "spiritual fraternity" consisting of all religions and people striving to live well and in line with their beliefs.

But Swedenborg himself never worked to create such a community. Five years after his death, the New Church was founded in England, a place Swedenborg often visited and where he died. The New Church was carried to America by missionaries and, under the umbrella of the Massachusetts-based Swedenborgian Church of North America, thirty-seven New Churches are now attended by fifteen hundred faithful nationwide. Internationally, sixty-five thousand belong.

I never heard of the religion before Googling while preparing for an annual teaching gig in the area. The Portland churches I'm familiar with are three Catholic ones I went to while attending art school here in the late 1970s. Considering my alma mater, it's a cool coincidence that the arts will be featured today. I think back to the grandeur of last week's house of worship. This small, plain, gray-clapboard church on a busy residential street has the glitz of a shoebox. It does have age over Times Square Church, having been built way back in 1910, but not a flake of gold glows in the sanctuary measuring maybe twenty-five by fifty feet. A bare wooden floor shines beneath a white ceiling spanned by two white pipes from which philodendrons cascade. Nine gray metal-framed maroon-padded chairs have been set in a semicircle facing a small stage where a dark wooden table carved with the alpha *A* holds an open Bible on a gold brocade cloth. Four candles await lighting. To the right, a piano of dark wood promises music.

Seven women, one man, and a ten-year-old boy take their seats. The boy rings a pair of bells joined by a cord and Patricia and I choose the fourth and fifth seats from the left, between the boy and his mother, and the man. Age of the adults is middle and up, skin is white, dress is very casual, clogs, jeans, fleece tops, ethnic jewelry. We're handed fat white plastic binders titled *Joyful Noise, Songbook of The Swedenborgian Church, Portland, Maine* that include a run-through of the service, and music and lyrics for approximately eighty songs. In keeping with the religion's intent, selections cover traditions including Quaker, Hebrew, Christian, and folk in general.

The Reverend Lorraine Kardash, who doubles as choir director, triples as player of the guitar, quadruples as this morning's leader of a church with twenty members, stands at the white wooden pulpit next to a woman she calls Elkie.

"You can call out any you'd like for us to sing," Pastor Lorraine says as Elkie adds, "If we know it!"

"Do you know 221?" the woman to our left asks.

"No."

We settle for number 3, "Canaan's Land." The boy is now coloring, so it's only ten voices attempting the song that repeats *Where the soul of man never dies.*

Emanuel Swedenborg thought those souls formed groups that comprised the most amazing human ever known. But there's nothing about that in the song, or in the next, "Peace Is Flowing Like a River," which we follow through all four verses, the subject switching to hope, joy, and then love. Pastor Lorraine suggests we try 713,

"Song of the Soul," but it's a flop. She smiles anyhow from a face framed by gray hair. In spring-bright clothing this early January morning—white sweater, yellow scarf, green corduroys—she's a joyous-looking sixtyish Swedenborgian, now starting 714, "Turn, Turn, Turn," adapted from the book of Ecclesiastes, words by Pete Seeger.

A time for peace, I swear it's not too late, I hear Patricia singing in a way that makes you believe her.

We sit and sing for fifteen more minutes. Then the man and Elkie light the candles on the stage. "The open Bible is one of the many sacred books in the world and is a symbol that God's love is bound and open to us all," Elkie reads, adding that we honor Emanuel Swedenborg in this open, safe place.

Pastor Lorraine stands and announces, "Instead of a children's talk today we're going to do a dance!"

One of my Portland experiences of nearly thirty years ago was a Harry Chapin concert during which Harry choreographed the audiences' moves to the band's music. I loved Harry, but have never loved a forced dance. And do not now. Patricia whispers that if there were more people here, we could easily sit this out. But with only ten of us, nonparticipation is noticed. We join the others as Pastor Lorraine strums and Elkie leads us in a circle. Yes, we have to both dance and sing. *Wade in the water, children, wade in the water . . .*

We wade, clap in time, circle in awkward weddings-only Hava Nagila. I watch Patricia intently following Elkie's lead and I thank my HP for such a good sport of a friend. And for the conclusion of the experience, which, for me, held no particular spiritual element other than the reminder of Patricia's nature.

Announcements follow, including the date of a talk comparing Emanuel Swedenborg and Martin Luther King Jr. The flyer I picked up at the door mentions others: "Spirituality from India," and "Healing with the Moon."

For now, there is a drawing to make: the tree of life from the mystical Kabbalah, the ancient Hebrew text that has influenced both pop singer Madonna and Emanuel Swedenborg.

"The tree of life is the main symbol in the Kabbalah," Pastor Lorraine is telling us. "I've seen it for years. I even had a business called the Tree of Life. But I never knew what it was."

What it is isn't a tree but a diagram of ten connecting circles that illustrate the beginning of the universe, and man's place in that universe. To create this, drawing boards, pencils, paper, and tiny plastic cups are passed around as Pastor Lorraine tells us, "Each sphere relates to an aspect of the divine." We'll trace the ten over an outline of a human body because, she says, all ten emanations of God are also represented in us. "Some are on the more negative side, some on the more positive side. You don't try to shut them off; you try to find a balance.

"Say you're compassionate, in excess. Your restraint is not as developed. A beggar asks you for money and you give him the one hundred dollars in your pocket. Then you have no money to feed yourself or your family. You need balance."

We're directed to trace the cups in correspondence with a drawing at the pulpit, circles hovering over different areas of the body. "If there are problems in your head and neck area, emotional problems, one in the top three is out of whack," Pastor Lorraine tells us. "What is your spiritual life? How are you feeling about yourself? As you meditate on the spheres, you have to ask yourself, 'Where am I?' "

The breathy sound of pencil on paper is all that can be heard as we work away, coloring our circles. Pastor Lorraine tells us that the Kabbalah goes hand in hand with the Torah. Then she instructs us, "Go inward, become mystical. The tools are singing, music, praying, meditation, affirmation."

We draw lightning bolts from one circle to the next. "What are you feeling as you see the lightning strike each sphere?" Pastor asks.

My unspoken answer is that it's just nice to be doing some art, an annual line on my New Year's resolution list that gets nowhere near the attention it should. I've never drawn in church, and doing so makes me wonder why. I think of Susan, who always has a sketchbook in her bag, and draws everywhere: at concerts, on trains, in the intensive care unit. It's part of what she does and who she is. It's part of me, too, but it's fallen to the roadside as I've steamed ahead with other forms of creativity, including writing. If nothing else happens this morning, I will be grateful for the reminder of that, and for these moments spent quietly in that zone entered through making something, which I visited regularly in those four years of study across town.

"You can feel right in your body where you are," Pastor Lorraine is saying. "Unless you can feel, you won't heal. Ask God, who is your partner, to enlighten you in some way. To correct you, tell you what changes you can start to make."

I don't know which represent the need to do more art, but I guess it might be the top three emotion ones, and color them in my favorite green.

Then we're on to chanting, repeating the consonants making up the name of God in Hebrew: *Yud Hay Vav Hay.*

"Breathe in the sacred name of Jehovah into the areas of your body where you need healing," instructs Pastor Lorraine, who's playing a CD of crackling fire followed by voices chanting those letters. It's another experience similar to that down in Newport, the sounds transporting the mind to an ancient cave, and it's over too soon as we stand in a circle again.

We're asked to hold hands, and I take Patricia's right and the man's left. We're asked to speak our needs and pray for them. Members mention a business decision, the anniversary of a daughter's death, a son's new path in life, the earth, the weird weather. A voice to the left says, "For a woman, I don't even know her name, she was killed in South America, she was a nurse." I remember the story on the front page of the *Portland Press Herald*. A city nurse on a humanitarian trip dies after a road accident. I think of her. I think of Dominick. I think of Tommy. I think of Patricia. I think of the gift of being here. Of course I don't say any of that.

A basket is passed. Dollar bills pile. Our hour is over.

The boy is allowed the thrill of extinguishing the candles. The door of the church is open. Our trees of life sway in the wind.

At a breakfast place in which we each indulge in one enormous pancake, Patricia tells me she enjoyed the morning's unorthodox form of worship. She says she'd think of returning. I shouldn't be too surprised; this is a soul as open as the pair of small sculpted hands we find in the window of the New Agey giftshop she takes me to next. It's a duplicate of the sculpture she sent me a few weeks ago for Christmas. Filled with tiny multicolored nuggets, it arrived with this legend: "Life is a gift from God. Day after day, he showers us with His most precious stones. Beauty, Love, Abundance, Life!" The idea is to pour the stones into the hands daily, to be reminded of what we are being given. I don't have my pair along with me this morning, but I have received reminders aplenty anyhow.

HOLY CROSS POLISH NATIONAL CATHOLIC CHURCH

HAMTRAMCK, MICHIGAN

At the conclusion of this morning's service, a congregation member spots my party of three and offers to answer any questions. My friend Lil asks her about the elderly man who's remained in his pew after everyone else has gone home.

"Oh, he's wonderful," the woman replies. "I went to school with his daughters. His wife died several years ago."

These facts could be any man's. But they fascinate me. Because this man is wearing a Roman collar. He's a priest, retired from assignment here at Holy Cross Polish National Catholic Church, one in a denomination riding many rails paralleling Catholicism, but veering off when it comes to following the pope (no connection to Rome), running a church (parish members hire clergy and own the church buildings), and requiring priests to be celibate (many, as was the case with the previously mentioned elderly cleric, are married with children).

Looking at him and hearing that he has daughters and once had a wife is like looking at water and being told it's sand. It's hard for me to compute all this while standing in a very Catholic-like church.

Not surprisingly, the Polish National Catholic Church was begun by a Catholic Pole, immigrant Franciszek Hodur, who was ordained the year he arrived, 1893. His parishioners included fellow immigrants and, on their behalf, Father Hodur unsuccessfully petitioned the Vatican for cultural inclusion, including the naming of a Polish bishop. Dissatisfied, he started the PNCC in Scranton in 1897 and was excommunicated in 1898. Nine years later, he was consecrated as a bishop by the Dutch Old Catholics, one of several national churches disconnected from Rome.

For about one hundred years, the PNCC was part of an international league of non–Roman Catholic churches known as the Union of Utrecht. But recent disagreements over issues like homosexuality and the ordination of women led the liberal-leaning union to expel the conservative-leaning PNCC in 2003. Today it remains this country's only Catholic Church that does not recognize the pope but maintains relations with the Roman Catholic and Orthodox churches, and belongs to the World Council of Churches. Accurate membership figures are unavailable, but estimates range anywhere from 30,000 to 250,000.

There's long been a Polish National Catholic Church in the town next to mine, and Calvary's Light–like damnation threats to any of us who might venture inside, but as I researched the faith, I found a dynamic suburban Detroit pastor whose story drew me here.

You might not automatically attach the adjective "dynamic" to the Reverend Jaroslaw Nowak, who during today's 9:30 a.m. Mass seemed shy and unsure. But for the past year he has driven to Toledo, Ohio, once a weekend to say Mass for thirty-five people in a basement cafeteria. The congregants of Resurrection Parish lost their regular Roman Catholic church home in 2005, when Toledo bishop Leonard Blair closed seventeen houses of worship.

A native of Poland who, like founder Hodur, originally was a Catholic priest, Father Jaroslaw joined the PNCC in 1994, five years before emigrating. Home base for the forty-two-year-old husband and father of two is the sturdy red brick church on Pulaski Street in 2.2-square-mile Hamtramck, just north of Detroit. Poles flocked here in the early 1900s for work at the Dodge Brothers factory, and it's still a city of immigrants, with Stan's Grocery ("The Best Polish

Food"), Bengal Masala Café, Beirut Hair Salon, and Aladdin Sweets vying for customers. Late last year, the Polish American community watched as its Our Lady Help of Christians Catholic Church became a mosque.

Inside Holy Cross, I take the second seat from the back in the left-hand set of fifteen blond wood pews with maroon vinyl kneelers. There's something Newark-homey and very Old World about the cream-colored sanctuary, its large altar, crucified ray-encircled Jesus suspended above, stained glass windows with illustrations of John baptizing Jesus, Jesus as shepherd, and a bearded Arlo Guthrie of a God. Chalk taps as hymn numbers are written on a board in the choir loft. Each seatback offers hat clips a good fifty years after President Kennedy killed the American haberdashery market by deciding to go bareheaded at his inauguration. Christmas decorations including a tree and a crèche remain displayed despite this being January 28. A polka hit at this time of year is "I Wanna Be Polish for Christmas," the lyrics of which express envy over the length of time Poles spend celebrating Christ's birthday. And even though volunteers will remove decorations today, the celebration is not yet over: the stapled six-page black-on-white Holy Cross bulletin mentions the Polish custom of the parish pastor blessing homes between January 6 and February 2.

In the wooden seat pocket I find a pink booklet titled *The Sacrament of Penance—General Confession for Adults, Private Confession for Youth, Prayers and Examination Of Conscience*. A lamb on the cover raises its head from its barbwire entrapment and *baaas* at a cross. There's a *Good News Bible*, "Today's English Version," and a black hardcover titled *Modlitwnik PNKK*, its contents in Polish. Inside I find 188 pages of familiar hymns: "Ludu Mój Ludu," "Przybieżeli do Betlejem Pasterze," and the "W Żłobie Leży" that started every Midnight Mass of my childhood.

At eight forty-five, Pastor Jaroslaw enters in a green cassock with a gold cross on the front. He is of medium height and build and his dark hair with its rounded widow's peak is worn short. He is attended by a pair of altar girls, a taller dark-haired girl and a shorter blonde. Parishioners bless themselves, reach for the pink booklets for the penitential litany. Father asks, "Please make an examination of your consciences and confess your sins to God."

After allowing enough time for this all-white, largely sixty-and-up saintly looking crowd of sixteen to silently admit the infractions their souls bear, Pastor Jaroslaw begins the confiteor, in which each of us admits that, by our sins, "I have broken the bonds uniting me with my Creator." The booklet instructs us to strike our breasts as we continue: "By my fault, by my fault, by my own great fault."

We are absolved and given the penance that must be universal: one Our Father and one Hail Mary, which we recite in Polish.

The confession completed, Father Jaroslaw walks to the pew of the old priest who will later catch Lil's attention. There Father kneels in the aisle as the elder makes the sign of the cross over his head and says, in Polish: "*Wymię Ojca i Śyna i Ducha Świętego, Amen.*" He prays as Father Jaroslaw taps his left breast three times. Here is a priest publicly saying that he, too, has fallen. That he, too, needs forgiveness and absolution. Watching this, I get the sand and water feeling for the first time today. I've known good priests and I've known bad priests. I have never seen any from either category publicly admit a wrong.

As for me, I admit that I did not keep holy the two previous Lord's Days. But it wasn't for lack of trying. Two Sundays ago I missed my date to worship with the Jehovah's Witnesses while still in Maine because I not only got locked out of my car but did so while it was running, and in an ice storm that prevented swift rescue by the AAA. Last week, I traveled to West Virginia and was able to keep my car keys in hand but the same type of storm kept me off the road leading to a service at the preeminent Pentecostal Signs Following (read: snake handling) church in all of Appalachia.

But I've made it to Michigan, where the Mass begins with Father Jaroslaw saying, "The Lord rebuilds Jerusalem, gathers the dispersed of Israel." We reply, "Heals the brokenhearted, binds up their wounds." I wonder where Lil and Dave are. Having recently moved to Detroit from Philadelphia for newspaper work, these friends whom I met through Tanya are unfamiliar with Hamtramck, but wanted to meet me this morning, Patricia style, for both church and breakfast. A mid-fifties man in dark jacket, gray shirt, metal glasses, and comb-over walks to the pulpit. He reads from Nehemiah, Ezra's "Today is holy to the Lord your God. Do not be sad, and do not weep." This happy-day message ends with the good news that Lil and Dave have arrived. They pull into my pew, Lil in neat woolen suit and Dave in blazer and tie, and the reverence of clothing choices is touching.

They join me in listening to the second reading, one of my biblical faves, mentioned during my visit to Brown Memorial CME, 1 Corinthians' reminder of all the gifts we have to share. Pastor Jaroslaw then takes the pulpit to give us the Gospel from Luke 1, which, like the previous readings, is printed in the bulletin, this particular passage also translated into Polish. Luke unrolls a scroll written by the prophet Isaiah and finds the words "The Spirit of the Lord is upon me, because he has anointed me to bring glad tidings to the poor. He has sent me to proclaim liberty to captives and recovery of sight to the blind, to let the oppressed go free, and to proclaim a year acceptable to the Lord."

The idea of it is wonderful but daunting. It might be hard to get through five minutes acceptable to the Lord, what with looking around in jealousy or judgment or any of that other stuff we're not supposed to do. A whole year?

"Niech będzie pochwalony Jezus Chrystus!"

We answer this "Blessed be the name of Jesus" with *"Na wieki wieków, Amen."* A version of "For the ages."

The altar girls take seats on the altar steps. Pastor Jaroslaw begins his sermon, speaking very slowly.

"Jesus was the Messiah who came to save the world," he tells us. "We know what happened. He was rejected. He is in front of us on this table. He will be present here on this altar. He will wait for us. What kind of decision will we make? Will we recognize him as God or will we reject him?"

Father Jaroslaw reminds us that today many do not see Jesus as the world's savior. "My sisters and brothers, we call ourselves Christians, Catholics, we believe Jesus is the Son of God, we have this opportunity today and every time we participate in the holy Mass, we can receive him. And his blessings. We really need that. We know how to follow this day the teachings of Jesus. How hard it is to confess to others the teaching of Jesus Christ. Not just by word but by our lives."

Father uses no notes but sounds like he could have borrowed Pastor Carter's from New Year's Eve Sunday: Be an example. In our neighborhoods, in our countries of origin. Maybe just beneath our own roofs. I liked the idea a few weeks ago, and I like it again. I wonder what Lil and Dave got from the message but when I do take a peek at them, I just get the kind of smiles that say how happy they are to see me after a year or two. They're newspaper people, so I know they're also busy observing.

The brief sermon is followed by a few bits of housekeeping. The second collection is for the Music Scholarship fund. The Superbowl party will be held next week, complete with big screen, fitting for the big interest in this football-mad state.

The Nicene Creed is recited, and includes a genuflection between the lines "He was born of the Virgin Mary" and "And became man."

Away in the manger, the choir sings as two men with baskets begin to walk down the aisle.

An altar girl rings the bell and Father turns to remove the Communion chalice from its nook in the altar.

Everyone but Lil, Dave, the choir, and me walks to the front and kneels at the railing with its closed gate. Though I'm in such a familiar setting, this still isn't a church to which I belong, so I again refrain from receiving. But I do watch—mainly because I haven't seen this posture for receiving since Vatican II removed the railings in the '60s. The taller girl holds the paten in gloved hands and a long white cloth is draped over the rail. Each communicant places his or her hands beneath the cloth as the priest approaches and places a wafer on each tongue. I find the scene poignant, from another era. Father Jaroslaw next brings his chalice to the back of the church and upstairs to the singing choir. I'm struck by this room service, another thing I've never seen a priest do except for delivering a host to a disabled person in the first or second row.

A bell is rung each time a wafer is given, making it easy for me to count ten people in the loft.

A Polish hymn is begun by a man and answered by the women.

I'm not familiar with it, but do know the words *do Bethejem*—"to Bethlehem." Where I can say I've been. As I now can say I've been to a church that is very much like the one I know best, yet in my community once was considered different enough to have fallen under the long-ago warning to stay away.

After the service, my friends and I linger. Lil has traveled a lot for work in the past few years and tells me she often found herself entering Catholic churches along the way. She was raised Catholic but her divorce prevented her from participating in the sacraments. "I knew I couldn't take Communion," she says. "I didn't want to be a part of something in which I couldn't be accepted completely." She's now comfortable in Dave's Presbyterian faith, which she finds more intellectual and respectful. But both Lil and Dave enjoyed this church's decor, which they say reminds them of the interiors of small churches they've visited in Italy. They want to get a closer look, so we walk to the crèche, to the flickering votives in their heart-shaped holder. We receive the impromptu tour from the woman who had attended school with the older priest's children, who tells us that even though she's living far away now, this church remains her home. She's glad we've visited, and invites us to return. I'm glad I visited. If only to dispel another myth, to learn that this church, these people, like so many of the other churches and congregants I've visited this year, aren't so different after all.

KYKOTSMOVI MENNONITE CHURCH

KYKOTSMOVI VILLAGE, HOPI NATION

Don't use your camera—you could have it taken away."

I wonder if Wallace knows gullibility when he sees it. This clerk at the Tsakurshovi Hopi Arts and Crafts Gallery might trade in jokey DON'T WORRY, BE HOPI T-shirts, but he assures me he's not kidding about the warning.

Proof comes later via the big blue sign at the entrance to the village where I'll be going to church. While in Kykotsmovi, I read, there's to be no photographing, sound recording, hiking of foot trails, removal of objects, or sketching. These rules have nothing to do with the cliché of stealing a soul. They have everything to do with respect. Kykotsmovi, like the communities on the rest of the three hundred reservations within the United States of America, is not a theme park. It's someone's home. I, the guest, stash the camera and continue driving.

These 10.7 square miles of ochre rock are unlike anything my used-to-greenery eyes have ever seen. The village was founded in 1890 by a group from nearby Oraibi, the oldest continuously inhabited settlement within America, established in approximately 1100. Kykotsmovi, sometimes called New Oraibi, translates to "Mound of Ruined Houses." I don't see ruins as I roll my rental car to a stop a five-hour drive north of Phoenix. Mary's younger sister has just moved to that area, so Mary and I made the trip. She guided me through the Sunday morning Greek Orthodox service in Newport but I'll give her a rest this morning, as she, like me, knows nothing about Mennonites, whose pale pinkish-tannish church stands just before the Kykotsmovi General Store.

Mennonites are often shelved next to the Amish by many who picture members with simple wardrobes and without modern conveniences. But the approximately twenty American Mennonite groups range from those in line with modest simplicity to those who more resemble your average tube-watching car-driving stuff-accumulating neighbor. All see Jesus as the center of life and worship and consider the Bible the inspired Word of God. All are part of a community of 1 million in sixty countries following a faith founded 475 years ago by people who didn't believe Martin Luther's reforms were extreme enough. In 1525 they began rebaptizing one another. A Dutch Friesland priest named Menno Simons disconnected himself from Catholicism in 1536, plugged into the Anabaptists, and eventually inspired the name of this new faith.

Many Mennonites refuse military service, and protest related costs and/or delete from their tax payments the percentage funding defense. They often volunteer locally and internationally and in times of disaster. The church's missionary work is one of their trademarks, and the church in Kykotsmovi, here since 1941 but in its second building, is an example of the work of converting Native Americans to European religious traditions.

Hopi tribal beliefs based in the natural world have been the target of missionaries since the first—a group of Catholic priests—arrived in 1592 and spent the next ninety years in conversion efforts. Not much of what they had to say matched local doctrine. For starters, in the Hopi religion, Taiowa the sun-father and nephew Sotuknang created the world, and it was a spider woman named Kokyangwuti who came up with the great idea of humans. Those humans caused such problems that Sotuknang annihilated the surface of the earth. Some escaped by heading inside the world, and belief in the link between the upper and lower realms remains key in stories and ceremonies marking events from birth to death.

On this Superbowl Sunday morning at 9:30, twenty-four people are seated in the church's brown metal-framed chairs for a service that will be solely in the Mennonite tradition, with not even a nod given to a spider woman or sun-father. Several hymns will utilize the native language, but that'll be it for any hint that we're in a totally different country, the Hopi Nation, which is located within the Navajo Nation, which is surrounded by the American state of Arizona. The sterility of the liturgy makes me sad. A glance out the windows at the surrounding Spartan village underlines the fact that the Hopi don't live lives of excess. Why not leave them their faith? There are no statistics revealing what percentage of the tribe's twelve thousand members practice either native or Christian religions, but even if it's a sliver who've switched, the presence of a white church seems wrong. And, as I'll come to learn when members testify later this morning, it's a source of spiritual and community strife—even for converts. Natives might come to believe in and love the Christian God. What does that say about their connection and commitment to their embattled culture?

It doesn't look like many of Kykotsmovi's younger members have to worry about such conflicts. This morning, worshippers' average age is sixty. Dress is very casual—more fleece and hoodies. Males are scant, only three men and one boy, as are Caucasians—one of the men, a teen girl and her mother, and I. My seat in the last row is covered by a copy of *Hopi Gospel Songs for Church and Street Services in Hopi-Land*. Compiled by the missionaries under the division of the Mennonite and Baptist Mission Boards, the majority of its songs are hybrids created, the book tells me, "by the native Christians to some tune they learned from the missionaries at home or away in some Government Indian School. They made them when they were alone with God all day, either behind a flock of sheep or at some other work where they could meditate on the things of God so dear to the heart."

On the little shelf below the seat in front of me is a brown book with the golden words *Loma' tuawti- ta ta'wi* on its cover and a small design that looks like a candle. I also find a red hardcover Bible not unlike that from a hotel room nightstand drawer, this one indeed marked with PLACED BY THE GIDEONS.

A short dark-haired woman in her late forties wearing a white long-sleeved shirt and dark slacks walks to the front of the cement-floored room and stands at the wooden pulpit with its silver microphone. Behind her is a wall covered by white draperies. On a riser, an altar table is carved with IN REMEMBRANCE OF ME and holds an open Bible and a fake flower arrangement. Similarly artificial trees grow at the altar sides. I see no crosses.

"Saying 'I'm just human' is an easy way to get out of things," the woman begins. "I need to show others what a Christian should be."

I don't know how I pick up on it but this woman's name is Zelda. She directs us on Christian conduct, asking God to help us "follow your way, come into our lives, work through us."

Now Lorna Epp, wife of Pastor Larry Epp, dressed in red sweater, red plaid skirt, black stockings and shoes, walks to the piano and plays expertly the intro to number 574, "If My People's Hearts Are Humble" and the room sings gamely *If they pray and seek my face, If they turn away from evil, I will not withhold my grace.*

We go from that to number 539, "O That Will Be Glory," to number 526, "All That Thrills My Soul." I do OK with these, but it's a different story as we move to hymns in the Hopi book. There's no translation for "I tam hak tumalaiyunwni," or "Pam Nuyhurs Nua," but I love hearing the hard-consonanted language. The second hymn is over too quickly and Zelda is saying, "Now let's meet everybody." There is a circular routine, those from the chairs on one side walking against the movement of those from the other, no hand going unshaken.

Pastor Larry is up front announcing the collection, and a basket is passed. I hand it two seats to my right, to the white teen wearing jeans and holding a copy of *The Jesus Bible* in her lap. Larry prays in thanks for the small basket that overflows with so many bills that some fall to the floor. With his salt-and-pepper hair swept to his right side, in wire-rimmed glasses, maroon-and-black-striped button-down shirt, and dark pants, Larry has a question: "What is worship?"

Zelda says, "Spending time with God." Someone else ventures "Praying," another "Singing."

Larry doesn't give a right or wrong, just continues with the power of a motivational speaker. "Let me ask you: Do you ever come to church asking what am I gonna get out of this?"

This past year I have asked myself that many times. The hope has been that I'd get lots—of inspiration and insight regarding what the many branches of Christianity this country has to offer. The year has taken on a life of its own as I tick off a church visited only to read about or hear of fifteen more that sound compelling. I return from these long weekends or weeks to find my side of the dining room table piled with pertinent newspaper and magazine clippings Tommy has saved for me—on religious trends, unusual beliefs, the latest on one of the more well-known churches I've already visited. The volume of ideas reminds me of a comment made by a veteran New York City restaurant critic, who said there were so many eateries in existence, and opening each and every day, that she could eat five times a day for a lifetime and still not hit each one. The same could be said for religions of any type. Worship on the hour every hour still wouldn't cover every building or branch. It can be overwhelming to choose which to visit next, so I'm not joking when I say that I rely on Southwest, but also on divine guidance. I'd wanted to include Mennonites in this year, and then Anne moved to

Phoenix, and Googling found me this church on this reservation. If venturing into other Christian churches has given me the feel of being very far from my Roman Catholic roots, today I truly am.

But I don't feel unwelcome, and I'm enjoying listening to Larry, who's easy talking, smiling, gesturing with wedding ring shiny even though Lorna put it on his finger way back in 1960. I appreciate his positivity as he talks about the energy of the disciples. "They changed the world! You know what? You and I can change this world, too. If we follow God, we can truly make a difference in this world."

He asks, "How many of you got up this morning and thought, 'I want to go to church today and I want God to speak to me?' " He gets no answers. "It's the best place to be on a Sunday morning. But sometimes when we do things out of habit, it becomes rote. We need to come with eagerness: 'I can hardly wait to get there to see what God has to say!' "

Larry has another question, and says the answer is between God and each of us. "What is he asking you to do this morning? Did he get your attention? Did he stop you from something you're doing? Don't ignore God."

Then he quotes Christian author Max Lucado: "God loves you just the way you are, but he refuses to leave you that way." Then, to close, adds one of his own: "God is in the business of changing lives and he uses his Word to do that."

The Longer I serve him, Lorna leads, *the sweeter he grows, the more that I serve him, the more love he bestows.*

The ninety-minute service is over, but the testimonies have yet to begin. Zelda is up front again, encouraging the sharing of how God has worked in our lives. Ivan, a middle-aged man in a blue fleece jacket, praises Pastor Larry who, along with Lorna, soon will be leaving the village after nine years of service. Ivan is concerned that the new pastor will be Hopi, and how he will be regarded by the tribe. "Hopis don't support one another," says Ivan. "We must put a shield around him."

Then he begins to speak his native language. He gestures, spreading his arms wide and moving from side to side as if being pulled in either direction. His eyes meet mine at some points and I think, of course, he's got to be talking about me.

But he's not, as I learn when he soon apologizes for speaking Hopi, saying there are some things so close to the heart that he can only say them in his native language.

"Some of the older ones, we know how you came here," he says. "Not to belittle the others, but white people came in a boat over the oceans. Some for freedom of religion. We did not. And when you hear the drums, like we did last weekend, it pulls at your heart. You feel pulled from one side to the other." He does the open-arm gesture again, and his dilemma is clear. He now adores an imported God, but the ties to his original religion are in his blood. He might easily be someone who'd attended one church her entire life but who wants to explore others. And often enough feels a homesickness for the faith of her youth, often enough wonders where is the right place for her heart and soul. A woman to the right of me raises her hand to tell how her native language helps her understand the Bible of her adopted religion. "I've been a Christian a really long time," she tells us. "But I didn't get what I was supposed to get out of a sermon. I finally came to my senses. Read the Bible in Hopi. Read it from Matthew to Revelations. I dream in Hopi. Read the Bible in Hopi and you'll know what the Bible really means to a person . . . Because you all think in Hopi, right?"

To her right, a woman in her fifties says: "I know that God/Jesus is the only answer. But, like Ivan, I'm torn with our Hopi culture. It's like you're being pulled in two ways. You're not sure what to become. Prayer is the only answer."

Zelda has advice: "You just have to let God do his work in your life. It's not just Hopi tradition, it's other stuff. Sometimes, if you are on a fence, let God do his will in your life. If you're always in control, it's hard."

The half hour of testimony concludes. But like at The Riverside Church, we remain seated, and we remain focused. The honesty that's been revealed in the room is as real as the rock beneath this building.

Nam I tano God u mu ma, the congregation sings, and I recognize the melody to the hymn with the hopeful wish of "God Be with You 'Til We Meet Again."

I leave town without making a sound recording. I take no photos. I don't even venture a quick sketch. I won't need any of that to remember what I've seen and heard here today in this country within a country within my own.

KINGDOM HALL OF JEHOVAH'S WITNESSES

MILWAUKIE, OREGON

Normally, the Jehovah's Witnesses come to my door. Today, I will go to theirs.

I've chosen to visit this notoriously dogged religious group here in Portland, Oregon, because both the city and the state are among the least churched in America. I had planned to visit them in Maine three weeks ago when I had the accident with the keys and the ice storm. But here on the other side of the country, Kingdom Hall—the name for the building in which the Jehovah's Witnesses worship—sits in a quiet suburb not unlike the thousands that many of this religion's 5.6 million members crisscross while evangelizing and distributing copies of the magazines *Awake!* and *Watchtower.*

Known as Jehovah's Witnesses only since 1931, the Watch Tower Bible and Tract Society originated in the Adventist teaching of Pittsburgh evangelist Charles Taze Russell, who believed Jesus Christ had returned to the earth invisibly in 1874 to prepare for the Kingdom of God anticipated to arrive in 1914. Russell had been raised Presbyterian and during childhood chalked Bible verses onto sidewalks, warning of the fires of hell. At thirteen, he switched to Congregationalism, and at sixteen questioned his faith altogether. In the tradition of so many of the leaders I've learned about this year, he scanned the religion menu and ordered up teachings on faiths including Buddhism and Taoism, but nothing satisfied his spiritual palate until, at age eighteen, Russell heard Adventist preacher Jonas Wendell.

The year 1874, which Wendell had preached was the year of Christ's return, came and went. But that didn't dampen Russell's new fervor for the Bible, and Christians' responsibility for spreading the word.

That spreading has always confused me. Believers say only 144,000 righteous will be resurrected to heaven, along with an unnumbered "great multitude," leaving the rest of us sleeping in death until we're resurrected to nowhere greater than the earth we already were done with. I don't know about you, but if I believed that only a few were going to get the greatest reward, I don't think that I'd eagerly be selling more tickets to the lottery.

But the Witnesses do. Their door-to-door ministry is one of the few facts most of us know about them, along with their refusal to honor symbols of nationhood and to accept blood transfusions, and the lightning speed with which they build their halls, often in as little as two or three days.

Unknown by most nonmembers is the faith's contribution to First Amendment freedoms. The group's legal clashes over proselytizing resulted in twenty-three Supreme Court rulings from 1938 to 1946 alone. I'm all for the First Amendment, so I'm curious to see what goes on in a Kingdom Hall.

Half an hour before the 10:00 a.m. service of the North Congregation (the 4:00 p.m. is *en Español*) cars arrive at this one-story brick-and-clapboard building twenty minutes outside Portland.

My greeters to this morning's Public Meeting and Watchtower Study are three women my age who ask, "What hall are you from?"

Uh-oh.

"Well, I'm from Massachusetts," I start, and that's enough to change the subject.

"Massachusetts! That's so far away!"

They welcome me to the blue sanctuary area, where I join sixty-two congregants chatting quietly. It's fifty-fifty male/female, average age a youngish forty-five. Only one worshipper, a woman behind me, is black. Only nine appear to be under eighteen. Each and every person is in Sunday best.

The three sections of teal pews with light-hued movie-theater armrests can hold approximately two hundred. The side walls are light blue. With no windows, and a low acoustic-tiled ceiling, the room feels close. Up front, against a powder-blue curtain, a stage-like area holds a pair of teal-upholstered chairs, a wooden pulpit, and a floral arrangement. A panel at the left informs that "The Great Day of Jehovah Is Near—Zephaniah 1:14." I see no cross.

"Welcome to this morning's public talk and Watchtower Study," announces a man at the pulpit. He's about forty-five, in a dark suit with light tie and shirt. He doesn't introduce himself, but it's not because he's the assigned pastor—there are no such things in this religion. All baptized members, including children, may participate in services, though they're traditionally led by elders.

This elder announces that congregant John Sheer will be speaking on "What Is Behind the Spirit of Rebellion?" But only after a governmental-sounding hymn, "Loyally Submitting to Theocratic Order."

I don't have a book, and there are no seat pockets, but a woman to my right offers to share, introducing herself as Debbie. She tells me she can't sing, then proves it as, to recorded music, we do our best with the first of three verses: *As Jehovah's people sound throughout the earth / Truths about the Kingdom, of such priceless worth / Theocratic order they must all obey?/ And remain united, loyalty display.*

The man up front praises God, and the "wonderful illustration you've used in setting up your organization." I've never heard the world, or heaven, or whatever this man is referring to, called an organization. It sounds like something TV mobster Tony Soprano should be running. But I do like the compassion of his request that we be loving and kind to one another because "people are truly skinned and thrown around in life."

Brother Sheer, salt-and-pepper hair, bushy mustache, wire-rimmed glasses, olive suit with yellow shirt and print tie, takes the microphone and tells us about antitax demonstrations in Bolivia in 2004 that left twenty-two dead and more than one hundred injured.

"That's just one of the ways a rebellious spirit manifests itself," he says. "Through protests, even violence. Right now, we're living in what you could call an era of rebellion . . . children against their parents, against authority, engaging in sexual activity, smoking marijuana, involved in lewdness, drugs, shootings . . ."

Brother Sheer traces the problem back to the 1940s. "After World War II something broke down in child rearing," he says. "Those born after the '40s can't accept authority." History proves this is not a good thing, he adds. "The first human couple on the earth rebelled against Jehovah. They lost the eternal life they had a chance for. Change is not always good."

He says that rebellions have always happened, but "it's a bad alternative, a bad inclination to want to rebel against authority and do your own thing." He mentions the '60s and says that today there's something in the air. "A kind of moral decline. No faith. The average person wants peace out there, but Satan doesn't want us to have peace on earth." He says rebellion, while sometimes for a good cause, almost always gets out of hand.

"In the Middle East we have people who blow themselves up in crowds of people, trying to change something. It doesn't really make sense."

As for those of us here in Milwaukie, "We need to check ourselves," Brother Sheer says. "If we find ourselves rebelling against Jehovah or his organization, or the Bible in any little way, nip it in the bud."

There's no segue to his next topic. "The women's lib movement," he starts, "while its initial points were good for some people, by making things better for women, there were a lot of bad side effects. Women want their own careers. There is less attention on the family and husbands. The families fall apart and it's a sad state of affairs."

I look around. No one in here is rolling their eyes, women aren't elbowing each other as if to say, "Get a load of him."

"Whether or not they're sincere," Brother Sheer continues, "rebellions are not solving mankind's problems. True Christians don't get involved in rebellion against government."

I look around again. Nothing.

Brother points us to Proverbs 24, verses 21 and 22: "My son, fear the Lord and the king; have nothing to do with those who rebel against them. For suddenly arises the destruction they send, and the ruin from either one, who can measure?"

"That's a scripture to always remember," Brother Sheer says. "To not get involved in any kind of marches or demonstration. Because they're downright fruitless."

I'm glad he next asks the question: "So, what's the solution? The Bible points us to Jehovah God and his Kingdom. Submitting ourselves to that king is the only thing that will solve mankind's basic problems.

"Among Jehovah's Witnesses worldwide, the worldwide brotherhood, even in times of war, are neutral to these things. They will never go and pick up arms and kill a fellow man. It's wonderful to see Jehovah's instruction of his people is working."

He extends an invitation to associate with Jehovah's Witnesses. "What group would you want to be in? I know the guys that sound good to me."

Applause follows his nearly fifty-minute talk, then the pulpit is given back to the original speaker, who reminds us, "Our opportunity to learn more and give praise to Jehovah is only half over." It's time to join with Brother Thorne in the Watchtower Study.

But I'm not ready to move on. My head is still spinning. Keep quiet? Don't make waves? Change is bad? How did Brother Sheer's people get here? Probably as mine did, as immigrants fed up with their lot in another country, so they marched. What about the rights that keep him and his fellow Witnesses free to walk door to door and say whatever the heck they like? How easily does he think those —including the ones gained by his own religion—were won? And don't get me started on the rights of women. This weekend's travel partner is longtime friend Margaret. She holds down a job, but that wasn't what ended her marriage. It was the alcoholic spouse who struck both her and whatever child was on his radar. She had to rebel. She had to end the marriage. Would Brother Sheer tell her to remain in it?

The religion's *Watchtower* magazine gives an answer: "The Christian apostle Paul wrote: "*If she should actually depart*, let her remain unmarried or else make up again with her husband" (1 Corinthians

7:10–16). Since the Bible does not forbid separation in extreme circumstances, what a woman does in this matter is a personal decision (Galatians 6:5). No one should coax a wife to leave her husband, but neither should anyone pressure a battered woman to stay with an abusive man when her health, life, and spirituality are threatened."

Copies of the *Watchtower* are in the hands of the congregation as Brother Thorne and Brother Star, both in their forties, step to the front of the sanctuary.

Brother Star reads an Old Testament passage about a feast that brought together the community. Brother Thorne plays teacher—"What issues did this raise? Let's see—Sister Hebert?" Two teen boys in suits rush a microphone to her, in the style of the old *Phil Donahue Show*.

"Satan said humans would only serve Jehovah out of self-interest," answers Sister Hebert.

"Sister Crocks?"

"The angel spent 13 billion years with Jehovah and calls him a liar."

I have no idea what they're talking about, but it's impressive that Brother Thorne knows the name of every one of the people in here, and they all know the back roads of the Bible. The question-and-answer session continues, with congregants as young as six citing scripture like they're contestants on *Jeopardy!*

I'm zoning out. After another hour, Brother Thorne encourages us to hit the pavement: "If there's a street or two in the territory on which you haven't found someone home, remember that Sunday's a good day!"

The final hymn begins without a collection plate ever passing. The Jehovah's Witnesses follow the edict of 2 Corinthians 9:7—"Every man according as he purposeth in his heart, so let him give; not grudgingly, or of necessity: for God loveth a cheerful giver." Any cheerful folks may open their pocketbooks at the unobtrusive donation box at the rear of the room.

Debbie is back next to me with the hymnal and together we begin "Joyful All Day Long," a state of being that, in any religion, is a blessing.

I spend an hour calling for and awaiting a taxi that never arrives. And in that time before I walk down the hill to find a bus stop and a bus that appears instantly, I watch the departure of the morning's worshippers, headed off to ring doorbells and spread the Word. Eight of them pull over and offer me a lift to wherever I need to go. "We'll take you back to Boston!" cheerfully offers the woman who'd asked me the name of my hall. I've no reason to believe my cab won't find me, so I pass on the offers for that reason, rather than for any of the cautions I'd been given by a few I'd told of this weekend's destination, like those I'd received before visiting the Mormons. I found the Jehovahs to be friendly and, despite their home delivery of their faith, not at all pushy toward a visitor. The only thing I feel they have in common with the Mormons is the blandness of their liturgy. Yes, they certainly know their Bible, as I witnessed in the lesson portion of the morning. But, when interpreting it, they turn me off by fostering more beliefs that fall into the categories of outdated, even dangerous, than talking up those, like their admirable pacifism, that could benefit the world. Starting with the immediate unchurched city.

NORTHAMPTON VINEYARD

NORTHAMPTON, MASSACHUSETTS

Go straight to the counselor's office, take a left past the trophy case and the computer lab, then head to the music room. Monday through Friday, this space is Northampton High School's Little Theater. Sunday mornings, it's Northampton Vineyard.

Should the ground beneath this beige concrete floor prove fertile enough, the Vineyard might one day have a building of its own. Until then, this is church for the thirty-one worshippers now filling the ten rows of ten blue plastic chairs facing a baby stage before which a baby grand is being played by a grown woman singing *I could worship your name forever!*

Most of this congregation looks to be of college age; nothing unusual, as this is the Five College area, home to Smith, Amherst, Hampshire, and Mount Holyoke colleges, and the University of Massachusetts. Many are adept at flipping the chairs' folding desktops and setting down cups of Deans Beans 100 percent organic and fair trade coffee, and even on a Sunday morning they lend a lively feel to the room. On the stage, band members ready electric guitar, mandolin, bongos. To the left of the piano, a staffer checks a board of electronics next to which a bright green cloth holds sacramental glasses of wine. To the left of that stands Pastor Brent Alderman Sterste, whose ecclesiastical garb consists of jeans, layers of shirts, a gray cap, and—an image that's a first for my year of church visits—a chest harness holding a small baby. "Good morning!" Pastor Brent enthuses as he begins this morning's service at the church he four years ago felt called to found.

Northampton Vineyard is the newest of the fifteen hundred churches under the umbrella of the Texas-based Association of Vineyard Churches, which weaves traditional biblical teaching with today's realities. The main founder was the late John Wimber, who got the call for this undertaking at age twenty-nine, when life found him, in the words of *Christianity Today*, a "beer-guzzling, drug-abusing pop musician, who was converted while chain-smoking his way through a Quaker-led Bible study."

The fruits of his efforts provide a spiritual home for those seeking enthusiastic renewal. "We actually believe that the thing God cares most about in the world is your life," says Northampton Vineyard's Web site. "We believe that Jesus wants and is able to give you a life that is actually worth living."

Though a permanent home is somewhere on the wish list, the dreams of this young church include stressing the importance of the arts, and working on issues of social justice, local outreach, and connection to the land.

Back in early 2002, Brent and future wife LeAnne were enrolled in a class called Discovering Your Gifts and Ministry at the Vineyard church in Cambridge, at the eastern end of the state. When the question of what he might do for God if he were able to do anything in the world was posed, Brent found the answer to be the planting of a church in this city that's a sort of Cambridge West. Four years later, he and a contingent of a dozen Vineyarders moved from eastern Mass to start the church.

A story about this church was among the clippings Tommy left on my side of the table months ago, and the details of the Vineyard Churches' fast growth, and the fact that a group of young people had moved from Boston to my valley to start one of the newest communities in a very collegiate hippy-holdover area, piqued my interest. Add to that the fact that the reporter, my good friend Holly, said it was a church she enjoyed, and she is not much for much church.

So here I am in a baby blue seat two rows from the back, very near the last of the three square clear-glass windows that make up the theater's right-hand wall. The 10:30 start is too early for Holly, who sleeps in on Sundays, so I'll have to fill her in on the details, including Pastor Brent reminding us that today is the deadline for submissions to *The Gregarious Monk*, the church zine. Also, a new small group is being started by church member James, who stands and says, "Hey, everybody." Pastor Brent tells us that Northampton Vineyard already has two small groups meeting, on Tuesdays and Thursdays. "We'll try to discuss, experience, and pursue God in his Kingdom," he says. "We'll be looking at the Kingdom of God through the Gospels. What that means for Christians today."

Pastor LeAnne is on the stage now, and Pastor Brent is thanking God that she was called to lead within this church he once described as "a place where secular liberals can come and think about faith in a safe way." Female pastors are A-OK in this church, and this one will be speaking from the book of James. Her husband places his hand on her back and their baby watches from the harness as Pastor Brent prays that Pastor LeAnne will deliver a good sermon. It's a sweet family portrait and adds to the intimacy of the celebration.

Pastor LeAnne faces her congregation, most members from late teens through their thirties with a couple of young families and a few grandma types, three children under eight, everyone white except for a black man in his late thirties. The area's standard-issue fleece, jeans, and clogs is their attire. As for Pastor LeAnne, a shortish bespectacled brunette who looks to be in her late twenties, in the same week the *Boston Globe* features an article on how female preachers should dress, the pastoral closet has yielded a light jacket over brown sweater and shirt, and dark pants. She begins by talking about having just finished maternity leave and her return to work at a nearby college. She and Pastor Brent and the baby had relied on her health insurance and income, and she'd been putting off the decision to return or stay home. Then she tells us, "God said to quit the job."

Pastor LeAnne follows that with, "A new era in life requires a shift in perspective." She comes off as sweet and nervous, speaks rather quickly as she describes her love of reading. "The number one reason I ended up living in Massachusetts as an eighteen-year-old," she says, "was because you have a lot of great writers—Emerson, Thoreau."

But she says that in a work of literature, beliefs without actions are empty. And that actions have to have meaning. In the hard times of her life, she says, "It was tempting to take the road of not using God. I'd say, 'If I just work hard enough and think hard enough, I could just pull myself up by my bootstraps.' "

Don't we all feel that way at some point? Don't most believers at times neglect the fact that God is on their side?

Quoting author Anne Lamott in her collection of essays *Traveling Mercies*, Pastor LeAnne reads, "Trusting in God is like waiting for that next lighted circle to step into."

Pastor LeAnne asks us to trust God, saying that, "He wants us to have good lives now, in the present moment." I feel the same appreciation for her upbeat message that I did for Pastor Larry's back in Kykotsmovi. She continues that feeling, reading from James that "wherever you are in life, there might be a place where God is calling to you.

"We must learn to depend on God and community when we are trying to fill the voids in our lives. Lent begins on Wednesday. What will we be doing during that time? There's always fasting, but even smaller actions count toward sacrificing at this time. I might pass up a piece of cake, or not go on the Internet when I'm bored."

She also will be thinking, and invites us to join her in figuring out, "How do you want God to move in your life in the next forty days?"

I think of my usual Lenten practice, the forgoing of chocolate, such a widespread choice among Catholics it has to be in the Bible somewhere. By the time I refocus, Pastor Brent is on the stage, baby-free, saying that he moved here a year and a half ago and since has marveled at what Vineyard has, well, harvested even in that short time. "Some are seeing Jesus, often for the first time; we want to minister to them, worship in the arts, do social justice, healing.

"God, I just asked you if you would come touch our hearts," he prays with eyes closed. He's genuine, comes off as good, with none of the smarmy or mean feel I have witnessed in some of his contemporaries, including Pastor Mark in Seattle. "Heal the sick, the worried, come and fill us up," he adds. "We want to get to know you the next forty days. We seek inspiration for our church. Come, Holy Spirit, come, into this time of worship."

The woman at the piano begins to play and Pastor Brent says, "We'll talk to God in that manner."

Come, now is the time to worship, she begins, joined by a young guy on bongos and another on acoustic guitar. A boy of about six hits the windowsill as if it were a drum. We follow the white-on-blue words displayed on the hanging screen. Pastor Brent and Pastor LeAnne sway to the left of the piano. The baby is sleeping in her mother's arms. The piano player's powerful voice asks *Come, let us sing for joy.* A few in the congregation lean forward in prayer, others clap to the beat, the black guy raises his arms, a slender curly-haired Mariane Pearl–looking woman to the left kneels on the concrete, kids run down the blue-carpeted aisle. *Better is one day in your courts, in your house, than a thousand elsewhere.*

"We trust you and your promises for us," Pastor Brent prays. "Give us more hope. Joy in facing what we have to face. Giving up control can feel like a failure. And it's frightening. But so much good can come from it."

It's Communion time, with Pastor Brent telling us that we eat, then drink the nonalcoholic wine, in memory of Jesus. "If you're considered a good follower of Jesus, you're welcome. If you're not yet with this Jesus thing, everybody's in a process and that's OK. Then the Bible suggests maybe this isn't a meal for you today."

I'm in a process. So I decline as one of the two blue-tinted wineglasses is brought around, as is a plate of what looks like broken matzo, the pieces of which are dipped into the liquid.

"Behold the Lamb of God who takes away the sins of the world," Pastor Brent prays. "Friends, let's keep the feast. Let's eat together."

A slight crunching is the only sound.

Soon, offertory baskets are passed by the same pair of women who distributed the bread and wine.

"If you're a guest," Pastor Brent says, "we prefer you don't donate. We prefer you fill out the blue card telling us about you." Some reach for a pen from the cups set on every few desktops.

Leaning, leaning, the piano woman sings. *I have blessed peace with my Lord so dear, leaning in the everlasting arms.* At the hymn's conclusion, Pastor Brent asks us to carry throughout the week the thoughts that have hit home for us today. I fill my imaginary souvenir bag with the reminder about Lent and the question of where we'll be during it; Pastor LeAnne's line about it being tempting to take the road of not using God; Anne Lamott's about stepping into the lighted circles of trust.

As we close the hour-long service, Pastor Brent invites us to take advantage of assistance from the Prayer Team, identifiable by their sheriff's badges, maybe a strange crime-linked motif for people of faith, but, in this largely college town, a cheeky choice that'll stick in minds.

"If there's anything at all we can do, come on up," says Pastor Brent. "It's a risk coming up for prayer, but you're safe here, and you'll have an encouraging if not miraculous experience."

Some are up for the risk, standing before the sheriffs with bowed heads and whispered prayers. Hands are not raised but suddenly I get it, the theme of surrender. That whole Let go, let God thing. And isn't that what it's all about?

CALVARY CHAPEL

FORT LAUDERDALE, FLORIDA

The band blasts into the opening number. A spotlight throws dizzying patterns across a stage on which two guitarists, a pair of bass players, and a drummer wail. Fake (I hope) smoke drifts ceilingward. Audience members hoot, hold cell phones aloft. The lead guitarist steps to the microphone and shouts, "You guys look so eager to praise the Lord!"

Rocking religiously is this worship-starting performance by students enrolled at Ocean's Edge School of Worship, a sort of ecclesiastical School of Rock located on the grounds of evangelical Calvary Chapel, Florida's largest megachurch and, with eighteen thousand attending each weekend, the nation's eighth-largest church of any kind.

Hailing from a religious background that, with the exception of the annual polka Mass at the parish picnic, was all organ all the time, I have been fascinated by the presence of electrified bands in most of the churches I've visited since Resurrection Sunday. And here at Calvary, the rock is not only righteous, it's educational. Since opening two months ago, Ocean's Edge has attracted twenty-one students to its ten-month program training those who will one day lead services in word and music, and enrollment is expected to almost double next term.

The seventy-five-acre campus and satellite churches in Plantation and Boca Raton are headed by Pastor Bob Coy, who in 1985 founded the Fort Lauderdale location that is a big part of what lured me here. It's February—a brutally cold month, and air miles will give me a chance to hit the beach while visiting my *Cioci* Yvonne, who lives one town north of here, and my mother-in-law and sister-in-law, who are vacationing one town south. I spend this very sunny Sunday morning indoors, checking out Calvary, part of a fellowship of approximately one thousand nondenominational Protestant churches, the first of which was started in Costa Mesa, California, by Chuck Smith, former pastor of a Foursquare Gospel congregation. They state their exact position on the evangelical map as being in the "middle ground between fundamentalism and Pentecostalism in modern Protestant theology." That boils down to applauding fundamentalism's unwavering belief in that inerrant Bible, but feeling that fundamentalists are now "rigid, legalistic, and unaccepting of spiritual gifts." Pentecostals are viewed as "enthusiastic and emotional at the expense of the teaching of God's Word."

Delivering that middle ground in Fort Lauderdale is chatty, witty, neighbor-over-the-fence-style Pastor Bob, another megaleader who got a coffee-table start. Four friends were seated around his at the beginning, and he now preaches to 16,996. Assistant Pastor Stephan Tchividjian, Billy Graham's eldest grandson, is among the seven hundred staffers, and guest preachers have included Pastor Stephan's grandfather and Uncle Franklin, former prime minister of Israel Benjamin Netanyahu, and former teen-heartthrob-and-aetheist-turned-believer-and-award-winning-religious-broadcaster Kirk Cameron.

Several hundred of those nearly seventeen thousand faithful right now are seated in the Calvary Chapel gymnasium, where a fourth hymn is beginning and hearts are beating fast both for the Lord and the hiply dressed Ocean's Edge band members, all of whom are white and male except for the Asian guitarist. My chair in the twelfth and final row of the front section, just to the right of center court, offers a perfect view of the band, and the space where Pastor Bob's sermon soon will be simulcast from the main sanctuary up the sidewalk.

A white female vocalist has joined the band. She consults a lyrics sheet and has a pleasant voice when it's not shouty, but then, she is singing about doing just that: *When I think about the Lord, how he picked me up and turned me around, set my feet on solid ground, it makes me want to shout!*

A fortyish man walks onto the stage when she's done. He's dressed in a brown jacket over a blue button-down shirt hanging outside his jeans, white sneakers.

"Let's pray," he says, and heads bow as he invokes open hearts for the upcoming message, mentioning in conclusion, "I'm Pastor Dallas. Anybody need a Bible? Jason will bring them around."

Hands raise, including one of mine. Jason hands me a blue

paperback of the New King James Version as Pastor Dallas instructs us to "turn around and shake hands with somebody and tell someone you're glad they're here."

My only neighbor is two seats to my right, an elegantly dark-suited black woman in her twenties who takes my hand and gives me the scripted line. Pastor Dallas is now asking us to take out our copies of the *Calvary Connection*, a folded brochure listing church info including the March 3 Beach Baptism: "Bring a Bible, a change of clothes, a towel, quarters for parking, and a ready heart!" Pastor Dallas also wants us to look at the cover feature, on "His Caring Place."

"We live in a society where babies are disposable," he says, reminding us of the church's pro-life stance and explaining this abortion alternative, a home environment in which mother and baby may live for six months of teaching "how to be a mom." We're digesting that as Pastor Dallas announces, "Let's go to the Lord in prayer! You've prepared our hearts with music. Thank you, Jesus, as we gather here today." An enormous screen that takes up the entire stage descends. The band has disappeared.

On the screen is a giant Pastor Bob, slight, fortyish, salt-and-pepper goatee and brown thinning hair combed to tentative bangs. In dark suit with open-necked button-down blue shirt, he leans on a big dark wooden podium bearing a gold outline of a dove, Calvary Chapel's logo.

"If you're joining us for the first time," he tells me, "you need to know we are fanatics!" Whoops and cheers respond to this fact. "I'm convinced if there's anything to be fanatics about, it's our friend and savior, Jesus Christ."

He wants us to open the Bible to Ephesians, chapter 3, and 1st Samuel, chapter 17. "The subject matter is spiritual warfare."

It's too dim in the gym, I can't read the small print. But I listen as Pastor Bob tells us that Calvary Church Fort Lauderdale received an award for the best TV teaching program of the year from the National Religious Broadcasters.

"That's a very cool thing," he says as he shows off a diamond-shaped glass award on a stand. "It's kind of like the Oscars, so I'd like to thank my mom, my dad, all the little people."

That brings laughs and he waves the award. "I really do want to thank my savior Lord, Jesus Christ. When I think of where we were when I was in that all-girl revue in Las Vegas . . ."

There are more laughs. I make the note to look up what he indeed used to do. But the only info I can find is what's on the official Web site: "At the age of twenty-four, Bob Coy left a coveted position in the music industry to serve as an associate pastor with Calvary Chapel of Las Vegas. In 1985, Bob and his wife, Diane, moved to Fort Lauderdale and began Calvary Chapel of Fort Lauderdale."

I don't know what that coveted position was, but Pastor Bob indeed is showbiz-savvy. As pastors love to do, this one is now posing a question: "What is that something that bothers you or bugs you or infuriates you, reduces you to someone you don't want to be? What is it? That, my friend, is your Goliath. We don't know him as Goliath. We say, 'That's my anger,' 'That's my lust,' 'That's my fear,' 'That's my anxiety.' Those are the feelings that follow. He is so in control, you're embarrassed."

Pastor Bob doesn't consult notes on the pulpit. I wonder if there's a teleprompter. He talks easily, jokes. Smiles with today's very white teeth, but doesn't appear smarmy. Refers to "the enemy" as if we're at war, which his camp believes we indeed are.

"Are you missing a mission trip to the Mideast?" he asks the students in the crowd. "Do you say, 'I'm not gonna go because the government says it's dangerous to go there'? But God wants you to! The enemy's in control of the Body of Christ.

"I love that we change up the worship here at Calvary Chapel. Some say, 'It's too happy here, too up, not what I'm used to.' That's the battle, the war. If he can take away our worship, or joy, he's got more space than he can have."

I like happy, but references to "the enemy" and "he" are denting the effect. At times the words seem to mean Satan, and at other times your local newscaster—or you, if you're not in total tune with teachings.

Pastor Bob mentions Ted Haggard, though not by name. "When a national evangelical leader was found to have some serious sin, my heart broke for him," he says. "It was the start of a long heartbreak. I knew he would be mentioned on Leno and Letterman.

"He gave the enemy of the Lord great occasion to blaspheme

God," Pastor says. "Do you understand the war? The enemies of the Lord have greater occasion to blaspheme him. What we don't want to do is give the enemy fuel for that fight."

Pastor Bob says intimidation is a weapon, one that the enemy uses all the time. From behind the pulpit, he draws a wide sword that reaches to his chest. The show-and-tell is unexpected and very effective.

"The enemy loves to intimidate," Pastor Bob reminds us. "James says we ought to be slow to wrath, quick to listen, because the anger of man does not produce the righteousness of God.

"The enemy knocks us down: 'You think you're gonna be a missionary? Give me a break!' And you say 'I could never do that.' "

Pastor twirls the sword. "May I remind you God is in the business of saving the least, saving the last, saving the lost?" He uses himself as an example, someone who never attended Bible college yet who is running this massive church.

"They say, 'Then how do you know how to do what you do?' I don't. Most of you guys know half the words I use I make up. If you're an English teacher, you labor through this. Talk about funny . . ." He holds up the award, to more laughter.

"If I know I'm a child of God and I know he wants to work in my life, that defeats the enemy," he says. "Some of you right this very morning, you're just about to fight your spiritual enemy. My fight is one I battle daily."

He doesn't elaborate on his personal challenges. What he does is ask, "Will you join with me in a word of prayer? Help me help us to be those people of faith."

The ushers and deacons will be distributing what Pastor Bob calls the "Communion elements." He adds, "I don't know what your religious background may be, but hold the elements in your hand and consider them, sing the song, and we'll come back in a moment."

Our band takes the stage again, now only the young woman and the two guitarists. *Broken I run to you, for your arms are open wide.*

A silver hubcap-type plate containing pieces of more matzo-like bread and edged with polio vaccine cups of wine is passed around the gym. *I know your touch restores my life,* sings our young woman.

Pastor Dallas is up front again. "The Bible tells us to examine yourself," he starts. "Do that. Examine your life. Let the Lord look deep into your heart as you have with the Communion elements. Remember what Jesus has done for us by the cross on Calvary."

As we remember that, we also remember we're in a rock venue. "We'll play you one last song and hope you enjoy it," shouts the blond guitarist. "You all have a wonderful day!"

I will. But not because of this service. Pastor Bob had tried, putting a smiley face on the fear talk, but it was fear talk nonetheless. And it was relayed in an enormous space where I felt no particular link to my fellow worshippers. A high ranking among the nation's largest church does not impress me. Refueling me for the week, reminding me of God's presence, making that presence palpable, that's what I'm looking for. I did appreciate the opportunity the students had to showcase their musical talents. But I'm not on a music quest. So I leave Calvary, off to lunch with my loving aunt. I know already that breaking bread with her, despite the busy Sunday-afternoon chain-restaurant setting of the Olive Garden, will be a richer and more spiritual experience than was this morning.

HARVEST CHURCH OF THE NAZARENE

LAS VEGAS, NEVADA

I came to Las Vegas because of its Sin City moniker. The idea of a Lenten visit to a metropolis built on the shifting sands of vice seemed perfect. As did my choice of companion—my mother, whose many pastimes include passing time in front of the slot machines her gang occasionally visits at the Native American–owned casinos a few hours from our town.

This morning, she's doing her thing while I'm doing mine, oddly enough for the second time in three weeks, in a public school. But the Irwin & Susan Molasky Junior High School, tucked into a placid and pricey neighborhood of mountainside homes, is a very temporary home for this church. God has called Pastor Bill Williams and his Harvest Church of the Nazarene to Las Vegas's inner city, and his first service there will be next Sunday.

On the church's final Sunday at Molasky, I attend the service crafted for the busy. As I read upon locating the church's Web site, "Harvest Express is an in & out Service for busy people who want to get to the point and get going. There are 2 songs, a prayer and the message. People of Vegas have varied schedules so we have varied times, varied days & varied locations to meet to worship God and hear what He wants to tell us."

It's great that everything is in the open. This church knows we don't want to be there all day. Well, some of us, at least, and it makes no bones about that. I feel comfortable here already. All the more when Pastor Bill's wife, Margaret Williams, greets me with a hug as I step from my cab half an hour before the Express. I'm the only worshipper so far, and help her and Bill and their daughter and son-in-law carry in music stands and a pair of two four-by-fours that will be screwed into the shape of a cross. As we lug, Margaret explains that Nazarene is from Jesus's full name—Jesus the Nazarene—and that the church's roots are in the Wesleyan tradition, one that is often characterized by a devotion to service to others and with early social justice roots including campaigning against slavery and for women's rights. The unloading done, I cross the parking lot and stroll the sidewalk bordered by low bushes. Rosemary is everywhere. I run my hand along the plant, where tiny flowers a peaceful blue are attracting small bees. The spiny leaves are a gift. As is the name of the plant. Yesterday, twenty-five years to the day on which I lost my very dear friend with that very dear name, my mother and I walked the Strip in search of the cathedral she'd attend today and came upon a long line of the same bushes. I stepped across a few feet of very green Astroturf and crouched at the very real rosemary sending up arms of woody scent. I am here, it was saying. In the middle of this Disneyland for adults, a couple feet of fake grass between me and the sidewalk littered with business cards bearing pictures of hookers guaranteed to arrive at your hotel in twenty minutes. In this crazy, fake, furiously weird place, I am here.

This morning the rosemary was reminding me of that again. I'm carrying that gift—and a stolen frond—as I enter the school theater, where Margaret introduces me to a woman named Becky, who, with the fast stride you'd expect on somebody who's here for Express, leads me to the right place.

Express is not held in the theater where the big cross has been assembled for the 10:30 service. We travel down a hall lined with watercolors of sheep and beaver and then make a left into an art room. That's where I find Pastor Bill, seated at a square made of two six-foot wood-grained plastic veneered tables surrounded by eight chairs, a church bulletin with the cover photo of a dogwood blossoming in an otherwise foliage-free forest awaiting at each place.

The room holds four such sets of tables, but two are covered with chairs stacked upside down, their legs stuck into tennis balls. The third table holds coffee, a basket of chocolates, and more bulletins. Everything in this room—the primitive masks on the walls, the pottery wheel, the storage niches for drawing boards, the row of sinks, the poster of a Wegman dog with the legend "Nobody can do everything but everybody can do something"—takes me back to my high school years. I spent every possible moment in the six basement rooms that made up an enormous and impressive art department, where teachers intensely passionate about creativity directed so many of us into lives of making some form of art. And right now, in what is Mrs. L. Coston's art room thousands of miles away, my first prayer is of thanks for those teachers. I'm feeling that it might be heard. In a city where odds are everything, the fact that there are only four people at this table makes the possibility of our voices being clearer to God than, say, from a building packed with seventeen thousand all the greater. Pastor Bill's daughter and son-in-law enter, and the young man begins to strum an acoustic guitar. He's dressed in khaki shorts and a blue polo, his wife in a blue jersey top and dark blue pants. Becky and the woman to my left, Beverly, wear jeans. It's Richmond-come-as-you-are, and *Come, just as you are to worship,* the guitarist sings in a clear and powerful voice. The four of us at the table are moved to join in. It's early, it's an incongruous setting, it's a tiny congregation, but already I'm glad I've come all this way. I feel a surprising Philadelphia Deliverance–type piety at this table. I pick up the three-by-six sheet of paper titled "SONGS for TODAY" and chime louder, dropping all my inhibitions about singing even though everyone can hear me very clearly.

I glance at Pastor Bill, a short and stout sixtyish man with white goatee, salt-and-pepper hair, and wire-rimmed glasses. He looks dressed for winter in a woolish gray button-down shirt, and already is getting a bit pink in the face as with intensity he closes his eyes on the last few lines, stabs the air with his right pointer finger. *One day every tongue will confess You are God.*

The second of the two promised songs is slower, the proclamation *for we cannot say enough about You* followed by eight long alleluias.

Then, just as swiftly as they arrived, our musicians exit, and we move on to the one prayer. A fourth worshipper enters, the only male and the only non-Caucasian. He's in his fifties and Asian, and wears a black leather jacket that he keeps on as he listens to Pastor Bill gently tell God that "we fell so short of experiencing what you are like. We're seeing what you do for us but then we pass it off to luck or life or whatever. Thank you for how you are working in our lives and have allowed us to live another day."

Some of us don't get the next day. The frond in my pocket reminds me of that.

After a few breaths, it's housekeeping time and Pastor Bill tells us that NASCAR will be in town next weekend, so traffic is sure to be thick. Becky nods, takes a sip from her paper Starbucks cup. To my right, Beverly is breakfasting on a chocolate pastry and opening an Aquafina bottle.

How do you see church? Bottled water and jeans, fit into any available space, worth the effort for just one more worshipper than attended the spiritualist service back in October? I'm beginning to see this as one of the most rewarding mornings of the year.

Twelve minutes in, Pastor Bill introduces the topic of perspective. "One can see with the eyes of faith, or with the eyes of fear," he tells us, moving straight into a story from the Bible. Moses had chosen a dozen spies to explore Canaan, which God had informed him would be a gift to him in the years following passage through the Red Sea. The spies returned with two different types of reports: ten negative, two positive. Sure, there was milk and honey, the ten agreed with the two, but the residents were powerful, the city fortified, a bad place to be.

"Ten saw with fear, two with faith," Pastor Bill notes. "Two with faith. Ten saw obstacles, two saw opportunities. Ten people caused an entire nation to die. Affected an entire generation."

Pastor Bill reads but is not stiff in delivery. He makes eye contact, gestures, knows when to turn up the volume or keep it down. Pastor Bob from last week, Joel Osteen, Rick Warren, each have more people using their restrooms right now than Pastor Bill might ever reach. But he is as effective and good as any of them.

"Problems never defeat you," he says, "your perspective does." He gives us three results of seeing with eyes of fear—discouragement, discontent, defeat—then tells us he was a senior in high school in Owasso, Michigan, sitting in the back of the class due to his surname, thinking the blackboard was supposed to look blurry. An eye test introduced him to eyeglasses. "I still remember the first time I put them on. I could see signs, the blackboard . . . it changed the way I could see the world. My vision changed."

Pastor Bill chokes up a bit. "I've had trouble this week finding what God wanted me to share with you," he says slowly. I buy the tears. It's an emotional time. "It's the last day here, it'll be the first day there," he notes of next week's urban location. "I found this old sermon I'm preaching today. I picked that out." He starts to cry. "I know this sermon is for you, but I needed to be reinforced. I needed to hear it again. This is what I needed to repeat: a vision of church that was to make a difference . . . I've had this hunger for the inner city. A more diversified place. The big churches aren't serving the people there. So we will. I've been looking too long with the eyes of a sixty-year-old and being afraid, and having a sense of it's not going to happen." He's very weepy now but manages, "God has awakened me. It will happen. Maybe in the last year of my ministry, but it will. Pray for me."

"Amen," the Asian guy says softly.

Pastor Bill continues. "Some of you. Some of you are looking at your job situation, and it's not looking too good. You're looking with the eyes of fear. In your relationships, you might be without a partner, fear is getting hold of your life. I understand the temptation to look with fear but you can't go forward with fear. As a church, every time we have taken a risk and moved forward in faith, God has blessed us. Our move is a major risk, but we believe God is with us in the Red Sea. He is in the water with us, and he will walk with us on dry ground."

I reach inside my pocket. The rosemary is new and fresh and fragrant.

"This is a message for you, for what you're going through—your perspective makes all the difference."

The service concludes here, at fifty-five minutes. Not quite the twenty-five-minute quickie Mass at the church my niece Kara attends, but not three hours at Foursquare. "Amen," the Asian guy says again quietly as Pastor Bill removes his glasses, wipes his eyes, and keeps them shut as he whispers a prayer.

"Each person here," he says, "you drew them here. You could speak to me in my backyard, in the mountain, in the desert. But there is something about coming to a place where others are. Help us to come to a place of faith."

Here in Mrs. L. Coston's art room, at a table surrounded by just five people, we're already there.

FULL GOSPEL TABERNACLE CHURCH

MEMPHIS, TENNESSEE

In the early 1970s, rhythm and blues of a secular nature made Al Green a superstar. But following a physically and spiritually painful period of his life, in 1976 he began concentrating on gospel music. Three years later he founded and began to pastor Full Gospel Baptist Church here in Memphis, Tennessee.

Green has sold more than 20 million records, watched six consecutive singles shine in the Top Ten and in 1995 was inducted into the Rock and Roll Hall of Fame. But nothing matters more to him than his faith, which he had shoved aside despite a teenhood spent in the family gospel group the Greene Brothers, but to which the now-fifty-eight-year-old returned after the aforementioned personal crises, which included having a boiling pot of grits poured on his back by a former girlfriend who then shot herself.

Blessed with a new direction, Al Green escaped the fate of peers including late greats Sam Cooke, Marvin Gaye, and Otis Redding. He lives peacefully and prayerfully in a house behind Full Gospel, located at 787 Reverend Al Green Road, which is just off Elvis Presley Boulevard and down the way from Graceland.

"I take more people to Graceland than to church, or anywhere else," says the cabbie who drives me down both the Boulevard and the Road. He adds that he's extra busy during the annual Elvis Week in August, when about fifty thousand hit town to mark E's 1977 passing. I'm a fan of both the King and Reverend Green, but Reverend Green is the one with the church—a church at which he preaches and sings each Sunday—so I've taken the opportunity of this church year to fly down here, staying on the banks of the wide Mississippi I stared at late into the night. Half an hour from that hotel, I find no King-like hoopla at Full Gospel, which, without the words REV. AL GREEN on the sign on the dry lawn, could be any white-block church in any town.

I stand in the parking lot and stare at the modest home and the adjacent garage-looking structure hung with an AL GREEN MUSIC CO. sign, all behind a sturdy iron fence. No fans queue for tickets, no souvenir annex glows, and when I enter the church only eight people are seated. It's the third Sunday in Lent but fashionwise we're back to Resurrection Sunday. A woman in a fancy deep aqua dress and blazer greets me and answers my question of how long the service might last. With a smile, she calculates, "We might be here until three or four. We stay however long the spirit moves us."

It's only 11:00 a.m. here in this circular sanctuary beneath eight huge beams that spoke toward the center of the white ceiling. I pick a seat on the left, toward the back of three sections of pews that combine to hold maybe three hundred. They're dark wood with royal blue upholstery, same color as the rug. The seatback pockets, two to each long pew, are empty, no books, no material, no nothing in the six pencil holes. Upon a red-carpeted stage area elevated by a few steps, a boxy wooden pulpit is decorated with a gold-fringed red sash, a gold cross and crown its insignia. Behind that await four comfy leather chairs. Three wide wooden choir seats are lined up behind a white wooden barrier.

No traditional altar or altar table, but the far wall holds a rectangular cutout in which a huge white wooden and rare cross stands. It's backlit by a modern triangular stained glass window of brown and blue. To the left hangs a print of a giant Jesus at a riverside as a crowd of tiny people stand ready for baptism. To the right of the cross hangs a painting of the Last Supper. The only other artwork is on the rear wall: a five-foot-tall primitive Jesus walking on water, and an almost-as-large horizontal painting of an unsettling urban scene. Skyscrapers crowd, one of them having been struck by an airplane. On the highway, four cars are mangled. To the right lies Peaceful View cemetery. The white-robed former occupants are floating toward a Jesus who hovers above the city. Similarly dressed souls are headed skyward from the car wreck, and from the remains of the plane.

I'm not the sole visitor looking around. Others are arriving, most notably a group of maybe twenty teens, most of them white, who file in looking around like, well, tourists.

Precious Lord, a woman standing in front of our section begins to sing, drawing out each syllable like taffy, *take my hand.* To the far right is the band area—baby grand, upright organ, drum kit—and a rustle of organ and drum begins there, ushering the imploring hymn that gospel music legend Thomas Dorsey wrote in 1932 after his wife died in childbirth, their newborn just hours later. *Lead me on, let me stand, I am tired, I am weak, I am worn. Through the storm, through the night, lead me on to the light. Take my hand, precious Lord, lead me home.*

A man in a dark purple armless robe walks up to the woman and asks us to stand for a brief reading and prayer. I'm distracted again, this time by the arrival of the choir, ten women and a man who, like everyone save for the twenty teens, their chaperones, a man and a woman in the center aisle, and myself, are black. They wear pink robes with gray yokes and arm stripes and, with the backing of a very loud organ, they jump into a rousing "I'll Fly Away." I know we're only inches into the liturgy, but I'm loving the morning already. And even without Reverend Green yet appearing.

"Sit back, relax, and let God be used today," a woman in a red blazer and white sweater is telling us now. "We kind of feel down when we don't see him," she continues, and as I take my notes I capitalize the H in "him." Because she means God. Then it sinks in: she means him—Al—Reverend Al. And I realize he's not going to be here.

The woman tells what is, essentially, my story this morning—about being disappointed that a pastor she'd looked forward to hearing wasn't at the service she'd taken pains to attend. A friend informed her, "You would have a problem if God, through the blood of Jesus, wouldn't be there!" This woman assures us that "God will be here with you today." We'll be hearing from Al's stand-in, whom she says is going on ninety-five and who must be the tall and boney older man in one of the chairs behind the pulpit. "The key," the woman tells is, "is getting a blessing from God to you today. He's sitting right now in your midst."

I know he's here. No, "he" isn't, but "He" is. I guess I'll take what comes, which next is what the black-on-green bulletin tells me is the Christian Creed. We then receive a greeting from choir member Sister Pat, who descends the choir steps to deliver "a great big hug and a kiss from us to you. We love you and God does, too!"

"Our God is a mighty God, children, and he's worthy to be praised!" It's the nearly ninety-five-year-old Bishop Albert Reed now at the pulpit as wildly joyful music pumps and few, including me, are able to sit still. A slight woman in her twenties and in a cream dress has removed her shoes and is spinning in the aisle. A larger woman in a periwinkle suit moves robotically, forward and back from the waist. She appears ready to topple now and then, and her seatmates steady her each time. It's full frenzy, some of the church members overcome and lowered to the floor, where, as at Pastor Elizabeth's Living Waters, white sheets are used to cover them. Ten minutes of rock/soul music blast, during which the Bishop speaks occasionally into the microphone but can't be heard over the tumult.

"Some here are from across the country, across the sea," the Bishop says as the music hushes. "We're glad for Jesus. God is good to everyone here."

"Right!" some shout. "Hallelujah!" A wad of bulletins is being used to fan the spinning woman, who's now flat on the floor. A young man in a jean jacket walks to the front, where a woman lays a hand on his forehead and he then is out, leaning into the arms of a man who'd handily been standing nearby.

"I'm about to see my ninety-fifth birthday," Bishop Albert tells us, and there are a few more shouts of "Hallelujah," including from the four men in the chairs to the left of the pulpit. "God is everything we need. He's a healer, sin forgiver, blesser. " Between his age and southern accent, the pastor is hard to understand, but the faithful here answer often with definite yeses and rights and amens.

We understand that he's inviting us up for tithing. Small white envelopes are given to anyone who needs them. "Anyone has no money," says the Bishop, "let the Lord bless them. We're sure glad to have you!" The organist and drummer play something soft and jazzy as the worshippers make their way to the front of the church, where a platter awaits donations. "All of you have to thank God for life," the Bishop tells us when the tithing is over. "It's a privilege we receive it."

He's not saying anything hugely profound, but his sweet delivery, and the attempt he's making to stand in for a star, is admirable. I feel like I want to hug him. That's after I get done hugging the choir's only male, large and bald with a voice that could power a DC-10. He begins a dynamic hymn: *No one else could do, could care as much—yet you thought my soul was worth it.*

"He showed us the pattern," Bishop Albert sums up. "He came, lived, died, and rose again. Just like he said. He didn't do it for hisself, he did it for us. All we have to do is repent of our sin. Some of us don't believe in repentance. We believe in putting our name on the check. But a name on the check ain't worth nothing if you're not saved."

Salvation arrived for the Bishop at age thirteen. "I thank God that eighty-two years ago he sanctified me. I feel good every minute of the day. He said, 'Ask and it shall be given, seek and ye shall find.' Members of the church, be loyal to one another—God is loyal to you. God bless you every moment!"

"Amen!" and "All right!" come from the pews. Then the Bishop tells us that nearly thirty years ago he assisted Reverend Al in purchasing the building in which we sit. As he puts it, "I took the pastor's money and bought this church—he paid cash for it. I met him, and fifteen minutes later we went looking for a church." He tells us he's been a member of the Memphis-grown Church of God in Christ for eighty-two years, and currently is a senior bishop. He has fifteen kids. Last week, the baby of the fifteen bought him a new car. The Bishop tells us, "God is good, trust him. If you live for God, he'll pay your debts. Children, put your trust in God and love one another."

Up now is a woman identified as Sister Green, Reverend Al's brother's wife, who, a cappella, delivers what sounds like a spiritual: *Soon I'll be gone with the troubles of this world / Troubles I'll be gone / Soon I'll be gone with the troubles of this world / I'll be going home to live with God.*

Slow soul music follows, and we sit for what feels like meditation. But the service is over, even though it's only 1:10.

"Let the doors of the church be open," someone calls out. They are and I exit, despite the absence of Reverend Al, glad that I entered for this celebration of the God that he and I have in common.

ALL SAINTS PARISH

BROOKLINE, MASSACHUSETTS

Not often does pub music waft from a church's open door. But today is Saint Patrick's Day, and this church is in an area plenty Irish, Jack Kennedy's birthplace right up the road, so I guess it's not too shocking to hear "The Star of County Down" as I approach the sanctuary of All Saints Parish.

The folk tune shares the same music as some old English and American hymns, but it's the contemporary rocking and racing version mumbled by the brilliant Shane McGowan that springs to mind, rather than the one that gently glides from the cello, flute, and guitar trio at the rear of the sanctuary where the Celtic Eucharist is about to be celebrated.

This 111-year-old Episcopal church offers the service each Wednesday and Saturday evening as part of a Celtic spirituality focus that began in 1989.

"Celtic worship returns us to a time before the split between Christians and hence is profoundly ecumenical," All Saints rector Rev. David A. Killian writes in the twenty-page black-on-gray liturgy booklet. "Celtic worship seeks to heal the wounds of centuries. Celtic Spirituality is committed to caring for the earth, promoting equality between men and women, securing justice and freedom for all, and working for peace in the world."

All that will happen in a stately rectangular meeting room tucked into the right rear wing of the neo-Gothic church a quick ride on the T, as the subway is known in these parts, from downtown Boston. A dozen chairs, most of them topped by red upholstered cushions, are lined on either side of the room lit by clear glass windows and six brass chandeliers hanging from the dark-beamed ceiling. The second and final row of seating on each side consists of assorted couches and armchairs set onto the rust-colored rug dotted with blue, tan, and white flowers. I choose the front row, second seat in from the wooden altar table with its white crocheted covering and big lion-claw legs. This is not my usual back-of-the-room location, simply because I hadn't seen the table prior to sitting down. But now the altar is nearly my neighbor and I have a clear view of both its contents—three fat white candles and a pewter Celtic cross—and that of the seats across from me, where the white-robed man who must be Pastor David sits awaiting our start.

My search for artwork finds that the only things hanging on the white walls above the dark wainscoting are four certificates in the corner near the back door, and the red exit sign above it. I browse the literature from an info packet I collected at that back door. "This Week at All Saints" tells me about a Lenten series of talks on a pastor's trip to Israel and Palestine, and an upcoming mission trip to Tanzania. Another trip will be made to Washington to lobby for affordable housing and healthcare reform. A "Family Sabbath" event will encourage a refreshing twenty-four-hour period during which work, errands, and general everyday craziness must cease. The church's Ruah Spirituality Institute is planning a Women of Wisdom series for those of all faith backgrounds. A Lenten collection of a mile and a half of pennies will result in twelve hundred dollars for a local food pantry. The projects and offerings are right up my alley. This might be a church to further investigate if I didn't live ninety minutes away. Then again, King's Chapel member Elsie makes a weekly trip of similar length to this city from her home on the Cape. I wonder how far would be too far if I really and truly were sold by a church not in my immediate area. Then I remember how hard it always was for me to be on time for Mass right around the corner, as was the case in college, or a mile up the street, as is the case in my hometown. Suddenly, ninety minutes seems out of the question.

Even so, I'm happy to be here today, at a church that has grown an entire ministry from ancient Celtic roots. Tommy's parents came from Ireland as teens and the older of his two sisters lives there, as do an endless supply of relatives. I married into that culture and enjoy visiting it whenever possible. Today I'll be there spiritually as I fish from the packet a sheet of readings, an eight-page booklet of music, and a double-sided sheet bearing a lengthy "Commemoration of St. Patrick, Apostle of Ireland," Saint Patrick, who rocketed from toiling as a teenage slave in Britain to establishing in Ireland a powerful church that shaped the culture in ways that, for better and for worse, still reverberate. His delivery of Catholicism in 450 AD is considered history's only bloodless conversion of a country—if you leave out the fact that in the process Patrick stabbed King Aengus in the foot with his crosier, receiving no complaint because the victim believed impalement to be part of ceremony. That celebration of the saint has come to include contests involving mass consumption of green beer is stymieing. Nonetheless, I've chosen to spend Saint Patrick's Day here, where, right now, further reading of the life story of the former Patricius Magonus Sucatus must wait. The woman who's been skillfully alternating between cello and piano now stands before the music area in kilt, black sweater, and boots, a silver Celtic cross on a chain around her neck.

"I can't do that Irish accent, I wish I could," she tells us with an apologetic smile. "What a glorious thing to have you here, and all these musicians coming out to lead the celebration." She gestures to the worshippers first, twenty-five of us, dressed in casual layers after last night's foot of snow. I count several nods to the holiday in a trio of green shirts, one green boutonniere, and a pair of shamrock antennae. Seventeen in our crowd are female. Everyone is white except for an Asian man. Only two look to be younger than forty.

I consult my stack of information and determine that the kilted one is the Reverend Kim Hardy, aka Celtic Liturgical Coordinator, now telling us there might be chaos in this worship. "I'm sure God will be pleased, because he loves chaos."

Pastor David steps to the front of the altar. Over the long white robe is a green scarf with gold cross embroidered onto each end. A white cord cinches his waist. Pastor is white, late sixties, and with a gray beard and receding hairline. He's accompanied by a graying white woman maybe in her late fifties, in blue plaid blazer, white turtleneck, and black slacks. They light the altar table's three candles and read a prayer at each, one lit in the name of the Maker, then the Son, then Spirit. We join them in the conclusion, "We will light three lights for the Trinity of love: God above us, God beside us, God beneath us: the Beginning, the End, the Everlasting One."

Confession is next, five brief lines that speak of the misery we've brought into the world one way or another. Pastor David's prayer is like a painting, as nice an absolution as I've ever heard: "You have lowered the canopy of night and its gentle shadows cover us with your peace. May the dews of heaven heal our wounds and wash the tears from our eyes. And may the burning light of Christ banish forever the darkness from our souls, that we may be at peace."

"Kyrie eleison," the two words repeated, makes up the hymn that follows and I think back to St. Spyridon, which seems like ages ago. We move to the readings for this fourth Sunday in Lent. The first from Joshua, the Israelites celebrating Passover in Gilgal, eating for the first time from the land of Canaan. The Psalm response is "Sing for joy to the Holy One!" and then we're at the second reading, from 2 Corinthians, in which we're told, "Everything old has passed away; see, everything has become new!"

We stand for the Gospel reading, about the prodigal son living high on the hog and, after having squandered all his riches, returning home poor, starving, in need of work, even willing to tend to the literal hogs on his father's estate. What an image of forgiveness and love: "But when he was still far off, his father saw him and was filled with compassion; he ran and put his arms around him and kissed him."

When we take our seats, Pastor David tells us that he's saving the prodigal sermon for tomorrow. "Today, I'd like to talk about a young Brit named Patricius, who died in Ireland as Patrick."

Pastor's reference is *How the Irish Saved Civilization: The Untold Story of Ireland's Heroic Role from the Fall of Rome to the Rise of Medieval Europe* by Thomas Cahill, master of making history accessible and fascinating. You'd be caught up in his work even if you're not of the particular ethnic group, though he still might get around to yours: He's so far also published *The Gifts of the Jews: How a Tribe of Desert Nomads Changed the Way Everyone Thinks and Feels* and *Sailing the Wine-Dark Sea: Why the Greeks Matter* as part of a seven-title series on Western history. But the Irish came first with him, and today they also do with Pastor David, who recounts Patrick's six-year enslavement in an Ireland that still practiced human sacrifice.

"Patrick had been a slave, and was the first in history to speak out about it," Pastor tells us. "For most of the world it was not until the nineteenth century that it was seen as wrong. We could call Patrick the patron saint of the disadvantaged, downtrodden, marginalized, excluded."

After Patrick, slavery and human sacrifice ended, Pastor David says before adding, "But they never stopped warring." The laughter that comment brings seems odd.

"He is a saint for everyone—believer and non, Christian and non—because human life is valued. My life is valuable and worth living. He thought all life was indeed precious."

A saint for everyone is a great concept and title. That my life is valuable and worth living is yet another of the strong reminders I've picked up along the way on these visits. I'm grateful for that, and wordlessly voice that as we begin "Thanksgivings and Concerns." *Lord, draw near* is sung after each intercession. We pray that the church may have rest from dissention and strife, for those walking in a global warming event this weekend, for those in Darfur, China, Haiti, Iraq, and on the Mexico/U.S. border. Curiously, during a liturgy of this type, nobody adds Northern Ireland.

"Christ, Lord of Tenderness, bind us with a bond that cannot be broken," Pastor David says and the sign of peace is shared as "Peace of Christ." *How can I repay the Lord for his goodness to me?* we sing, and answer in a way as we tithe into a pair of small round natural-color reed baskets.

Pastor David and the woman in the blazer have ready at the table a pair of blue-green pitchers, a blue-green chalice, and a matching round plate holding what looks like a big sugar cookie. The familiar "Holy, Holy, Holy" begins the consecration that in form and wording is also not foreign to me. Pastor David and the woman read the prayers and lead the responses from pages in a red binder, right up to the Our Father and the proclamation by Pastor that "the bread of heaven is broken for the life of the world."

"Body of Christ, bread of heaven," he says to each communicant as a new tune begins to the beat of a *bodhrán*. I remain in my seat, watching the drummer, appreciating that added bit of musical authenticity.

"Until the eternal day dawns," we pray at closing, "which Christ as morning star bore witness to, may we catch sign of the signs of glory all around us, O God."

I don't know the very complicated melody that follows, but I'm familiar with some of the words, translated from Irish and known by several names, including "St. Patrick's Breastplate" due to the protection so much of the prayer seeks. As does this portion we sing at the service's conclusion: *Christ be with me, Christ within me, Christ behind me, Christ before me, Christ beside me, Christ to win me, Christ to comfort and restore me, Christ beneath me, Christ above me, Christ in quiet, Christ in danger, Christ in hearts of all that love me, Christ in mouth of friend and stranger.*

ST. MARY'S CONVENT

GREENWICH, NEW YORK

My Confraternity of Christian Doctrine teacher was always telling me I'd look good in black. He didn't mean cocktail dress. He meant habit.

He went on to become a priest, and now sports the color nearly 24/7. I never ran off to the convent. Until this weekend. But it was TV, rather than Father D, or *G-O-D*, that inspired me.

Specifically, our local PBS affiliate's broadcast of the Emmy Award–winning documentary *The Hidden Life*, an insider's look at America's oldest indigenous community of Episcopal nuns. Sisters were shown at prayer, of course, but also tending their farm and, among other things, nailing the lid on the coffin of one of their own. My heart was won by these women who didn't need any man but the one upstairs.

I have a soft spot for nuns, anyhow, despite the fact that, for four of my eight years in parochial grammar school, I was taught by sisters who regularly hurled massive geography books across the classroom, locked us in broom closets, and smacked us on the backs of our heads with the final stick from a croquet set. But for the other four years—including the formative first two grades—I was taught by sweethearts. Sister Tobia in first and second excited us about reading and, because I'd arrived at school already equipped with the skill, made me a proud tutor of kids who hadn't yet cracked the alphabet code. Young Sister Mary Jane, fresh from her vows, was the kind of guitar-playing ice-skating pizza-eating fun nun who had even the toughest among us considering the convent for a few minutes. Sister Consolata's sixth-grade classroom was the scene of impromptu afternoon-long spelling bees and unprecedented dance classes, this rotund ball of energy in floor-length habit leading a line of embarrassed boys around the edge of the room in a hula lesson in preparation for a school play.

My great-aunt Sister Benecia, though far more serious than my teachers, was known to be up for creative mischief. She visited from

Buffalo for several weeks each summer, and if during that time neighbors up the street phoned, as they were wont to do, alerting us that Mormons or Jehovah's were going door to door, as they, too, were wont to do, we'd take down the three-foot-tall crucifix from above my *babci*'s bed, place it in Sister's arms, and send her to answer the door with a polite smile.

In adulthood I have come to greatly admire a local community of Sisters of Saint Joseph, including several who twenty years ago took a donation of five hundred dollars and purchased a decaying gray Victorian in Springfield's North End, the poorest neighborhood in the Commonwealth of Massachusetts. After rehabbing what they would name the Gray House, they began a food pantry, a thrift store, an after-school program, a kids' summer camp, English as a Second Language classes, and computer lessons.

"Every time I've visited a convent or interviewed a sister for a story," my friend Holly says, "I want to become a nun. No worries on how to dress, play some softball, and enjoy quiet time. Doesn't sound bad." I'm thinking of Holly as I drive through the flooding countryside of western New York on this gloomy Sunday morning, trying to locate Saint Mary's Convent. I have clear directions, thanks to MapQuest and Compunun, the latter being the nom de screen of Mother Miriam, head honcho of St. Mary's, who responded to my e-mail asking if anyone could walk off the street (or, in this case, the 620 surrounding acres) and into their chapel for a service.

The Community of Saint Mary includes two other independent provinces besides the Eastern one that I will visit: Tennessee (Southern Province) and Wisconsin (Western). Five nuns founded the order in 1865, but they didn't get much support from the Episcopal Church until four of the five died tending to yellow fever patients during an 1878 epidemic in Memphis. The church now celebrates the lives and sacrifices of the "Martyrs of Memphis" each September 9.

Greenwich convent life is Benedictine, mixing prayer and labor. Sisters' work includes leading retreats, designing greeting cards, serving on the board of a children's hospital, and assisting the path of a newly completed convent in the African country of Malawi. There's also the farm, with goats and chickens and bees.

Seven years ago, the community moved from its quarters in Peekskill to the grounds of a proposed spiritual life center here. In 2004, construction began on the Christ of King complex, which includes a conference center, youth camp, theological study center, and healing ministry. The convent sits on the opposite hillside, its driveway winding past beehives and a barn.

A woman is crossing the small parking lot, calling out that Mother Miriam is away this weekend and had asked her to look out for me. I'm disappointed that I won't meet Compunun in person, but Betsy makes me welcome. She's around sixty and dressed in dark pants and a tan sweater, a cross and oval religious medal on a chain around her neck. I ask her if the convent has any visitors this weekend (only one other car is in the lot) and she tells me that one is in residence and that she'll be in the chapel. Her route to the chapel is through the kitchen, through a hall, then another, as the sound of voices singing a cappella grows louder. No, sorry—it's chanting. Betsy whispers that I must hang my coat and I tell her I'd rather keep it, in case the chapel is cold. "No, hang it," she says. Her tone is gentle but I snap to it, nun-conditioned to obey despite not being certain if Betsy indeed is one. I give her the coat, which she hangs just above a croquet set, which I quickly note holds both final sticks.

The chapel is behind us, a bright white-walled and ceilinged space occupied by a dozen people. We pass a board noting who is observing silence. The name Pat has the note "almost" next to it.

Nine of the twelve inside are the nuns, who sit Shaker-style, in two rows of heavy dark wooden seats facing one another, four to the left, five on the right, which is where Betsy directs me, to a space just behind herself and another woman maybe close to seventy. I remember this chapel from the documentary's funeral scene, and another in which a rare new member takes vows.

The nuns are impressive in their traditional habits, the kind my grammar school teachers and Sister Benecia wore, black and down to the ground, white starched bib providing a bright backdrop for a hand-sized cross of ebony edged in silver, a silver lily in the center. Their heads are covered by black veils reaching just past their shoulders, a white band edging their faces. The exception is a nun on my side, front row, with a light-blue veil and mid-calf navy dress. A newbie, I guess, though this one is graying; at middle age she is still the youngest of the group, which includes two in wheelchairs and a pair with canes.

Their voices are clear and constant as they take turns reading what Betsy has told me are the matins that lead up to the Mass, and that she points out for me in a book.

"Praise the LORD. Sing to the LORD a new song, his praise in the assembly of the saints," the nuns recite. "Let Israel rejoice in their Maker; let the people of Zion be glad in their King."

I want to look at them, but I don't want to. Like at St. John Will-I-Am Coltrane, or Kykotsmovi or Sabbathday Lake, this is not entertainment. But, really, how often are you in the presence of such an assemblage? The last time I was around this many nuns in traditional garb was Sister Benecia's funeral, when they packed Motyka's to pray before her white coffin.

There is an old feeling to what we're doing here and I'm again shot back to nearly a year ago, to St. Spyridon, that chanting making it seem another world. This is another world, too, another time. Who does this anymore? Apparently, at least nine women.

Silence hangs when matins ends. Betsy and one of the nuns approach me with all the books I'll need for the service. The hymnal, and its 960 pages, plus another 1,001 pages inside the red *Missa Penitentialis,* open to "Holy Eucharist Rite II."

"Is this what you're used to?" the nun asks, pointing to the page. I want to say that I'm not used to any of this. But I see familiar words and responses, so I nod. I know where I am today, here with my feet on the pink linoleum, back comfy against a counted-cross-stitched cushion that cries out WORSHIP THE LORD!

We formally begin to do that when a door to the right opens and a priest enters via the aisle splitting the nuns' pews. He's an aged hippy with graying hair pulled into a ponytail and wearing glasses of the giant lens size last popular when Jimmy Carter was teaching Sunday school in D.C. His vestments are Lenten purple with some gold and white, worn over gray trousers and black shoes. The woman who'd been Betsy's seatmate disappeared during the matins and has reentered the sanctuary in a white garment that has transformed her into an altar girl, one with tight gray curls and small lips she's colored a vivid red.

The priest—Father Curtis, Betsy whispers, retired for two years, comes here each weekend—stands before an altar table simply set with a pair of lit candles, a chalice, and a Bible on a stand. Above the altar hangs a carved dark cross, a saintly figure to either side. Four long rectangular stained glass windows illustrate the Annunciation, Nativity, Baptism, and something I can't make out because the three top panes are blank, awaiting repair. Along the side walls run very ornate carved and painted Stations of the Cross. To my right, Jesus is being sentenced, next to a fire alarm.

A cappella, the nun in the front row on the left begins to sing. Her voice is skilled and can scale the most Alpine notes. *Bless the Lord,* she begins and we try to follow along.

We sing *Lord, have mercy* and Father Curtis asks that "our hearts might be fixed where true joy is found," then sits to apply Chapstick while a nun from my side of the room steps to the big wooden pulpit to read from Isaiah.

"Remember not the former things or consider the things of old," she says, "I am making a new thing, do you not perceive it?"

Here in this Old World setting we chant the happy Psalm 126, "When the LORD restored the fortunes of Zion, we were like those who dream. Then our mouth was filled with laughter, and our tongue with shouts of joy; then it was said among the nations, 'The LORD has done great things for us.' "

The altar girl woman comes forth from her chair to read, "The righteousness from God that depends on faith. I press on to make it my own." I hear Bob Dylan's "Pressing On" in my head but it's run over by the start of "Jesus Christ Our Lord." *Were the whole realm of nature mine, that were an offering far too small. Love so amazing, so divine, demands my soul, my life, my all.*

And that's what they give here. All. Everything. Could I do that? I try to picture living here, relaxing here after a hard day in the goat yard, joining Holly in the sitting room that Betsy and I passed, with its magazines and spinning wheel and absent television.

Father Curtis reads from the Gospel of Luke, the parable of the vineyard workers. "The owner of the vineyard said, 'Who shall I send? My son? It may be that they will respect him.' "We know what happened: the very son God sent to become the cornerstone was rejected. Killed. Easter isn't so far ahead that this parable seems out of place.

He turns his attention to us. I notice a golden ring on his left hand, wedding ring finger, another on his right.

"I just want to make one thing clear before I make my remarks," he says, and, jumpy since Living Waters Foursquare, I wonder if he's going to yell at me for writing. But he tells a story about falling in the mud as he was leaving for the chapel. "I apologize for being late," he says. "There was a small matter of cleaning up."

There are laughs and Father Curtis smiles. "Here we are," he announces, "the fifth Sunday of Lent."

Lately, even my Jewish friends are asking, "Aren't you nearly done? Isn't Easter in a week or two?"

Father Curtis tells us it's today. "Every Sunday is a little Easter," he says, and I like the term. It reminds me of Little Christmas, and the Irish custom of giving women a break on January 6, the same day the rest of Christianity is marking the Feast of the Epiphany.

But this is Little Easter. "This is a day to be happy!" Father Curtis proclaims. "This is a day to rejoice!

"I'm amazed all the churches I go to, you just don't see anyone getting down on their knees anymore," he says. "This is a time to get down on your knees and say thank you."

Father Curtis is dramatic, but not overly, as he pauses. "A small thing. Take a moment. Look at Psalm 126. What did he tell us? Take five minutes to look at this."

He sits. The sermon itself has taken maybe five minutes. Father Curtis would be a hit with the Catholics.

I do as he's asked, reading: "The Lord has done great things for us and we are glad indeed."

Indeed.

We stand for the Nicene Creed, then continue on to the Prayers of the People. The nun who did the reading leads these, a variety of intentions, including "all who are in danger, sorrow, or any kind of trouble," and that makes me think how each and every day, nuns around the world are doing all this praying away for souls in need.

Today's needy include the congregants at the church in Malawi, and the Archbishop of Canterbury, who is ill. There are whispered names after that: "Alicia." "Danny." I whisper "Dominick," who this week feels so horrible that he won't take visitors. He certainly has had his ups and downs, but each down is frightening, cause for worry. And prayer. There is a mention of one sister's birthday, and another's anniversary.

A confessional prayer is led by the priest, who includes the sin of "what we have done and left undone." Father gives an absolution and begins the sign of peace. "We're glad you're here," Betsy tells me with a handshake. *Thou didst give thyself for me,* the nuns sing, *now I give myself to thee.*

During consecration, Father faces the altar like in the days before Vatican II, back when Sister Benecia wasn't allowed to stay in a private home on vacation, even that of her own sister, lodging instead at our church's convent. Despite that old touch, the all-female population of the rest of the room gives a modern feel and I like that it's just us, and him.

The nuns approach the altar for Communion, lining up along the step. I can see their shoes, most of them sensible black things, though the singing nun wears Birkenstocks and the young nun wears sporty clogs. The other three visitors line up in their pants, sweaters, hoodies. "The body of Christ, the bread of heaven," Father Curtis says, echoing the Celtic Eucharist's wording.

"The blood of Christ, the cup of salvation," the altar girl says as she offers the chalice to each communicant.

Father Curtis concludes the service by asking God to "send us out to do the work you have given us to do, to love and serve you as faithful witnesses of Christ our Lord."

The nuns, whose dress makes them the most obvious witnesses in the room, exit row by row, two by two, bowing first at the altar. Returning to their world, one I've felt privileged to visit and could see myself returning to if, as was the case last week, it just weren't so darn far away.

I get my coat. I see that the croquet sticks remain in place. From a self-service counter near the spinning wheel, I buy two containers of convent-made honey packaged in a plastic angel-shaped bottle. Betsy leads me out.

I have to ask. "Are you a nun?"

She shakes her head. Smiles. "I aged out."

Despite the shortage of sisters here, no one over forty-five is allowed to apply. You can, however, become an associate, which is what Betsy is, included in the community through a relationship of support and prayer.

Or, as I did this morning, you can just visit.

REVOLUTION CHURCH

BROOKLYN, NEW YORK

I'm no Tammy-come-lately when it comes to following the saga of Tammy Faye and Jim Bakker, evangelists who, long before Joel Osteen was knee high to a TV set, led the nation's largest church, reaching 13 million a week via broadcast of the PTL (for Praise the Lord) Club before the scandal-fueled crash of an empire that included the six-hundred-acre Heritage USA, the nation's third-largest theme park.

Tammy Faye, who went on to become a drag-queen idol and a costar to porn icon Ron Jeremy on TV's *The Surreal Life* reality show, is now, in early 2007, dealing with recurring cancer that has her down to the weight of a fourth grader. As for Jim, he's moved on from the literal big house, where he served time for fraud, to a private home in Branson, Missouri, where he heads yet another television show and promotes his memoirs. But I can say I knew them when.

OK, I didn't know them, but I watched them. Faithfully, if you will. Every weekday morning in the mid-1980s, at 6:00 a.m. as I ate my breakfast and dressed for work. Baby-faced Jim, who'd been ordained in 1964 by the Pentecostal Assemblies of God and that same year started working with none other than Pat Robertson and his Christian Broadcasting Network, prayed and wept throughout each broadcast. At his side, huge-haired Tammy Faye prayed and sang and wept and wept and wept, smearing eyes mascaraed to trademark tarantulian appearance. They begged God for blessings, they begged viewers for money. They were shameless at both, and they were incessantly entertaining. I watched for that reason, rather than for spiritual gain, but I did pay special attention to Tammy Faye who, unusual for a conservative evangelical of any era, and for most celebrities of the time, shone part of her spotlight on AIDS victims. Both Jim and Tammy Faye held affection for the high life, including rumored gold-plated lavatory fixtures and air-conditioned doghouses. As a tune by country singer Ray Stevens asked at the time, "Would Jesus Wear a Rolex on His Television Show?"

Jim passed the PTL pulpit to Jerry Falwell in 1987, hoping to save the ministry after word leaked that he was connected to an alleged rape seven years earlier. But that wasn't the worst of Bakker's problems. The following year, he was charged with embezzling millions from PTL. In 1989 he was found guilty of twenty-four counts of fraud and conspiracy and faced forty-five years in prison. By 1995, both his marriage and his sentence had ended.

Kids Tammy Sue and Jamie were there for it all, and life hasn't been for a picnic for either, either. Tammy Sue married at sixteen and has suffered from depression but has made a career in North Carolina as a singer and minister. Jamie rejected his faith. As he wrote in his 2001 autobiography, *Son of a Preacher Man: My Search for Grace in the Shadows*, "If anyone had an excuse to lose faith in God, it would have been me." He began drinking, dropped out of high school, and mucked about the world of punk rock, singing for a time in a group that covered the music of Social Distortion. But now thirty and known as Jay, he's become a star in his own right, thanks to the Sundance Channel broadcasts of the critically acclaimed *One Punk Under God*, a documentary series on his unlikely path to the pulpit.

Produced by the same folks who filmed the 2000 RuPaul-narrated documentary *The Eyes of Tammy Faye*, the series focuses on Jay Bakker's life in Revolution, a church he and two friends founded in Phoenix in 1994 in order to " show all people the unconditional love and grace of Jesus without any reservations due to their lifestyle or religious background, past or future," according to the Web site.

Just ask and Revolution will give you a free sticker that is the church's apology to those hurt by religion. "As Christians," it reads, "we're sorry for being self-righteous judgmental bastards."

Revolution offers cybersalvation, too, posting sermon recordings on its Web site "for people who have given up on church." And Pastor Jay, one wrist tattooed with the word "Broken," and the other with "Outcast," will travel to speak to groups anywhere in the country to give the message that God loves you, no matter what.

But wherever he speaks, don't expect to see Pastor Jay talking up church. "Religion Kills" is a theme of Revolution, which defines religion as "a false perception of holiness that focuses on law and kills the true message of Christ" and stresses that Jesus, rather than Christianity, is the savior. The Web site asks: "Are we driving people to Christianity or leading them to Christ?"

What's driven me here this Palm Sunday is Jay Bakker's story. On Palm Sunday, Jesus was hailed and adored. The following week, he was dead. Jay Bakker once had it all, thanks to parents who were pressed by adoring crowds. With those powerful parents, Jay lived a multimillion-dollar existence, had life on a string. Then lost it all, only years later to find a faith that truly sustained him. It's a replaying of the story of the prodigal son, the mighty having fallen, but it feels more authentic because I observed the path of his high life and fall. Along with Tommy, who had been up early with me all those mornings long ago and who has an interest in storefront churches, seeing them as a very real way that the faithful are served, congregations consisting of those who might not be your regular churchgoers but who still have that desire to be connected spiritually. On the next-to-last Sunday of my year of church visits, the idea of attending a service that explicitly rejects "church" is really intriguing. And yes, I'll admit there's a curiosity factor. So both of us are here to listen to Jay Bakker.

Our destination is Pete's Candy Store, which every Sunday at 4:00 p.m. hosts Revolution New York. Until the 1960s, this small storefront in Brooklyn's Williamsburg section indeed sold sweets. Now a bar, restaurant, nightspot, and community hangout, it offers concerts, book readings, and Jay Bakker beneath the curved wooden roof of a narrow back room the size of a train car. Five small red tables are set along each wall, eight or ten chairs scattered along them. No seat is a bad seat in this intimate space ending in a tiny white-lightbulb-crowned stage on which a trio might not fit. But it's plenty big enough for the one man who walks through the aisle lined with approximately forty thirty-somethings reading *The Onion* and using the Wi-Fi.

"Hello, hello!" says the man who drops a leather bag onstage at four on the nose.

Jay Bakker wears a watch cap above his father's round face framed by long thin sideburns and punctuated by a piercing on his bottom lip. His glasses are dark rimmed, his socks are white, his jeans are black, as are his sweatshirt and the lace-up shoes. Gold is the wedding ring that links him to the medical student wife whose studies in the area brought the couple from Atlanta. Pastor Jay asks for a friend on whom he'd played a joke, earlier having texted a plea for the friend to preach today because Jay supposedly couldn't. "Because it's April Fools' Day," he points out. "My parents, well, they're not normal anyhow, but they got married on April Fools'. They were doomed from the start."

That brings laughs from some as Bibles are dug from backpacks. There's no music here, no housekeeping, no public-service announcements, just getting down to business. "Um, well," starts Pastor Jay, "we've been going through Galatians for ten weeks, and we're not even close to finishing it." He notes that he'll be using Martin Luther's commentary. "Half of us don't know what the Bible says, much less Martin Luther, myself included."

Sitting on a barstool, knees askew, his bag now on a nearby piano seat, Pastor Jay tells us that Galatians was written by the apostle Paul and that it is the closest to the truth in telling of Christ's life, having been written ten to thirty years after, as opposed to the typical thirty to fifty. As for Paul, he was a work in progress. "Some think he screwed everything up, some think he was better than Jesus," Pastor Jay says, adding his own two cents. "He's a cool dude. He's basically saying, 'What are you doing?' "

Pastor Jay tells the story of Abraham being informed by God that he would father a child. Abraham, whose wife, Sarah, was unable to bear children, used a slave, Hagar, as her stand-in, and Ishmael was born. "I think we do that a lot when we're waiting on God. We sometimes use our own attempts. But he had a son." I'm reminded of Pastor LeAnne back at Vineyard Northampton, who in tough times found it "tempting to take the road of not using God. I'd say, 'If I just work hard enough and think hard enough, I could just pull myself up by my bootstraps.' "

The couple eventually allowed God to work, and when they were ninety became the biological parents of Isaac. Pastor Jay says that "with Christ, salvation's a free gift. But we try to do things on our own." He reminds us that "we are God's masterpieces."

The service is not without additional references to his famous background. "For me, growing up, it was all about how many people did you get at church," he tells us. "It's the same at Revolution—how many do you get? That shows we have success! The point being, sometimes we try to please God through works, and sometimes we end up being a mess."

He advises that we check our motives. "When we started Revolution, we got in a circle to pray," he recalls. "I hated it. Who said 'Father God' fifteen times?" His congregation laughs. "We all grew up charismatic. I wouldn't hang around with certain people. I was depressed. I'd go to pray, I'd go to the balcony and walk back and forth so people would see me. I was praying to be delivered from my misery. I hated myself."

Pastor Jay tells of leaving Revolution early in its history and telling his friends that he wouldn't be returning. "I felt like I couldn't do it anymore. Even though I started a church reaching people no one else cared about, I was a hypocrite."

He talks about those unwanteds, those similarly tattooed, those who are gay. He mentions Internet boards with hundreds of postings about the sin of homosexuality and only a handful about Darfur and Iraq.

"I personally don't think homosexuality's a sin," he tells us, touching on one of the controversies illustrated in the *One Punk* series. "If you're putting that in front of children getting killed, you're making a new law." Prioritizing preaching against homosexuality over trying to end poverty or disease does not follow the real teachings of Christ. Not ending poverty, not ending AIDS are the real crimes, he tells us. "God forbid we send condoms to Africa," Pastor Jay adds sarcastically, "because that would only promote having sex."

He has to stop himself, acknowledging that's his soapbox. "I want to get on there and say who are you judging? That's how we decide you're a brother/sister of Christ—is your morality." He uses his hands, white against his black-clad chest, as he quotes God reminding us to love. "So when we're being persecuted, we've gotta love our enemies," he affirms. "Love those who persecute, that's the taking up of the cross daily. That's how we're going to change things."

He adds that the human inclination is to revolt, and I'm hoping he's not going to get all Portland Jehovah's Witnesses on me, though it would be hard to imagine this renegade telling us to not rebel. He simply says that "love and peace can conquer. When you're loving your enemy, their true nature will come out."

Pastor Jay thanks Martin Luther for helping him see all this, then throws in the fact that he's almost done with his talk. "If you're confused: law bad, grace good." We're saved by Christ and not by the laws created by men and women, Pastor Jay tells us. Then he adds another personal story. "I was drawn to Christ. Most of my life, I was driven there, pushed there. I didn't want to go to hell. I was afraid of God."

Perfect love, he says, casts out all fear. "Church is not a safe place. It's supposed to be a hospital. It's an American gladiator." A reference to yet another television program, but this one giving an image of the church as a battleground, its members fighting the odds and sometimes actually coming up victorious. Or at least, as is our pastor, at peace. "So that's it. We're done. Think on these things, look for yourself and see if it's true." His concluding prayer is brief, asking God to be with us this week, confidently adding, "We know you will be."

There is a mention of a donation box at the bar—"We can all use it to keep the church going"—but no mention that today is Palm Sunday, one of the most auspicious days on the church calendar. The omission doesn't bother me. Pastor Jay is the illustration of what some of this day is about, a Gospel story being played out in our times.

Against the tide of young people filling the space for the open mike that follows this one-hour service, we follow this iconoclastic preacher from the dimly lit performance space toward the front room, and the light.

INTERFAITH CHAPEL

DENVER INTERNATIONAL AIRPORT, DENVER, COLORADO

"Have you closed your doors to make a beggar of a prince?"

"I'm the beggar, Moses! Begging you to hold me in your arms!"

I eat up this bit of Old Testament flirting between skirt-wearing, pre-NRA Charlton Heston as Moses and Anne Baxter as black-banged Nefretiri while I munch contentedly on a Cadbury's Fruit and Nut bar. An annual viewing of Cecil B. DeMille's 1956 version of *The Ten Commandments* is my Holy Saturday night tradition, as I end those forty days of Lent by gorging on chocolaty treats and watching a cheesy classic. No, it's not Easter yet—technically. Lent continues until dawn tomorrow, when the stone is rolled from the tomb and he's not inside. But at some point on Holy Saturday, the regulations are magically lifted and whatever you've chosen to forgo for the previous thirty-nine days can be enjoyed once again.

"You're no beggar, my love. You're a conqueror, and I am your captive for life!"

The resumption of candy consumption always has been the high point of my Holy Saturday, which always seems extremely and quietly sad. Jesus is dead so what is the point of anything? Back in my childhood, in the dreariness of the usually gray and damp and snowy New England early spring, we'd clean for Easter Sunday, get our clothes ready for the 6 a.m. Sunday service, and begin cooking whatever we could of the next day's big meal. In the afternoon we'd stop at the church and walk on our knees the length of the aisle, at the end of which awaited a crucifix on a red velvet pillow. We would press our lips to the cold plaster feet and then continue on to the right, to the papier-mâché cave in which a nearly life-size statue of a dead Jesus lay in state. We'd kneel at the Communion rail separating us from him and marvel about how, less than four months before, a foot-long baby version of him had rested placidly among Mary, Joseph, shepherds, sheep, and camels in this very same cave. Now, all because of our sins, including my coveting of Dede Duda's pony back in second grade, look what had happened.

The magical Lent-lifting hour has passed here fifteen miles west of Denver, in my B and B chosen for its location right down the road from Morrison, site of tomorrow's sunrise service at Red Rocks Park and Ampitheatre. A pair of three-hundred-foot monoliths have created perfect acoustics for the concerts held at Red Rocks since 1906. The Beatles performed the first big-name rock show there in 1964, and the stage since has hosted U2, the Allman Brothers, and, multiple times because it's their favorite venue, the Grateful Dead. I've seen it only once, on my television screen, when PBS ran a fundraiser featuring a broadcast of a Yanni concert. I remember shots of the soft orange rock walls, the packed rows of ten thousand seats, Yanni's tresses flying as he pounded the piano keys. I'll see the place in person tomorrow at 4:30 a.m., when gates open for the Fifty-eighth Annual Easter Sunrise Service. Wanting to conclude my year with a big, bold, memorable morning, I had researched sunrise services on beaches and mountaintops before deciding on dramatic Red Rocks, the geology of which made it a perfect match for a holy day hinged on a visit to a cave.

So that was the plan. Then the freezing drizzle through which I drove from the airport on Holy Saturday afternoon layered on the seats, on the aisles, and on stairs constructed by hand during the Great Depression by the Civilian Conservation Corps. So no booming music, no prayers from the multitudes, no enormous cloud of white doves released, no 2007 version of the grand nondenominational sunrise service that holds the designation of the event that has played most often at Red Rocks (Willie Nelson is in second place). The TV news gives me the bad news about the service I've traveled nearly cross-country to attend, the one I thought would so glowingly end my church visits with all the metaphors a sunrise can evoke.

It's that whole thing about God laughing at plans: "You want an unusual place for the last visit? I'll give you one!"

So I got up early anyhow, navigated the slick highway, dropped off the rental car, and went to the airport. And to church.

Airport chapels have existed since 1950, when Our Lady of the Airways was built at Boston's Logan Airport to minister to the needs of the city's many Catholic employees and travelers. The second was created soon after, at what is now John F. Kennedy International Airport, then Idlewild. One hundred and fifty airport chapels now serve worshippers around the world, including at Denver International Airport. This fifty-three-square-mile city unto itself, completed in 1995 at a price tag of nearly $5 billion, offers both a Jewish/Christian Interfaith Chapel and an Islamic *masjid*, the Arabic word for mosque.

DIA employs 23,000, and 106,000 passengers daily pass through to eighty-nine gates and 1,450 flights. But in the hour I spend at the chapel, I am joined only by a woman who stays the entire time, a man who drops in for five minutes, and a security guard who passes through to check an inner door.

Maybe people just can't find the place. The chapel is on a sleepy upper level of the southern end of the Terminal East atrium, fittingly one floor above the security department and just before the lost and found. The door to the chapel is to the right of that for the *masjid*. Both rooms were created, informs an adjacent plaque, with the involvement of the Colorado Council of Churches, the Archdiocese of Denver, the Colorado Muslim Society, and the Rocky Mountain Rabbinical Council. A sign outside the *masjid* instructs one to PLEASE TAKE OFF YOUR SHOES UPON ENTRY AND PLACE INSIDE THE DOOR. There are no rules posted at the entrance to the chapel, which is isolation-booth quiet.

A fake Easter lily on the gray marble altar is the only nod to the day. It, and a carved wooden cross, stand between plaques marked as were Moses' Ten Commandments last night on TV, with Roman numerals I to V on the left, then VI to X on the right. A book with gold-edged pages lies open before the cross. A blue Kleenex box rests to the left.

I haven't seen Kleenex in a church since last Resurrection Sunday, and I think back to my friends at New Mount Zion a year ago. They'd certainly enliven this space, though they'd have to take turns. There are only twenty-four light-wood-trimmed peacocky-covered chairs facing the altar, three rows of eight on the gray carpeting, and two on each side. The pair on the left contain my fellow worshipper —Caucasian, scarlet-haired, reading a small magazine—and her stuff—a red case on wheels and a dark tapestry bag.

Three walls are adorned with bland pastel prints of waterscapes. The ceiling is firm acoustic tile that doesn't look like it's going anywhere. Four tall clear glass windows make up the wall behind me. It's 9:20 a.m. and the Transportation Security Administration area below is an ant colony of searchers, searchees, fellow travelers of maybe every race and ethnicity, and maybe close to every religion in the world, though that might be stretching it as the total number of religions is estimated at approximately forty-two hundred—and those are general categories that don't include specific subgroups. But it's not hard to imagine a good portion of the majors being represented in the travelers moving ever forward through the lines.

I look down from my seat in the center of the back row to a version of what I saw in that queue awaiting seats at Times Square Church: the entrance to heaven. All ages and types, and so many soldiers also getting in line, moving through the stanchioned alleys, their documents being checked, possessions rummaged through, all being pointed toward their destinations across the state, worldwide. Announcements can be heard through the chapel wall: reminders from the TSA regarding procedures for dealing with suspicious baggage, and someone being paged. Voices from above giving direction.

My path brought me here. To sit with these chairs before this altar across from this woman now moving a rosary through her fingers. Two of us are gathered, and isn't that the minimum number? "Wherever two or more are gathered in my name, there I am."

Isn't God in a canyon? Isn't God in this room? Wasn't he in Mobile and Seattle and Omaha and Kihei?

I've seen a lot of him this year as I took the time to pass through those doors I long ago was warned against entering. At a concert one year ago, I was telling my cousin Jim about the journey I was about to begin. He's done his share of touring Christianity over the decades and gave a show-and-tell of his findings. "I see it like this," he said, and on the music hall table lined up four water glasses. "People who believe one thing, they're going this way." He moved a glass forward. "People who believe the other thing," another glass was moved, same direction, "they're going this way." He slid a third forward. "Other people, they believe something else." He made all the glasses meet. "But we all want to go to the same place. We all want heaven."

A year later I realize that the feisty Pastor Elizabeth at Living Waters, and the gentle elderly priest in Hamtramck, and the culture-split congregant in Kykotsmovi might be taking very different paths, but as Christians their goals are the same.

No disrespect to the rich and diverse traditions and histories and doctrines of the many churches I visited this year, but maybe I should have listened to Jim and realized then that the finish line at which the drinking glasses met was the simple truth. We all want to end up in the same place, we've just taken different routes. What I have observed in this past year behind all those doors and beneath all those ceilings (or lack of ceiling, in one case) were faiths that looped down lanes of love, or trod the tired trail of blandness, or dwelled on demons, damnation, and discrimination. The frequency with which I saw that third route chosen by churches that also called themselves houses of a loving God was disturbing, and again and again made the case for the many engaging in some form of the pilgrimage I've made in the past year. And not just as a tour. They're looking for a new spiritual home.

I don't know what the others are finding in their travels, but the past year has distilled for me the qualities I'd need in a new church home: a community that welcomed me warmly, didn't give a whit about my politics or lifestyle, gave tons of whits about the social justice needs locally and beyond, contained little-to-no hierarchy, allowed congregants a say in decisions large and small, offered a spiritual message inspired by love rather than by fear, and did all this in an art-filled space that rang with awesome music.

As Pastor James in Columbus noted, there are no perfect churches. But that would be mine. None of those I visited contained all those points, but several offered lots of what matters most to me.

Arch Street, the Quaker meetinghouse in Philadelphia, historic not only in American history but in my personal one—I got so much from just sitting and being quiet.

As I did, surprisingly, from sitting in a basement. I was struck by and would return for the love and joy lavished at Richmond's Metropolitan Community Church, and in the more traditional setting of Baltimore's St. Sebastian's, both offering nothing but acceptance and involvement to the traditionally outcast community and anyone else who happens by.

I felt drawn to a community meeting in another unusual setting, and to another church catering to those who might feel out of place in a traditional congregation: the candor of Jay Bakker and his Revolution, which puts the focus on God rather than religion.

Jazz, a form of music I'd never really followed, was the backbone of the storefront church of St. John Will-I-Am Coltrane, and fueled the pastor and the worshippers-turned-bandmembers, and me.

Harvest Church of the Nazarene in Vegas, and its tiny but dynamic gathering in a junior high school art room, might have been a "quickie" service but it wasn't short on illustrating the power and connection to be felt in a circle of five worshippers.

Much larger but somehow just as intimate was Chicago's Trinity United Church of Christ, one of those destinations to which I was led by the membership of a celebrity and at which I found much more than a chance to ogle. I was reminded literally and spiritually that God indeed woke us up this morning.

These are truly come one come all, no-questions-asked churches that move forward with reality and goodness in a modern word. Would I join any of these? If I lived closer, I might ponder getting more than a single impression.

As for the ones in which I balked at some or all of the theology, I'd feel drawn back only to revisit the members who showed kindness. Ruby, sharing her pew and her friendship at First Baptist Spartanburg. Nancy and Howard, telling their story as they drove me to the train station after worship at Saddleback. Cowboy David, who gave me a Cowboy Bible. Pastor Laura, who stayed behind to pray for Tommy. As I think back to these good people, I see again the bits of gold that shone in most every church, regardless of the name on the sign outside. The building doesn't make a church. The people do. And not just on Sunday, I was reminded, watching the weekday devotion of volunteers who gave up their weeks of vacation to travel to Mississippi and kneel in prayer posture as they connected plumbing for a storm victim they did not know. Church can be everywhere. God certainly is.

On this Easter Sunday, the *Washington Post* runs an essay by a former atheist who would agree with that. Carol Miller of Rochester, New York, who was born into a family of unbelievers but whose uncle's near-death experience got her thinking. "I now have a real relationship with God," Miller writes. "I have asked for the impossible, and it has come to me—and there is no way that I could ever believe that God is not right here with me. I thank Him every day of my life." But, she adds, "I will never be a part of any religion. Every religion is 'man-made' and distorts God's true message that love is all there is . . . I guess *this* is my religion. It works for me. My church or temple is wherever I am because I always feel that I'm in God's house. I think we all are if we would just realize it."

"What you need, baby?" the woman seated in front of me a year ago at New Mount Zion asked. A year later I can answer, "To remember these words: that we are always in God's house, wherever we find ourselves." He woke me up this morning and got me safely here. I am in a twelve-by-twenty-foot airport chapel, but I know where I am: Right where he wants me. On this day of his resurrection, and in my life. Very certain that I have my story straight, I say a prayer of thanksgiving, then pick up my pack. It's time to go home.

ACKNOWLEDGMENTS

So many people assisted me as I researched and wrote this book and lived this year. I thank them all and am especially grateful to Tommy Shea, Elinor Lipman, Julie Strempek, John Talbot, Helene Atwan, Julie Dias, Gail Fortune, Mary Bernat, Janice Polchlopek, Joanne and Jim Spence, Jane Magdalenski, Tanya Barrientos, Jack Booth, Susan and Dominick Pecora, the Grimanis family, Cindy and David Hamel, Betty Dew, Joan Connor, Kara LeFebvre, Mary Ellen Lowney, Tim Murphy, Rachael Raffel, Lil Swanson, Dave Warner, the Koss-Leland Family, Holly Angelo, David Bergengren, Maureen Shea, Mary Shea, Yvonne Milewski, Grazyna and Stan Kozaczka, Leslea Newman, Luanne Rice, Elizabeth Searle, the Masztal Family, Ted and Annie Deppe, Kevin O'Hare, Karen Parker, Sylvia Sepulveda, Janet Edwards, Rita Ciresi, Terri and Gary Hidu, Ann and John Iwanicki, Sister Jane Morrissey, Melissa Dobson, Dr. Stephen Holuk, Dr. George Baquis, Dr. Elizabeth Boyle, and JoAnn Murphy.

99
110
115
241
254